P9-DVJ-662

American Appetite

Also by
Leslie Brenner

THE ART OF THE COCKTAIL PARTY
FEAR OF WINE
ESSENTIAL FLAVORS
(co-author with Katharine Kinsolving)

AMERICAN

Appetite

The Coming of Age of a Cuisine

Leslie Brenner

AN AVON BOOK

Grateful acknowledgment is given to Garrison Keillor for permission to reprint an excerpt from "A Prairie Home Companion" (*Café Boeuf*, June 7, 1997).

AVON BOOKS, INC.
1350 Avenue of the Americas
New York, New York 10019

Interior design by Kellan Peck
ISBN: 0-380-97336-7

Library of Congress Cataloging in Publication Data:
Brenner, Leslie.
American appetite : the coming of age of a cuisine / Leslie Brenner.
p. cm.
Includes bibliographical references and index.
1. Gastronomy—History. 2. Food habits—United States—History.
I. Title.
TX633.B694 1999 99-10314
394.1'0973—dc21 CIP

First Bard Printing: April 1999

Printed in the U.S.A.

FIRST EDITION

QPM 10 9 8 7 6 5 4 3 2 1

www.avonbooks.com/bard

Acknowledgments

I owe a deep debt of gratitude to Jennifer Hershey and Lou Aronica for their vision, guts, imagination, and faith, and especially to Jennifer for the intelligence and skill she brought not only to editing the manuscript, but in helping me conceptualize it. Thanks to Nach Waxman of Kitchen Arts and Letters for his encouraging words and advice early on while this project was still a proposal. I'm grateful to Laura Fisher for assigning me the magazine piece that led me thinking in a direction that eventually became this book, and for keeping her eyes open for historical materials of value to me. Everlasting thanks to the wise and insightful Janet Capron, for reading the manuscript and giving great notes. My compliments to Saralyn F. Fosnight for her meticulous, thoughtful copyediting work.

Thanks, too, to a number of friends and professional acquaintances for their help during the research phase, particularly Chris Russell for fishing several years of vintage

Gourmet magazines out of the garbage and Gina Russell for putting up with them in her apartment; Alexandra Leaf, for generously sharing with me her expertise in French culinary history; Lila Gault, for putting me in touch with the right people in Seattle; Robert Lewis, Hillary Baum, Rozanne Gold, and Phillip S. Cooke, for going out of their way to make rare publications available to me; and Joanne Lamb Hayes, for digging into her own archives. I'm grateful to Ken Schneider and Judith Jones for answering desperate last-minute queries and to the staff of the Rare Books Room at the Los Angeles Public Library.

Heartfelt thanks to Sue Jamison and Richard Sykes and Ron and Christine Bass for generously opening their homes to me in northern California; to my mom, Joan Winston, for three weeks of marathon baby-sitting at a crucial moment and to Warren for his help and comic relief. *Merci encore* to Catherine Bernard for every kind of support; to Wylie, for sparing his mama from time to time so she might work; and finally, to Thierry, for his enduring patience, intelligence, acuity, and loving support.

Contents

Foreword

by Wayne Nish

I ASSUME THAT THE READERS OF A BOOK ON FOOD WITHout recipes would consist largely of chefs, restaurateurs, people in cookbook publishing, culinary historians, and other food professionals. Though gourmets, gourmands, and culinary Walter Mittys will make up another percentage of its readers, it is always those directly involved in a subject who will have the most passionately held opinions and the greatest emotional investment. But it's not always the doers in any given field who have the best perspective on what is developing and where it is going. Sometimes it takes a fresh view from someone who has observed from afar and is ready to step forward and comment on the fray. In *American Appetite,* Leslie Brenner has assumed just such a role.

When I first met Leslie some years ago—when I was executive chef at La Colombe d'Or—I told her about ideas that I had considered to be germane to the continuum of the development of food culture in this country. She then produced for my inspection an article she had published in *New York Woman* magazine in 1991 that outlined the contribution of America's new immigrants to the contemporary culinary landscape. Needless to say, we were both delighted to have found someone else of like mind. In the years that followed that article, she has committed more and more of her writing to the subject of food, the development of our food culture, and food history.

It is true, as she states in this work, that we Americans have a deserved reputation throughout the world for culinary barbarism. What might be added, however, is that our generation should not be held accountable for the sins of our fathers (and mothers), even if those sins involved unspeakable acts with a Blue Nun, Green Giant, or Cold Duck unnaturally coupled with James Beard, Julia Child, or Craig Claiborne.

Whereas much of America today remains a culinary wasteland, it cannot be denied, as Leslie suggests, that there is a movement underfoot, identifiable at least in American restaurant kitchens, that is defining a new, globally influenced American cuisine.

It isn't a stretch to suggest that the development of this new American form is being generated by the dynamics of our melting pot society. Where once French *haute cuisine* dominated both diplomatic circles and the pages of *Gourmet* magazine, its formerly unchallenged title as the king of western cuisine now represents only half of the story. Various Asian, Middle Eastern and southern hemisphere cuisines are in vogue throughout this country and are challenging French cuisine's position as the only authoritative food culture in existence in America. As documented in this book, fusion cuisine is a natural development of the movement of peoples. Nowhere else and at no other time in the history of the world has such a movement been more effluent and diverse than it has been to the United States during the second half of the twentieth century.

The flip side to the current work of young Turks in the culinary field is the integration and assimilation of new foodstuffs constantly being introduced by new immigrant groups to the already existing techniques the American home cook has at his or her disposal. Of course, not all of those techniques belong to any one country.

A mitigating factor worth mentioning, however, is the birth of the fast food industry in this country and its enormous growth since World War II. Fast food competes with home cooking. Without the need to cook, the development of a deep food culture is in danger of becoming stillborn. Unfortunately, it now seems to be an uphill battle as even France and Japan, two of the very cultures we have looked to as our culinary ideals, are becoming "Americanized," where small bistros and yakitori-yas are yielding to McDonalds, KFC, and Pizza Hut. The American convenience food industry is poised to invade their homes as well as it has ours. The globalization of our free market ideals will bring to the world some things we may not be so proud about.

The Finnish architect, the late Alvar Aalto, wrote "the simultaneous solution of opposites is the first necessary condition for any human achievement to attain the level of culture." As with trends in fashion, it takes extremes to effect change, and our food culture is no exception. The unusual and sometimes bizarre combinations that young, innovative American chefs are practicing today will make people notice (and sometimes retch). But the best of those ideas will eventually work their way into the American food landscape just as the ingredients and techniques of Northern Europe did here two hundred years ago.

For my part, I've never met a cuisine I didn't like. If it is well prepared, it will be good. More Americans have begun to come to the same conclusion, as witnessed by the explosion of new and diverse ethnic culinary trends documented every day in the ever-growing food media.

All of the world's cuisines converge in America. That is what will ultimately shape American cuisine into an identifiable entity in the twenty-first century.

—Wayne Nish,
Chef/Owner of March
restaurant in New York City

Introduction

American gastronomy has changed radically over the last fifty years.

Long crippled by Puritan-influenced attitudes that led to Domestic Science (the turn-of-the-century movement that brought us such sterile wonders as home economics and ubiquitous white sauce) and national Prohibition, by the 1950s, we had become a nation in which the ultimate in culinary sophistication was Green Giant frozen peas in butter sauce. For decades, gleaming heads of iceberg lettuce and waxy, watery cucumbers would line the aisles of supermarkets. Big, bright, shiny Red Delicious apples belied their bland and characterless interiors; gargantuan, perfect Sunkist oranges bespoke an ideal of cosmetic beauty and ease of transport—and flavor be damned.

As a culture, we learned to forget about the sources of our food. Farmers' markets around the country disappeared one by one until the few remaining became oddities—

quaint reminders of the past. Meat didn't come from animals, it sprang shrink-wrapped into existence.

Today, varieties of heirloom tomatoes vie for attention at farmers' markets everywhere; mesclun (something no one had even heard of twenty-five years ago) is available in supermarket produce departments alongside tropical fruits, bouquets of fresh herbs, and designer potatoes. Organic milk has taken its place in the dairy case right next to its bioengineered cousins tapped from cows fed with bovine growth hormone. Not far from that, little logs of domestic goat cheese from the boutique dairy in Vermont await marination in the extra-virgin olive oil from California available on aisle twelve.

Of course the majority of Americans care little about this bounty. And in many cities and towns across America, the gastronomic revolution has yet to arrive. If you want to make dinner in Luck, Wisconsin, iceberg lettuce will still have to suffice for your salad; you'll find nothing as exotic as balsamic vinegar; plain olive oil will have to do instead of extra-virgin. Forget about trying to find a decent bottle of wine.

But for a good portion of America—in large cities and their suburbs, as well as all over the West Coast and most of the Northeast, a wealth of produce and high-quality food products are available. Even those who don't regularly buy organic produce or seek out interesting cheeses or wines or imported pasta at least know about them—they've become part of mainstream culture. Arugula has become a joke in the American lexicon—a single vegetable that embodies culinary sophistication. "Tall food" has become a shorthand for culinary excess.

If many Americans—indeed a majority—haven't made the bounty of the food revolution (if revolution it was) a part of their everyday lives, if culinary sophistication has not crept onto their plates at home or in restaurants, that doesn't mean the impact on American life and culture hasn't been tremendous. One sees a parallel in the fitness movement: More than a third of all Americans are obese and wouldn't dream of taking a few laps around the block, let alone setting foot on a Stairmaster, yet fitness and the idea of being fit have a powerful grip on our imagination. The slice of American society that has gotten off its collective butt and exercised is relatively small, but that slice represents the way we'd like to see ourselves.

In much the same way, gastronomic sophistication has become very much a part of an emerging American ideal. Yes, we're modern; we're hip; we have mâche and frisée in our salad; we eat sushi and know good bread when we taste it; we're interested in wine. In California, my cousin's five-year-old daughter sits glued to the TV Food Network. She favors certain chef-stars—New Orleans chef Emeril Lagasse and Los Angeles' *Too Hot Tamales,* Mary Sue Milliken and Susan Feniger; David Rosengarten gets on her nerves. In the video store, the box of Henry Jaglom's film *Eating* proclaims: "In the nineties, women talk about food the way they used to talk about sex in the eighties." And though fewer and fewer Americans cook, cookbook sales are booming.

In the fall of 1996, New York University began offering a Ph.D. in Food Studies. Chefs appear on *The Late Show with David Letterman* and flaunt their skills at department store lecture series. Food has taken a place in our culture above and beyond the role of merely providing sustenance or even just gastronomic pleasure: It's serious business; it's entertainment. It's Important.

When I first proposed this book to a number of publishers and began to interview chefs and other food professionals, my working title was *The Coming of Age of American Cuisine.* I found, much to my surprise, that not everyone believed an

American cuisine existed—one book editor turned down the proposal on that basis. This led me into an investigation about what exactly is meant by the term "cuisine"—is it just a twenty-five-cent word for *cookery* or *food?* If so, of course there's an American cuisine. Or does it somehow imply a certain level of sophistication, tradition, and development? Does it depend on a proscribed number of standard preparations? And if those preparations derive from foreign dishes, does that invalidate them as American "cuisine"?

There are those who say that an American food revolution began in 1971, when Alice Waters founded Chez Panisse. Others say Julia Child started it ten years earlier when, with Simone Beck and Louisette Bertholle, she published her classic *Mastering the Art of French Cooking.* Of course, it's not that simple.

Whether or not what has happened to food in this country has been a revolution, in the lives of a generation of individual cooks there has been an awakening, a moment when a gastronomic lightbulb switched on, and a heretofore uncharted world of cuisine became illuminated. Thus, perhaps the American food revolution is more a series of minirevolutions, personal revolutions, that all add up to big change. Born in 1960, I've lived through the most tumultuous and energetic part of our gastronomic evolution/revolution. Of course I couldn't cook when I was five or six years old, but I do remember my mother watching Julia Child's *The French Chef* on public television. As I grew up, Julia's dishes were what we ate when my mom wanted to impress company, or even just please the family; plodding through Julia's sauces and poultry preparations were the way I taught myself to cook.

Like many Americans of my generation and the previous one, my gastronomic lightbulb went on when I first went to Europe, which I was lucky enough to do when I was nine years old. Today my most vivid memories of that family vacation involve a divine asparagus soup in Florence, wild strawberries in orange sauce in Rome, fresh cherries bursting with flavor eaten for breakfast al fresco in Venice, a raspberry tart in a tiny Paris bistro. Never before had I tasted food so delicious. It was only years later that I reflected that they all revolved around high-quality produce, all very simply prepared.

My palate reawakened years later, when, as a college sophomore at Stanford who dabbled in veal picatta and chocolate mousse, I first visited the six-year-old Chez Panisse forty minutes north in Berkeley. My childhood friend Julie was visiting from her eastern college; her father had invited us. When she told me what she had heard about Chez Panisse, that there was no menu—everyone ate the same thing—and moreover, that it would be a five-course meal, that was the most exciting news I had heard all year, at least. That must have been the first time I tasted *pigeon*, which horrified me a little, though I wound up loving it and roasted garlic. After that, nothing was ever the same.

Another light went on the following year, when I worked at a summer job assisting Vince DiBari, then vice-president of Local 47 of the Musicians' Union in Hollywood (whose claim to fame was being the youngest member, at fifteen, of Desi Arnaz's orchestra—Vince played trumpet). One Friday afternoon he called me into his office, disappeared into his washroom, and reappeared holding a big, sandy, floppy bunch of fresh basil—something I had never seen before. "Here, honey," he said. "Take this home."

"What do I do with it?" I asked.

He went to his desk, opened a drawer, and pulled out some homemade Italian sausages. "Make a tomato sauce. Cook these sausages, add them to the sauce, and chop up the basil and add it at the very last minute." It sounds pedestrian now, but the result was a revelation.

Thank you, Vince, wherever you are.

Having spent my entire life divided between two coasts, I've chosen to make them the focus—though certainly not the exclusive domain—of this book. I did so first because California and New York have been at the vanguard of the American food revolution since its inception, and second because I felt that by limiting it thus, the material would benefit from my personal experience. Culinary historians are often presented with a rather sticky problem: We look at popular magazines to determine when people were cooking a particular dish, or what restaurants were opening, but it's impossible to discern from them—or any publication—how popular a food or a restaurant was, or how ubiquitous an ingredient. If one experienced them firsthand, however, one can address such issues with confidence.

Still, I'm afraid there's been much I've been forced to leave out. The subject of this book is the cutting edge, as it were, of American cooking—I haven't attempted to chronicle what all Americans have cooked and eaten. And I've had to be satisfied with simply touching on many areas that would warrant a much deeper investigation: The specific contributions of particular ethnic groups, for instance, along with the influence of the health food movement and the rise of the cooking school. The nascent bread revolution bears looking into more deeply, as does the fairly developed coffee revolution. Today the American gastronomic landscape is so vast that many volumes beg to be written. I hope others will pick up where I've left off.

As with all love affairs, in America's love affair with food dangers have abounded. At times we've taken exotic influences too far, winding up with forms of fusion cuisine that one day we'll be embarrassed to look back on. Or food that is overly fussy and self-conscious, all in the name of attempting to be "gourmet" (a term so ill-used that many epicures have come to despise it). And as a country, we're in real danger of losing our regional cuisines. At the same time, we've gone so far in our explorations of foods from around the globe that now it sometimes seems as though there's nothing left to discover.

In their 1977 book *The Taste of America,* John L. Hess, one-time food critic for the *New York Times,* and his co-author and wife Karen Hess, the renowned food historian, offered the most succinct of food histories of the United States:

> . . . the earliest settlers, and the Indians before them, had a marvelous array of foods to choose from, and developed sophisticated and sensual ways of handling them. The foods were gradually homogenized by the Industrial Revolution, and good American cooking was gradually supplanted by the gourmet plague. Finally, the Pepsi generation of gourmet writers taught Americans to be ashamed of their own great food heritage.

The "gourmet plague" to which they refer was the tendency of Americans to embrace foods they perceived as *fancy,* rather than what was either simple and good. Perhaps that was the way things looked when they wrote—the book was published in 1977. Though in their preface to the third edition, published in 1989, long after the American food revolution was under way, they still saw things in much the same manner: "Americans are one more generation removed from the memory of real food." They continued: "It's not that nothing has happened. On the contrary, these have been years of turbulence, of obsession with food, and with change. But the more things changed, the more they were the same."

I believe it's more complicated than that. The Hesses themselves admitted that things remained hopeful. And the nature of progress is to take a few steps forward, a step in the wrong direction, a step backward, and another step forward. One continues to make progress, if gradually, in the right direction.

1

HOW WE LOST GASTRONOMY

SEVERAL YEARS AGO, ON A VISIT TO PARIS, MY HUSBAND, who happens to be French, and I went into a bistro near Les Halles, one that I selected by virtue of its lace curtains and the look of the Belon oysters and briny sea snails on ice in front. We were seated at a small table by the window, speaking English together as usual. When the waiter came to take our order, my husband ordered in French. *Poireaux à la vinaigrette,* followed by *confit de canard* or something of that ilk. "*Très bien,*" said the waiter, scribbling the order, and turning to me: "*Et pour madame . . . un* hahm-beur-gheur???" Such is the reputation today of the American palate.

That reputation wasn't slapped upon us unfairly, either: We earned it.

The New World started out as a land of bounty, bursting with glorious fruits of the sea—lobsters, salmon, crabs (sometimes a single crab was large enough to feed a family of four), sturgeon, abalone, oysters (including the now almost wiped-out West Coast Olympias), clams, terrapin—plentiful game and wild fowl (including turkeys), wild rice, beans, a wide variety of nuts, and fabulous fruits such as cherries, plums, grapes, and wild berries, including strawberries much superior to those in England. And of course corn. Yet somewhere along the way, around the end of the nineteenth century, we took a wrong turn.

The Native Americans ate well, especially on the coasts, and it wasn't only their ingredients that were wonderful; their clever cooking methods also went a long way to enhance them. Thus Native Americans roasted salmon on cedar planks in the Pacific Northwest and put together clambakes in the Northeast; they used ashes to remove the outer husk of the corn kernel to make hominy; they pit-cooked beans in maple sugar to make what later became known as Boston baked beans; they roasted peanuts and grilled meats. According to Waverly Root and Richard de Rochemont, authors of the classic tome *Eating in America,* once pigs were brought here from Europe, it was the Cherokees who invented one of America's finest contributions to gastronomy, Smithfield ham.

When the colonists came, they brought over the culinary proclivities of the English, including their sweet tooth and penchant for roast meats. They tried to plant English crops such as oats and peas, an endeavor that met with little success, so rather than starve, they were forced to learn the food ways of the Native Americans. After two years, the Puritans had come so far that they could afford to spurn clams, thinking them only fit for hog feed. Yet the Puritan faction that settled in New England was prevented by its faith from reveling in food, Thanksgiving notwithstanding.

Because of the Puritan influence, American food never attained the level in New England that it would in other parts of the fledgling union. Yet it may come as a surprise that Jean-Anthèlme Brillat-Savarin raved about a copious meal he enjoyed in Connecticut in 1794, including "a superb piece of corned beef, a stewed goose, a magnificent leg of mutton, a vast selection of vegetables, and at either end of the table, two huge jugs of cider so excellent I could have gone on drinking it forever."

In stark contrast to New England, Philadelphia boasted a rich food tradition; the colonists who settled there were not of Puritan stock. As the cultural and political heart of the colonies before the Revolution, Philadelphians enjoyed the best food of any American city. Epicureanism and entertaining were fashionable, and the city's chefs had access to a wide variety of spices, imported condiments, wines, and exotic fruit, as well as the excellent ingredients indigenous to the area. In the surrounding countryside, the Pennsylvania Dutch ate quite well—unlike the Puritans, their religiosity didn't require self-denial when it came to food.

But high-quality colonial cooking came not only from professional cooks; colonial housewives were dedicated cooks as well. ". . . In the eighteenth century housewives were more daring and imaginative than they are in the twentieth," wrote Waverly Root in 1976. (Admittedly, many American housewives were, as a species, less than imaginative in 1976.) The current fashion for flavored vinegars is not original: It dates back to early American housewives. Not only did they make their own vinegar, but they infused it with horseradish, shallots, basil, tarragon—and yes, even raspberries.

The colonists, however, were so overly fond of sugar that it would eventually become a detriment to American cookery. In the mid-eighteenth century, the colonies were consuming the second greatest amount of sugar in the world (England beat them out). The colonists' sweet tooth wasn't limited to desserts, either; "savory" dishes that may have lacked in flavor were also sweetened up, an urge that presaged America's later love affair with ketchup. According to historian Harvey Levenstein, the result of the colonists' fondness for sugar "was a cuisine which, even excluding desserts, relied more on sweetness than did any other major cuisine in the world."

Once the union was established, the Virginians were no slouches when it came to gastronomy. The mild climate encouraged the growing of Continental and Caribbean varieties of fruits and vegetables; gardening was a popular avocation. Thomas Jefferson was a great epicure; not only was he a first-rate gardener, he also stocked the woods surrounding his estate at Monticello with deer, guinea fowl, hares, rabbits, and "every other wild animal." In 1784 he went to France as the American ambassador and fell in love with French culture and food. As far as he was concerned, the French were far ahead of the Americans when it came to gastronomy. When he returned home, he had some of his favorite continental ingredients sent after him to Monticello: "macaroni, Parmesan cheese, figs of Marseilles, *Brugnoles,* raisins, almonds, mustard, *vinaigre d'Estragon,* other good vinegar, oil and anchovies." He was also an ardent oenophile, a fan especially of the red wines of Bordeaux. Half a century before the still-extant 1855 classification that ordered the best wines of the region into *grands crus,* topped by four *premiers crus,*★ Jefferson had singled out the same four—Châteaux Latour, Lafite-Rothschild, Margaux, and Haut-Brion—as his particular favorites. Jefferson's wine habit set him back some $2,000 a year, equivalent to $18,000 today.

Orchestrated during Jefferson's administration, the Louisiana Purchase in 1803 went a long way toward adding a

★A fifth was added in 1973, Château Mouton-Rothschild. Mouton was not among those singled out by Jefferson.

certain élan to American cooking, causing, as it did, the annexation of New Orleans. When the French had settled Louisiana, they brought with them a love and appreciation of good food that commingled with Spanish, African-American, and Native American culture, resulting in a vibrant Creole cuisine that has never been lost. Even though Louisiana was no longer part of France, French chefs didn't stop migrating to New Orleans during Jefferson's reign in the White House; they imparted an elegance and finesse to New Orleans cuisine.

It wasn't long before the French chefs made their way to New York City as well. In 1832 a French restaurant called Delmonico's that would be around for more than 150 years opened in New York, paving the way for a formidable French presence in kitchens all around the city. French chefs went to San Francisco also: Following the Gold Rush in 1849, gold-mining money demanded the finest haute cuisine. The prosperous citizens established a high level of culinary sophistication—a San Francisco tradition that endures today.

In the mid-nineteenth century, game was as important in American food as it had been to the colonists. The New York game market proffered a splendid array of wild turkeys, ducks, geese, pigeons, deer, bear, and raccoon. An Englishman visiting New York reported in his *A Diary in America,* published in 1839, that the food served in private homes in the "principal cities" of the United States was as fine as that in Paris or London.

Americans at this time were justifiably proud of their cuisine. When Samuel Clemens (a.k.a. Mark Twain) visited Europe in 1878, his reaction was opposite to Thomas Jefferson's: He complained bitterly about the food, comparing it most unfavorably to American fare. Before returning home, he composed a wish list of comestibles he desired upon his return, including Virginia bacon, soft-shell crabs, Philadelphia terrapin soup, canvas-back duck from Baltimore, Connecticut shad, green corn on the ear, butter beans, asparagus, string beans, American butter (he complained that European butter had no salt); predictably, apple pie, and curiously, frogs. (Who's calling whom a frog?)

The emergence of industrial canning signaled the beginning of the end of American gastronomy as it had been known. It played an important role in deciding what Americans would eat in the mid-nineteenth century; before the century's end, American eating habits would be completely changed.

The first patent for tin cans was taken out in 1825. When the Civil War broke out in 1860, canned foods became important for sustaining the troops; after the war, returning soldiers asked their wives to serve them the canned vegetables, such as peas and tomatoes, to which they had become accustomed during wartime. Canned foods now became status symbols, since they meant one could eat things out of season or locale, a luxury previously reserved only for the very wealthy. If tin cans broadened many people's culinary horizons by introducing them to new fruits (such as pineapples) and vegetables (tomatoes were newly popular), it simultaneously took Americans another step away from eating farm-fresh or garden-fresh produce, taking American cookery down a notch. The Mason jar was invented in mid-century, encouraging a home-canning mania, and major improvements in commercial canning in the 1870s made canned food commonplace for the first time in American homes.

Gastronomy was dealt another inadvertent blow in the 1870s, when bacteria was discovered, for the discovery led to a health craze that was detrimental to the cause of good eating.

In 1876 one Dr. John Harvey Kellogg, a vegetarian, natural foods advocate, and Seventh Day Adventist, opened the Battle Creek Sanitorium in Battle Creek, Michigan. Dyspeptic Americans flocked to it. Twenty-six years later, the now-famous Kellogg summed up his attitude toward food rather succinctly: "The decline of a nation commences," he said, "when gourmandizing begins."

Kellogg ardently believed in roughage, especially bran, and he insisted that Americans should not be eating meat for breakfast, as was the custom, but rather grains. To that end, he created a breakfast cereal in 1877 made of mixed grains and called it "Granola"; the invention of corn flakes followed in 1893. Inevitably, Kellogg turned American breakfast habits upside-down—which no doubt sounds relatively innocuous, except that gastronomically speaking, Cheerios, America's biggest-selling cereal today, is . . . well, it's not exactly an epicurean delight. And there actually exists a sizable population in this country that eats breakfast cereal for dinner, mostly for convenience's sake. Americans have increased their dinnertime cereal consumption approximately 30 percent from 1988 to 1997.

Another health faddist around the turn of the century, Horace Fletcher, advocated chewing food excessively—each bite, he insisted, should be chewed a hundred times. Philosopher William James and his brother, author Henry James, were among his adherents, though Henry was more convinced by Fletcherism than was his more sensible older brother.

Around the same time, in the late 1880s, a Wesleyan University chemist named Wilbur Olin Atwater brought the existence of calories and nutrients to the attention of the American public; he published tables of the nutritive values of a wide variety of foods, including the amounts of protein, fat, carbohydrates, and calories they contained. These tables were published by the Department of Agriculture in 1895. As far as Atwater was concerned, Americans' palates were the greatest barrier to their good health; we'd all be better off, he argued, if we paid no attention to our palates whatsoever. Atwater's legacy was that Americans learned to see food not as the source of pleasure, but instead merely as sustenance and fuel.

In this atmosphere, a Domestic Science movement sprung up, aiming to codify cooking and meal planning, eliminating spontaneity. Meals now became menu-driven, with the goal of providing a certain number of calories with plenty of attention to vitamins and other nutrients. The demands of the palate were shunted aside. "Elaborate methods of food preparation and dazzling combinations of ingredients were anathema to those who wanted to develop easy recipes whose nutritional content could be calculated," wrote Harvey Levenstein. "Since even the most imaginative cook would have trouble inventing more than a few truly unique dishes, let alone a whole new cuisine, the home economists naturally fell back on what they knew: a variant of the British cuisine dominant in New England before the upper classes began experimenting with French cuisine."

The New England Puritan esthetic came into ascendancy as the scientific food movement gained power at the end of the century; food magazines and cooking teachers emerged from the movement and the esthetic was disseminated throughout the country. "This was the era that made American cooking American," wrote food historian Laura Shapiro in *Perfection Salad,* "transforming a nation of honest appetites into an obedient market for instant mashed potatoes."

The basic tenet of the Domestic Science movement was that cooking (and indeed all of household management) could be approached "scientifically." This included the idea that household economics could (and should) be managed; charts were published on exactly what a housewife should prepare and serve over the course of a week in order to spend a specific amount of money (which represented a specific percentage of one's income) while ingesting the ideal amount of each nutrient. It was a real dollars-into-calories equation. "Peas and beans are the most nutritious of vegetables," wrote *The Boston Cooking School Magazine* in 1899, "containing as much carbon as wheat and double the amount of muscle-forming food." Another tip, under the heading "Diet of the Aged," suggests: "Bread should be toasted, whenever possible, as by doing this the starch is converted into sugar, and already partly digested." One is reminded of the greatest culinary killjoy in all of literature, Mr. Woodhouse in Jane Austen's novel *Emma,* whose favorite dish was thin gruel.

The Domestic Science movement was nothing if not an anal-retentive approach to homemaking and health. Its proponents seemed to believe that if a strict order could be superimposed over cooking, eating, and cleaning, one's whole life (and probably one's psyche) would be in better order. The movement's mascot, Fannie Farmer, author of the *Boston Cooking-School Cook Book,* was the first author to popularize standardized measurements in cooking, for which achievement she was dubbed "the mother of level measurement."

One of the legacies of the Domestic Science movement was home economics classes in public schools—a tradition that still continues and one that for the better part of a century has operated to the detriment of gastronomy. The approach of home economics was quite precise and antiseptic; not surprisingly, it has long had the effect of turning girls (and at some point, boys) off of cooking.

Just as Dr. Kellogg was urging people to eat bran, the rail system throughout the United States had just made enormous strides, contributing to the changing eating habits of Americans. Milk, meat, fruit, and vegetables, for the first time, were now transported to the cities from outlying farm areas, and even from faraway parts of the country. Refrigerated cars had just been put in use; the first boxcar of fresh fruit was shipped from California to the East Coast in 1869.

In 1894 the eighteen-year-old W. Atlee Burpee Company introduced iceberg lettuce, in answer to the long-running challenge of shipping tastier, more perishable varieties of lettuce. Before this, lettuce's fragility and perishability had made it expensive, accessible only to the relatively wealthy or those who could get it straight from the farm. Although the development of iceberg made lettuce available to the wider public, it was a dark day so far as American salads were concerned. And the old habit of eating what was fresh and local was rapidly disappearing.

At the century's end, a New Jersey canner had the idea to market condensed soups, and a brand was born in 1897 that would supplant homemade sauces and soups in America's kitchens, in large part, for the next century. Campbell's soup became so popular that by 1965 Andy Warhol was moved to paint the Campbell's tomato soup can over and over again as an icon of popular American culture. One wonders how many times undiluted Campbell's cream of mushroom soup passed for sauce in the 1950s alone.

In 1898 a young man named Henry J. Heinz started marketing bottled horseradish innocently enough, but another one of his "57 varieties" was tomato ketchup, the ingredient that has probably done more to blunt the palates of young Americans than any other in history. Most Americans don't think of ketchup as a sweet, but it's loaded with high-fructose corn syrup. In 1911, Fannie Farmer undertook to ruin the recipe for French dressing in this country by adding to it a spoonful of ketchup. Yes, it is she we can thank for that sweet orange goop.

This is not to imply that I, as an upstanding American, do not love ketchup. In fact my father's side of the family—good Midwestern Jews named Cohen—included a bottle of Heinz ketchup in their self-styled family crest (the other symbols were a poker hand of seven queens, symbolizing the seven sisters' penchant for cards; two women back-to-back, as the sisters frequently argued*; and a rack of women's clothing). A can of salmon stood next to the ketchup bottle because that was the family's seafood of choice. To the Cohen family, the definition of a good restaurant was one that had Heinz ketchup on the table. But obviously the Cohens weren't the only ones: Tomato ketchup was the top-selling condiment in the United States for most of the century, until it was overtaken by salsa in 1996.

Even ardent gastronomes can be guilty of ketchup worship today. An article in the high-toned food magazine *Saveur* in 1995 examined its production and rhapsodized over its deep tomato flavor ("It's got many of the attributes we'd all like to have: it's rich, bright, popular, dependable, adaptable, and well-respected.") and *Bon Appétit* celebrated all its glories in its November 1997 issue. We've come so far, and yet . . .

With fear of germs on the rise, bland purity became the ideal by the 1920s. Crisco shortening became a hot item, and a Crisco cookbook was even published. Home economists who were fond of white sauce were in luck. ". . . Finally," wrote Shapiro, "a pure and tasteless white sauce could be prepared by melting two tablespoons of Crisco, adding two tablespoons of flour, and stirring in a cup of milk." She concluded:

> With the Crisco white sauce, scientific cookery arrived at a food substance from which virtually everything had been stripped except a certain number of

*Across the top ran the motto *"Non valorium disputandum . . . non valorium est."*—"If it's not worth fighting about, it's not worth anything."

> nutrients and the color white. Only a cuisine molded by technology could prosper on such developments, and it prospered very well.

Ironically, the book that would kick-start the American food revolution half a century later, *Mastering the Art of French Cooking* by Julia Child, Simone Beck, and Louisette Bertholle, depends on vegetable shortening (what else but Crisco?) for its *pâte brisée* (pastry crust) recipe. Crisco would never make its way into a respectable pastry crust in France, but it had such a hold on American consumers that Julia must have felt compelled to use it.

The nation was headed toward homogenization in its cuisine. "The same forces—improvements in transportation, preservation, and distribution—liberating Americans from seasonality also continued to free them from the dictates of regional geography," notes historian Levenstein.

> Milk, cheese, and green vegetables poured into the South from the Mid-Atlantic states and Midwest. Practically the entire nation was blanketed with immature citrus fruits and indestructible iceberg lettuce from southern California, canned fish and vegetables from central and northern California, canned tomatoes and peas from New Jersey, Wisconsin cheese, western beef, midwestern ham and sausage, Florida oranges, Hawaiian pineapple, Central American bananas, and Cuban sugar. The shelves of an A&P in Louisville, Kentucky were hardly distinguishable from the shelves of one in Utica, New York, or Sacramento, California.

If health crazes, strides in canning, and the development of the rail system sent American cooking toward its decline, the advent of National Prohibition in 1920 finished the job. The Eighteenth amendment to the Constitution made it illegal to sell or transport alcohol; it also made it impossible for restaurants, which always depended on sales of wine and liquor to turn profits, to survive. All across the United States, they folded. With no stellar restaurants to further the cause, American gastronomy, weakened as it was, didn't stand a chance of surviving in any meaningful way.

Nor could American cuisine be recharged by influxes of new immigrants: Xenophobic immigration policies had already been enacted by the turn of the century, and in 1924 further restrictions closed off immigration almost entirely. The massive flow of immigration that had made this country so culturally vibrant throughout its history was cut off at its source, cutting off the possibility too of any foodways new to the United States.

By the time Prohibition was repealed in 1933, the Depression would have made it impossible for Americans to spend significant amounts of money in restaurants anyway. Now American gastronomy had been worked over to such a degree that it barely existed. General Foods introduced Birds Eye frozen vegetables to the market in 1930; scientist Clarence Birdseye had been developing them since he accidentally discovered, while ice fishing in Labrador, that a fish that froze immediately after being caught was delicious when thawed and cooked weeks later. (He soon learned that the Inuits purposely buried their catch in ice to preserve it.) While on one hand, frozen food offered home cooks a better alternative to canned foods, it was to become a regular, though often unnecessary, substitute for fresh food.

Six years later, there was a glimmer of gustatory hope in the form of the 1939 World's Fair in New York City. The restaurant in the French pavilion, headed up by director Henri Soulé, was eagerly attended by legions of New Yorkers and other visitors. Not only did the French pavilion spawn the famous New York City restaurant Le Pavillon, but it also brought young culinary talent (particularly French) into Gotham's restaurant kitchens.

Oddly enough, the advent of World War II offered another ray of hope. Since the war effort sapped the supply of canned goods, American consumers were urged to replace the lost canned foods in their diets by planting "victory gardens." The idea took hold in a big way: 20 million victory gardens produced 40 percent of the vegetables Americans consumed during the war. Among those who planted one were Pat and Margaret Waters, whose daughter Alice would go on to found Chez Panisse thirty years later. Suddenly the cultivation of produce (which incidentally happened to be far superior to its processed cousins) became a patriotic duty. In 1945 American consumption of vegetables hit a record high. I happened to ask my mother recently, in the presence of her best friend, if she had known anyone with a victory garden. "Sure," she said. "We had one." It seems that in Kearny, New Jersey, where she grew up, her father started one in an empty lot in the neighborhood when he got back from his wartime post in Fort Dix. It functioned as a community garden, worked by a number of neighbors, supplying them with peppers, corn, radishes, carrots, and so on. My mother's friend told me that her family had one too, in Boston.

The gardening boom, in the meantime, opened people's minds to vegetables they weren't accustomed to eating—broccoli, eggplant, and squash, for instance—and this new adventurousness was reinforced by returning soldiers who had experienced foreign cuisines abroad and wanted their everyday repertoires expanded as well.

Few had ever heard of pizza, for instance, before the war, but the American troops who had discovered it in Italy brought back home such a fondness for it that by 1948, it was already an American favorite.

Still, in the 1950s, the general state of American gastronomy continued to worsen.

The TV dinner made its debut in 1953. By the time I was eight years old—fifteen years later—it was an entrenched institution. I still remember my favorite, Swanson's Meat Loaf, quite clearly: two slices of meat that almost seemed to be predigested, smothered with sticky-sweet tomato sauce; a pile of little Tater Tots in the upper right-hand corner; a serving of dead string beans in the left, and in the top center, a "brownie." As far as I was concerned, the fact that someone at Swanson's figured out how to package string beans with the same cooking time as a brownie was the ultimate achievement of food technology.

The American housewife had been thoroughly persuaded, by this point, that cooking was a drag; new convenience foods offered a no-muss, no-fuss solution. Produce from the farm was now a distant memory for most Americans; farmers markets were a disappearing breed, and vegetable gardening, for most, became too quaint. The quality of vegetables and fruits that one could find in the now-ubiquitous supermarket was pitiable; farming had become so industrialized that concerns of shelf life and transport now overrode those of flavor and texture. Fruits and vegetables, which the consumer no longer thought of as products of the earth, but rather as perfect objects forming geometrical displays in the spotless supermarket, now had to look good. Softball-sized oranger-than-orange oranges, shiny bright Red Delicious apples, unblemished hard yellow-green bananas, tight bright heads of iceberg lettuce, perfect waxy cucumbers, and uniform green peppers all beckoned from their meticulous displays. But the flavor had disappeared.

As if that weren't bad enough, it was at about the same time that the nation's top restaurants—including Boston's renowned Locke-Ober's—began to use frozen foods.

And finally, Ray Kroc opened the first McDonald's franchise in Des Plaines, Illinois, in 1955. (The original drive-in restaurant was opened by the McDonald brothers, Richard and Maurice, in 1948 in San Bernadino, California.) Soon McDonald's would define American eating habits both within and outside of our borders.

"*Et pour madame . . . un* hahm-beur-gheur???"

2

WHY JULIA CHILD CAPTURED OUR IMAGINATION

DESPITE THE SORRY STATE OF AMERICAN GASTRONOMY in the mid-1950s, something better had started simmering beneath Americans' conformist and palate-deadening entertaining habits. Homogenous *Joy of Cooking* repasts were the norm, while cocktail and patio parties provided comic relief—perfect for a culture that embraced Frank Sinatra and Bobby Darin, Kool-Aid and Jell-O. Entertaining meant throwing cocktail parties or meat on the barbecue. The esthetic was a little cuckoo—pineapple centerpieces stuck all over with toothpicks and geegaws; pupu platters; anything flambé. In those years, the marshmallow reigned as queen and the maraschino cherry king. Rumaki—chicken liver and a water chestnut wrapped in bacon and broiled—was considered a chic hors d'oeuvre.

In what lay the appeal of the barbecue? In 1953, *Esquire's Handbook for Hosts* sung its praises as a boon to casual entertaining, as well as to families averse to "sitting primly at table for a staid and sober, indoor, formal meal." But *Esquire* continued in an even more telling vein:

> Another weighty vote is cast by the lady who usually presides in the kitchen. She gets damned tired of preparing and planning three meals a day for her family, and who can blame her if she approaches the routine task with no visible sign of rapture. Cooking, to her, is no longer an adventure. It's a chore, and she's sick of it. With the installation of a barbecue grill or fireplace, however, she enjoys a frequent respite from the normal kitchen drudgery.

In fact, there was little to inspire the homemaker in the kitchen. Popular cookbooks on the whole were rather dull: Beside the obligatory *Joy of Cooking* in every new bride's trousseau, *Betty Crocker's Picture Cookbook* sold well—more than 3 million copies from 1950 to 1955. These books did little to spark much excitement in the kitchen, nor did women's magazines, which focused on convenience rather than experimentation or adventure.

James Beard, meanwhile, stoked the fires of the outdoor cooking craze with his books *Cook It Outdoors,* which had been published in 1941, *Jim Beard's Barbecue Cooking* (1954); *The Complete Book of Outdoor Cookery,* written with Helen Evans Brown, an important California cookbook author, and published in 1955; and later, *James Beard's Treasury of Outdoor Cooking* (1960). Beard's books were serious enough: *The Complete Book of Outdoor Cookery* included a chapter on grilling game and one on grilling vegetables that presaged a 1990s trend. Outdoor cooking, of course, was the only kind of home cooking that any self-respecting man of the period would be caught dead doing, something *Esquire's Handbook for Hosts* chalked up to the incipient pyromaniac boy in every man; perhaps it had even more to do with a certain sense of adventure and fun that men felt was their due if they were to perform the otherwise lowly art of cooking. Women simply didn't allow it to themselves.

When it came to eating out, after World War II, people were in the mood to have fun. But as restaurateur Joseph Baum, who began working in the restaurant business at the time, remembered, "People didn't have anywhere to go because there was no travel yet. The world was sort of bombed out in great measure, and there was this enormous surge of resort business"—in Florida and California, for instance. Luxury trains such as the Florida Champion and the Silver Meteor came into ascendance at this time as well, offering elegant white tablecloth meals in their dining cars. "So there was all this bubbling," said Baum, "without anything specific yet. It was when the French chef was not the king; he was the emperor." Yet there was something unformed about Americans' attempts to dine. "People were making love, but not truly," recalled Baum. "And this beginning dating began to be boring. It was *boring*. Techniques were bastardized; there wasn't enough sincerity; there wasn't enough imagination. There wasn't enough of anything."

By 1957—a time when Beef Stroganoff was the height of elegance dining in or out—American restaurant cooking had sunk to its nadir. In September of that year, the headline of a *New York Times* article announced "Future of Chefs Is Served Up as Woe; Food Experts Find Few Taking Up Art." A spokesman for the American Culinary Federation complained, "There was a notion among youths that there was no glamour or excitement in cooking." The problem was that few Americans wanted to take whisk in hand in order to earn a living, and the supply of chefs coming over from Europe had dwindled. On top of everything else, in April 1959, *The New York Times* ran an article by its restaurant critic, Craig Claiborne, on its front page, bemoaning the death of elegance in cuisine. All the French chefs in the country were getting old, the argument ran, with the notable exception of Pierre Franey, who had recently left Henri Soulé's paragon of French food, Le Pavillon, which was then widely considered to be the best restaurant in the country.* Young chefs weren't coming up through the ranks to replace them. The whole culinary landscape looked pretty bleak. Le Pavillon and two or three other establishments aside, "Polynesian" restaurants such as Don the Beachcomber and The Luau in Los Angeles, and Trader Vic's in Oakland and San Francisco (and later in Beverly Hills, New York, Chicago, and all over the world) were about as serious as most people aspired to.

It seemed there was little hope of American gastronomy maintaining its already eroded standing, let alone improving.

What happened to change all that?

For starters, Julia Child happened.

But before Julia could mince and stir and sauté her way into our hearts, America had to be ready for her. After all, she and co-authors Simone Beck and Louisette Bertholle had to wait ten years to publish their seminal tome *Mastering the Art of French Cooking,* which was finally brought out in 1961 by Knopf after being rejected by its erstwhile publisher Houghton-Mifflin. Before America could embrace

---

*In their 1972 book *The Taste of America,* John L. Hess and Karen Hess took issue with the idea that Pierre Franey was a chef worthy of his exalted reputation, pointing out that before working at Le Pavillon his previous job was as Executive Chef of Howard Johnson's chain of restaurants. When Franey defended the practice, presumably common in restaurants, in the 1960s and 1970s, of using frozen foods, and stated in an interview that if he were still at Le Pavillon, he'd make large batches of sauces and freeze them, Hess and Hess wrote, "It may be doubted that the late Henri Soulé would have allowed Franey to do anything of the kind."

Julia to the tune of 100,000 copies in its first year of publication, the atmosphere had to be more conducive to Americans accepting cooking as something other than drudgery.

Meanwhile, as much of suburban America was caught up in its world of Formica and melmac, barbecues and tuna casseroles, another part of America was quickly growing in sophistication.

Culturally, few times in American history were as exciting and important as the period just after World War II, especially in the arts. In jazz, Charlie Parker played at the top of his game in 1947, treating fans at New York's Royal Roost to the wild improvisations of Bebop. Thirty-year-old Dizzy Gillespie, another Bopper, had his own big band by 1947. That same year saw the beginnings of Miles Davis's "birth of the cool," and by 1952 West Coast jazz took off in Los Angeles with Gerry Mulligan, Stan Getz, Chet Baker, and Art Pepper. By the mid-1950s Art Blakey, Horace Silver, and others would bring in hard bop, and in the meantime, John Coltrane had joined Miles Davis's group, Charles Mingus swung his groundbreaking music that foreshadowed free jazz, and Ornette Coleman came along two years later with his "Free Jazz" album.

In painting, the term "Abstract Expressionism" was coined in 1946; the Museum of Modern Art had moved to its present location the year before. In fact much of the excitement in art would happen in New York. Jackson Pollock painted at the height of his powers in the mid-1950s until he was killed in a car crash in 1956. Mark Rothko wowed the art world by reducing his worldview to a disc and a blob divided by a line, Willem De Kooning had returned to complete abstraction, and Robert Motherwell, Franz Kline, Adolph Gottleib, Robert Rauschenberg, and Jasper Johns—among many others—were all breaking new visual ground.

The clean, modern lines of the "international" school of architecture, with its flat roofs and expansive windows, were on the rise, with Philip Johnson's Glass House in New Caanan, Connecticut completed in 1948; Skidmore, Owings, and Merrill's Lever House office building went up in New York City in 1952. Frank Lloyd Wright worked on the Guggenheim Museum from 1956 through 1959, and Mies van der Rohe and Philip Johnson completed their important Seagram Building in Manhattan in 1958.

American literature couldn't have been more alive. William Faulkner won the Nobel Prize in 1949. The Beat Generation emerged in the next ten years: Allen Ginsberg wrote "Howl" in 1956, and Jack Kerouac published *On the Road* the following year; William Burroughs came out with *Naked Lunch* in 1959. Beat poets read their work at City Lights bookstore in San Francisco; Lenny Bruce delivered his sharp-witted routine at Ann's 440 Club just across the street.

The theater thrived as well. Cheryl Crawford, Elia Kazan and Robert Lewis founded the Actors Studio in 1947; Lee Strasberg joined them in 1948. Their "method acting" would find adherents in Paul Newman, Joanne Woodward, Montgomery Clift, Geraldine Page, and many others. Tennessee Williams's *A Streetcar Named Desire* went on Broadway in 1947, with a film version in 1951; *Cat on a Hot Tin Roof, The Glass Menagerie,* and *Sweet Bird of Youth* followed.

After a history of presenting primarily light entertainment, Hollywood—in trouble with the Justice Department for monopolistic practices and beleaguered by McCarthyism and a blacklist—turned more serious. Although it continued producing frivolous musicals and other escapist fare, in the 1950s it also gave us such important films as *Sunset Boulevard, On the Waterfront, East of Eden, The Manchurian Candidate,* and *Rebel Without a Cause,* satisfying American audiences' cravings for something more substantial.

So in the 1950s, Americans' Jell-O and luau mind-set coexisted with increasing cultural sophistication that included an appreciation of things foreign and, most important, an opening up of the American cultural imagination and a terrific optimism.

It was in this cultural climate that a number of innovative restaurants sprung up.

Forum of the Twelve Caesars opened in New York in 1957 in Rockefeller Center's U.S. Rubber Building; James Beard's biographer Robert Clark wrote that there, "food had indeed attained nearly epic seriousness." Despite a theme that seems kitsch in retrospect, Forum was the first really important restaurant to come along since Le Pavillon. Owned by a company called Restaurant Associates, and masterminded by its thirty-seven-year-old president Jerome Brody and vice-president Joseph Baum, Forum offered such specialties as "The Oysters of Hercules, 'which you with sword will carve,' " "Oysters in Senate Dress," "Fresh Truffles Herculaneum—Prepared 'Under the Ashes,' " "Fiddler Crab Lump A LA NERO—Flaming, of course," "Partridge BRITTANICUS—aflame in Gin and Juniper Berries, FORUM GAME SAUCE." A note at the bottom of the game section of the menu advised "Since the local 'Sumptuary Laws' have limited the netting of the Pink Flamingo, Lark, Thrush, et cetera—more than the usual number of days are required for our netmen to accomplish their task. The noble Peacock, however, is now arrived and our Archimigarius and his kitcheners stand ready with one of the most delightful recipes of their ARS COQUINARIA." The regular menu did, however, offer wild fowl of Samos, capon, "baby gosling" [sic], pheasant, quail, Scotch grouse, Mallard duck, venison, and alpine snow hare, all served with "maize" and wild berries.

Although one wonders reading the menu whether Forum took itself seriously, Joe Baum insisted much of it was in the spirit of hilarity. "We wanted to do something with a touch of humor," he told me in a recent interview on the 106th floor of the World Trade Center, where until his death in the fall of 1998 he reigned over a small restaurant empire that includes the enormous Windows on the World complex. If the choice of ancient Rome as a theme seems odd for a serious restaurant, it's interesting to note the serendipitous circumstances that gave birth to it. Baum said that because the restaurant was to be located in Rockefeller Center, a hub of communications—television, radio, advertising, and publishing were all represented there—Brody and Baum agreed that the theme of the restaurant should reflect that world. Accordingly, they came up with the idea of a "forum." In the meantime, William Pahlmann, the interior designer with whom they worked, had recently stumbled onto twelve huge seventeenth-century portraits of the Caesars of the Roman Empire that he felt would work wonderfully in a restaurant. Voilà—the concept was born.

And the kooky theme didn't exactly exist in a vacuum: Although serious films were finally being made in Hollywood, Technicolor casts-of-thousands extravaganzas were far more popular, and the flavor of the decade was the ancient world. MGM released director Mervyn LeRoy's *Quo Vadis?* in 1951; Victor Mature paraded around grandly in the first CinemaScope feature, 1953's Roman centurion epic *The Robe*; Cecil B. DeMille's *The Ten Commandments* was released in 1956. The Roman epic was picking up steam as Forum of the Twelve Caesars opened in 1957, and in fact the restaurant staff attended educational screenings of *Quo Vadis?,* in addition to taking in a Hunter College professor's lectures on Roman history and culture. Releases of the films *Ben Hur, Spartacus, Cleopatra,* and *The Greatest Story Ever Told* followed. The ancient Rome craze culminated in 1966 with the opening of the spectacular Caesar's Palace hotel in Las Vegas.

Roman epics notwithstanding, California had its mind elsewhere as far as gastronomy was concerned. Aware Inn opened in Los Angeles the same year as Forum, offering dishes such as filet of sole amandine, quiche Lorraine, and a gussied-up hamburger dubbed the "Swinger." Barbara Pascal, a native Angeleno, remembers eating there in 1963 or 1964. "It was a huge treat," she told me in an interview. "Very bohemian, very new and different, the harbinger of things to come." Southern California already had the Ranch House in Ojai (near Santa Barbara), where chef/owner (not a commonly used phrase in those days) Alan Hooker had been preparing single-seating dinners for an appreciative cult following that was awed by his use of herbs from his own garden in his cooking. Pascal, who recalls dining there in 1958, described her dinner, which included a crab dish with avocado and cream sauce, as "beyond belief wonderful." Still, Hooker, in his own words "a reformed vegetarian," recounted in his 1966 cookbook that when The Ranch House opened in 1950, Beef Stroganoff was the first meat dish he chose to tackle as a cook. If the choice seemed serious then, today it seems quaint. He couldn't help but confess, however, "Since I had never tasted Beef Stroganoff I had only my own ideas to go on, and so could not imitate." The choice of recipes and their conception revealed a cook who hadn't traveled or eaten widely and was really feeling his way.

Hooker's cookbook is an odd admixture of the very forward looking and the horrifically retro: A recipe for Chicken Poached in Champagne, for instance, calls for 4 leaves of lemon verbena ground in a mortar with other fresh herbs, salt, pepper, and—believe it or not—MSG. In fact many of his recipes, including most of the soups, call for MSG. Other recipes call for ingredients that would offend most modern serious cooks' sensibilities: beef extract, vegetable cubes, chicken cubes, canned tomato juice, Ortega brand canned red chili sauce, canned mushroom soup, red and green food coloring, frozen orange juice concentrate. At the same time, he advocated mincing garlic or crushing it with a mortar and pestle rather than using a press, and relied heavily on "silantro"* [sic] and fresh ginger, shallots, leeks—and even pineapple guavas.

La Côte Basque opened in New York City in 1959, and that was just the beginning of a string of classic French restaurant openings there: La Caravelle opened in 1960, Lutèce in 1961, and La Grenouille in 1962—and all are still open today. During and after World War II, French cooks had flocked to New York, opening bistros right and left, besides the fact that Le Pavillon helped seed New York City with a stream of French chefs and cooks for years and years.

Even more significantly, Four Seasons, which had ownership by Restaurant Associates in common with Forum of the Twelve Caesars, opened in 1959. Craig Claiborne, who had been hired two years earlier as the *New York Times*'s restaurant critic, called the Four Seasons "perhaps the most exciting restaurant to open in New York within the last two decades."†

A large part of what made the Four Seasons exciting was its architecture and design. Mies van der Rohe and Philip Johnson were the design architects of the Seagram Building that housed it, Philip Johnson the architect of the restaurant,

---

*Oddly, Hooker's cookbook distinguishes between two herbs, "silantro" and "culantro," which "though related in flavor, are not the same." Culantro he identifies as Spanish parsley, describing the seeds as being "the same as our coriander," and producing "a plant that is feathery and has a flower something like Queen Anne's lace." His recipe for guacamole requires 8 silantro leaves or 2 culantro leaves. He was apparently unaware that he was simply calling the same herb by two names.

†James Beard was under owner Joseph Baum's employ at the time as a wine consultant for Restaurant Associates.

and once again Brody and Baum engaged William Pahlmann for the interior design. With its dramatic yet soothing twenty-foot-square marble pool, outsized windows, and ceiling-high ornamental fig trees in the main "Pool Room," Richard Lippold sculpture floating over the bar in the "Grill Room," impressive Picasso stage curtain in one entry and Joan Miró tapestries in the lobby, Eero Saarinen–designed chairs in the ladies' lounge, and dining room chairs designed by Johnson, van der Rohe, and Charles Eames, never before had America seen a restaurant like it—so modern, stark, elegant. In fact four decades later, the restaurant design still feels modern.

Four Seasons was the first important serious *American* restaurant.

Like The Ranch House, fresh herbs set Four Seasons apart, for "Although herbs are used increasingly throughout America," Claiborne wrote, "they are not employed frequently in a fresh state." Four Seasons also offered its patrons wild mushrooms such as cèpes, morels, and chanterelles, which most Americans had never heard of. James Beard, in a letter to Helen Evans Brown, called it "the first really seasonal restaurant, where things are searched out all over the world." Says Michael Whiteman (who was Joseph Baum's partner in recent years), "If you go back and read the menu and you know the history enough, you know that people had their first cherry tomatoes at the Four Seasons; they had their first baby avocados in the Four Seasons; they had their first snow peas in the Four Seasons. . . . Wild flowers that were edible in the Four Seasons. And so there was this emphasis on product as opposed to the emphasis in a French restaurant, which is on *'cuisine'* and sauce." In fact a look at the Four Seasons's first spring menu turns up Periwinkles Mignonette, Prosciutto or Smithfield Ham and New Figs, Virginia

Blue Crab Lump, Calamondin* Crêpes with Ham Mousse, Consommé with Green Wheat, Muscat Consommé, Bisque of Smelts, Danish Plum Soup, The Queen's Grouse, Blackberries and Beignets, Nasturtium Leaves, Avocado with Sliced White Radish, Mangetouts, Dandelion and Egg, Stuffed Green Almonds en Brochette (a dessert), Primrose Beignets, Rose Petal Parfait, Kumquat Ice Cream, and Tea Granita with Lime (how nineties!). The fall menu offered Fall Terrine of Hare with Pistachios; Large Chincoteagues [oysters]; Chanterelles in Artichoke Coupe, Mornay; Grouse Roasted Rare—Traditional English Sauces; Autumn Gosling, Rosemary Leaves, for Two; Green Gage Plums in Almond Cream, California Teleme cheese, and Violets in Summer Snow.

Unlike California's Ranch House, Four Seasons had a trained executive chef: Swiss-born Albert Stockli. It was especially important that Four Seasons was not a French restaurant. The menu, like Forum's, was in English—but at Four Seasons there was no joke attached. And calling oneself an "American" restaurant in those days wasn't an asset; on the contrary, it was a liability, so doing so was a brave move.

Whiteman points out that Four Seasons was important in another way: "That was the beginning of the notion of restaurants having things grown for them, which the Four Seasons did," he says. Thirteen years later, when Alice Waters would open Chez Panisse, she'd be hailed as revolutionary for doing the same thing. "Our field greens are selected each morning and will vary daily," announced the Four Seasons menu. Presented to diners to select from a bounteous cart, many of the vegetables had been picked only that morning.

Yet if Four Seasons was ambitious, apparently it wasn't quite perfect: Claiborne complained of its use of iceberg

*A miniature orange

lettuce, pointing out that "Oak leaf lettuce, cos salad and Bibb are now available in this area." (Could they have been sold out of field salad that day? Perhaps customers requested iceberg?)

And the dish Claiborne singled out as the best? Beef Stroganoff. But the well-traveled Stockli was no Alan Hooker when it came to beef stroganoff: "I believe in making stroganoff the way they make it in Russia," *Fortune* magazine quoted him as saying in 1960, "and coq au vin as they prepare it in Paris."

Part of what happened in the 1950s was tied up with America's middle-class social mores—specifically, keeping up with the Joneses. The reigning image was that of the dutiful (and beautiful) housewife who could throw together a delicious spread at the drop of a fedora, when her husband called at four to announce he was bringing the boss home for dinner. Americans wanted to get ahead, and in those days it was actually possible. The postwar economy was strong, jobs plentiful, and climbing the ladder socially and materially was the order of the day. No longer was one satisfied with a chicken in every pot; there had to be cheese in every fondue set and two cars in the garage. As part of the ethos, one had to walk the walk and talk the talk—and perform in the kitchen for the boss.

The new economic prosperity, as well as the availability of commercial transcontinental air flights, began to make it easier for Americans to travel long distances, and travel they did—usually to Europe. France was a very popular destination, and if it wasn't accessible to every member of the middle class, it certainly held allure for anyone who could afford it. Paris became particularly chic in the late fifties, and soon Eiffel Towers, artist's palettes, and French poodles decorated everything from kitchen curtains to the circle skirts of bobby-soxers. *An American in Paris,* which had been released in 1951, and *To Catch a Thief,* which came out in 1955, went a long way in popularizing Francophilia; while the first international film festivals were born and art houses began to show foreign films for the first time. How many American teenage girls longed to be Jean Seaberg cavorting with Jean-Paul Belmondo in Jean-Luc Godard's new wave classic *Breathless*? Together with Audrey Hepburn and Leslie Caron, Seaberg brought the "gamine" look—pixie haircut, red lipstick, pedal-pushers or circle skirt, boatneck jersey, flats—to America. "I think France was the pinnacle of romanticized yearning for practically everyone who was in college," Judy Marcus, a retired high-school art teacher in Los Angeles, told me in an interview. Marcus herself was an art student at UCLA in the late 1950s; she recalled meeting the girl who would become her best friend, and who engendered in her an attraction to both France and good food:

> When I first met Joan I was eighteen, and she was nineteen and had just come back from living abroad. She lived mostly in France, a little bit in Morocco, too, but mostly in Paris. She had that really really straight silky blond hair with a fringe coming forward in front and a long ponytail. She wore a white men's shirt and a black full-circle long skirt just above her ankles and a really tight cinched belt and black flats. She looked very Parisian. I was very impressed with her.

As Americans became infatuated with France and things French, they began to try their hand at French cooking. If they were to spend all day in the kitchen making *duxelles* and whipping egg whites, they had to have someone to share their creations with, so they invited friends. People took pleasure in impressing each other with their endeavors;

and the competitive dinner party was born. Judy Marcus remembers skinning a goose, chopping it all up to make a forcemeat, and completely reassembling the whole thing in the shape of the bird; she also recalls attending a dinner party where the sister of architect Frank Gehry prepared an impressive cassoulet—a dish she'd never before tasted.

Never having traveled to Europe, Marcus and her friends had not eaten most of the dishes they were preparing; they dutifully followed recipes they found in French cookbooks or *Gourmet* magazine. How did they know the way the dishes were supposed to turn out? "If it tasted good," said Marcus, "you figured you'd done it the right way."

There were, at the time, a few good books to lead these intrepid fledgling Francophile cooks on their way—or at least put them in the mood. Samuel Chamberlain published *Bouquet de France: An Epicurean Tour of the French Provinces* in 1952; this book came out of a series of articles he had written and illustrated for *Gourmet,* which had been founded back in 1941. While *Bouquet de France* was not primarily a cookbook, it included a good number of authentic regional recipes, translated and adapted by Chamberlain's wife Narcissa. Also in 1952, Little, Brown had brought out James Beard's *Paris Cuisine,* a stylish volume based on recipes from Paris restaurants. (Incidentally, despite *Gourmet*'s presence on the market, in 1952 James Beard still thought there was a need for a "first-class food magazine.") In 1957, Waverly Root came out with *The Food of France.* Though not a cookbook, the food-centered travelogue created a cultural context for the dishes people were now cooking at home. *The Art of Eating,* the collection of five gastronomical works by M. F. K. Fisher, was published in 1954. It wasn't about France *per se,* but the work included enough references to France to feed the frenzied Francophilia.

★ ★ ★

While a certain segment of young, middle-class America was fixated on France and things French, James Beard (*Paris Cuisine* notwithstanding) had already become a champion of a different cause: American food. Besides his many books on barbecuing, fish cookery, hors d'oeuvre, and other subjects, the prolific author, journalist, and popular cooking teacher had also penned an important work, *The Fireside Cookbook,* in 1949. In this beautiful book, with its engaging, very American full-color illustrations by Alice and Martin Provensen, Beard offered recipes for Chicken Fricasee, American Style, Chicken Pie with a biscuit crust, Baked Beans, New England Style, Hashed Brown Potatoes, Pinto Bean Casserole, Jelly Roll, Old-Time Pound Cake, and the like, as well as a section on hams and one on American wines, with nods to Napa and Sonoma, as well as New York and Ohio(!).

Gourmet magazine gained popularity. It had been founded as an attempt to answer Americans' lack of knowledge of things gastronomic; its subtitle was (and still is) "The Magazine of Good Living." It purported to teach Americans, from its editorial offices atop the Plaza Hotel, how to live well, making the assumption that in order to live well one had to learn to eat well. By the late 1950s, *Gourmet* had become a sophisticated glossy with artfully photographed multicourse meals that piqued the American imagination. If no more than a handful of suddenly serious amateurs were preparing these feasts, legions were cooking vicariously, attempting a dish or two, and saving each issue.

This is not to say that *Gourmet* didn't have its detractors: In *An Alphabet for Gourmets,* M. F. K. Fisher lampooned would-be gastronomes who lived too much by the book: "They subscribe to *Gourmet* and its satellites," she wrote, "and even submit incredibly complicated recipes to the subeditors, which are discreetly rearranged before publication in some dutiful department as 'Letters to Our Chef.' They belong to local food-and-wine groups or their reasonable facsimiles, and bring back packages of musty filé powder from New Orleans, and order snails (packed, as a special inducement, with the shells wrapped separately) from a former maître d'hôtel who lives next to the airport in Lisbon. . . ."

One of *Gourmet*'s contributors was James Beard. Beard's first article appeared in 1942, and by 1948 he was a regular contributor. He very much wanted a staff job, and succeeded in landing one in the spring of 1949, as restaurant critic. An actor-turned-caterer-turned-cooking teacher/food journalist/cookbook author and the most visible food authority of the 1950s, James Beard attempted to bring his deep love of good food to the masses. According to Evan Jones's illuminating biography, *Epicurean Delight: The Life and Times of James Beard,* Beard's writing skills at the magazine weren't up to snuff; nevertheless, Beard supplied *Gourmet* with reviews and articles. By the mid-1950s he was known as the dean of American cooking. But in a typically Beardian turn of events, he lost the job less than a year later, ostensibly because he had committed a cardinal magazine sin. Returning from a press junket to five wine regions of France, Beard wrote almost identical copy for both *Gourmet* and another employer, the *Sherry Wine & Spirits* catalog, incurring the wrath of his boss Earl McAusland, the founding editor and publisher of the magazine. Beard wouldn't write for *Gourmet* again until the 1960s.

Beard had his hand in just about every angle of cooking and writing about food. He always had scads of projects going at the same time—he even wanted to open his own restaurant, scouting locations for years—and constantly struggled to scrape together enough money between his various gigs to keep himself fed in the manner to which he was accustomed.

Although the late James Beard remains a controversial

character since his fervent beliefs about food were so thoroughly mixed up with the aims of the various large food corporations for whom he worked as a spokesman, in today's culinary world James Beard has practically attained the statue of saint. (In fact, Jo Brans has called him "Saint Beard.") The Greenwich Village townhouse where he lived up until his death in 1985 has become the home of the James Beard Foundation, an organization that attracts chefs from all over the world to come and cook in his kitchen (which was renovated in 1990, when his notorious electric stoves were finally replaced by gas). The Foundation also bestows awards each year on chefs and food and wine writers, and throws itself a huge Oscars-style awards ceremony that is televised on the TV Food Network. Beard and the James Beard Foundation are spoken of with reverence by America's "foodie" community.

In fact, Beard represented not only what was the best in American cooking, but also the worst. At the same time that he was doing promotional work for Green Giant and Pillsbury, James Beard simultaneously offered Americans the notion, well ahead of its time—and in a recipe booklet for Green Giant, no less—that "No vegetable exists which is not better slightly undercooked." Beard was by no means the first to do so: Early American cooks such as Mary Randolph, author of *The Virginia House-Wife* (1824), recommended cooking vegetables briefly enough so that they retained a slight crunch. And in the first edition of *The Joy of Cooking,* Irma S. Rombauer counseled her readers to "Cook vegetables as short a time as possible. As soon as they are barely tender, drain them." However, it seems such proclamations should be taken with the proverbial grain of salt: A cooking chart on the facing page of Rombauer's book called for cooking green beans for thirty to thirty-five minutes. One can imagine how "barely tender" that left them.

For better or worse, Beard developed for Green Giant the butter sauce in which their frozen Le Sueur peas swim. (In my house, when I was growing up, these peas were a staple.) At the end of his memoir *Delights & Prejudices,* which he published in 1960, Beard described the way he liked to entertain friends at home, casually, and featuring foods not available in their own countries if they were from foreign lands. "Last year, for example," he wrote, "I had two friends from England to dinner who wished to sample the best of American beef. After a first course of razor clam bisque, made from the canned clams from Oregon and heavy cream, I served some succulent, grilled beef with tiny braised new potatoes and tiny French peas, which are now sold frozen with butter in bags, and delicious they are." This is Beard in a nutshell (or in a peapod, as it were): Although he advocated the freshest possible ingredients, he tried to impress guests with canned clams and frozen peas; in print he neglected to mention not only that he was paid by Green Giant for promotion, but also that he had created the recipe for the butter sauce.

Meanwhile, on the West Coast, one of *Gourmet* magazine's ardent fans in Sonoma, California, was feeling a little restless. In 1952 Chuck Williams was between jobs, so he did what any red-blooded American gourmand would have done at a time when transatlantic airfares were relatively inexpensive for the first time: He took a trip to Europe. Despite having served in the army, repairing aircraft in Eritrea, Iran, and India, he hadn't gotten a chance to see any "Continental" action where food was concerned—unlike the fellows stationed in France.

In France, he fell in love with the food and cookware; in Paris his favorite haunt was neither the galleries of the Louvre nor the nightclubs of Saint Germain des Prés, but rather the basement of the department store Bazar de l'Hôtel de Ville, "where mom and pop bistros bought their kitchen equipment." Though Williams had inherited a love of food and cooking from his grandmother during his childhood in Florida, his interest had somehow fallen away. But on arriving in Paris, the passion, unbidden, came back to him. "I was fascinated," he recalled when I interviewed him in 1995 as he was about to celebrate his eightieth birthday. Today Williams is a diminutive, wiry man with a runagate grin and twinkly blue eyes and as much energy as a Waring blender.

When he returned home to Sonoma, Williams, who never married, supported himself by building houses—entirely by himself, including plumbing and electricity—and reselling them. At some point he realized that it wasn't the most efficient way to be in the real estate development business, so instead, he bought a hardware store, with the idea of breaking it up into several smaller shops. Soon, however, he found that he didn't really enjoy selling lug nuts and chain saws, so instead he stocked the store with French sauté pans and other cookware.

In 1958, Williams made another trip to France—this time expressly to buy equipment he couldn't find in nearby San Francisco. "Within a couple years," he said, "I had a French cookware shop. All the copper and bakeware. Tart pans, the fluted ones with removable bottoms, charlotte molds and brioche molds, thick aluminum pots and pans and sauté pans, which no one had ever heard of. All the French knives and parers." Friends encouraged him that year to move the shop to San Francisco; he wisely heeded one friend's advice about "location, location, location," opening downtown, on Sutter Street, despite the expense. "The reason it was so good," he explained, "was Elizabeth Arden was in the same block—that was where all the ladies went to get their hair done. One block away were two medical buildings; everybody had to go to visit their dentist.

We were sort of right in the middle of it. We got all the ladies."

The timing couldn't have been more fortuitous, for the small new crop of enthusiastic cooks had nothing to cook with. "When I look back at what was available in stores at that time for the home cook, it was pretty meager," said Williams. "I remember going into the Macy's housewares section—it was half-empty, mainly because there was so much of it that wasn't manufactured during the war." What remained were a few thin aluminum saucepans and cast-iron frying pans. "Revereware was the best of the cookware then," Williams told me. "Stainless steel with a copper wash on the bottom. That was the dream of the bride." So Williams stocked French cookware as well as a few good imported ingredients, such as red wine vinegars and olive oils, mustards, and handmade preserves.

Somehow without sounding immodest—perhaps because he is not an immodest person—Williams attributes great significance to his own role in the remarkable progress that American cuisine has made in the last thirty-five years. "I would say that we had a great deal to do with it," he said. "I thought up the idea of a French cookware shop in the middle of the 1950s, and Julia [Child] was more or less doing the same thing in France with the cooking."

By 1960 a gastronomic light began to appear at the end of the tunnel. In their book *Great Restaurants of America* published that year, Ted Patrick and Silas Spitzer wrote, "Maybe French chefs are growing old and tired and their number diminishing. But it isn't altogether essential that a chef be of French birth and instruction. . . . There are already indications that the restaurant career is about to become, for young people in this country, the fashionable thing it has become for young people in England." They continued:

> The signs in this country all seem to us to be good. More and more people, men particularly, are learning to cook and regularly cooking, and young people no longer look to the kitchen as a den of drudgery. Fine food from all over the world has found its way into shops in every respectable-sized city and even into those citadels of food mediocrity, the supermarket.

On August 26, 1961, an apprenticeship program was announced in California, to answer the need to train American chefs, since European chefs could not keep up with the growing demand. "We can no longer depend upon the importing of trained cooks from Europe, but must systematically train our own," stated Charles F. Hanna, chief of the Division of Apprenticeship Standards in California's Department of Industrial Relations. Sanford Cohn of the California Restaurant Association complained that "when you get a cook now, he doesn't know the difference between sauce béarnaise and cherries jubilee."

Cohn's choice of béarnaise sauce and cherries jubilee—two preparations every chef at the time would have had to know—was indicative of the state of restaurant cooking in California. That sauce béarnaise—an emulsion of reduced vinegar, tarragon, chervil, egg yolks, and butter, recipe number sixty-two as laid out by Escoffier*—was important bespoke the supremacy of classic sauces, and indeed of standard preparations. Though any chef worth his or her salt today still has this sauce in his tool kit, it wouldn't be difficult to find accomplished cooks who didn't know how to put together cherries jubilee (though incidentally, cher-

*Master French chef August Escoffier published his monumental *Guide Culinaire* in 1903, standardizing some 3,000 French preparations, codifying and modernizing classical French cooking.

ries jubilee was resurrected last year at The "21" Club in New York—another bow to nostalgia).

Earlier that year the Kennedy White House had been implicated in a diplomatic skirmish that splashed across the front page of the *New York Times*. No, it had nothing to do with the Bay of Pigs; this was an affair close to the heart of the first family. The White House had been accused of trying to steal the French ambassador to England's chef. Ambassador Jean Chauvel's chef of twenty-two years was a Vietnamese man named Bui Van Han. As it turned out, even if Kennedy had indeed made a bid for the chef, Van Han preferred to stay with the Chauvels. Who knows, if the President had succeeded in luring him away, perhaps he would have had a different perspective on Vietnam and history might have been changed. . . .

Van Han's specialty was a staple of French cooking in America at that time—crêpes Suzette—a dish that had been on Henri Soulé's menu at the French pavilion's restaurant at the 1939 World's Fair in New York. It was this kind of sophisticated gloss that the Kennedys were looking to add to their state entertaining.

Six weeks after the Van Han incident, Craig Claiborne had a front-page story in the *Times* about the chef the Kennedys eventually did hire. "White House Hires French Chef" ran the headline; the subhead, "Macmillan [then prime minister of Britain] Treated to Trout in Wine—Verdict: Bravo." René Verdon, the Kennedys' new chef, was a *chef de cuisine* of the classic stripe. "The menu was seasonal," wrote Claiborne. To wit: trout cooked in Chablis with sauce Vincent (mayonnaise with chopped watercress, spinach, and capers); roast fillet of beef au jus, artichoke crowns Beauçaire (filled with "a fondue of tomatoes simmered in butter"); "giant-sized" asparagus as a separate course with sauce Maltaise (hollandise tinged with orange);

and a vacherin (meringue shell) filled with chocolate ice cream and raspberries. Francophilia had taken firm root in the American imagination.

At a dinner chef Verdon prepared for Indian Prime Minister Nehru and President Kennedy in November 1961 at Newport (while the first lady dined privately upstairs with Madame Gandhi), the meal began with New England Clam Chowder, served with an Italian wine, Soave Bertani. "Next came Cailles Véronique (quail in a special sauce, with its delicate touch of grape)," wrote Verdon in his cookbook,

> and with it a California wine, Almadén Pinot Noir. Glazed carrots and a Mimosa Salad accompanied this entree. Dessert was Bavarian cream mold with oranges, its sweetness tempered by the splendid champagne served with it, a Cuvée Dom Perignon 1952. Petits fours with almonds were also at hand, and demitasse followed.

Thus was the climate in 1961 as the nation read about the goings on in the suddenly fashionable nation's capital.

So when Julia Child came along later that year, America was finally ready for her. "I happened to come along just at the right time," Child told me in an interview. "If it had been a bit earlier, it wouldn't have gone over. People were ready, but nothing had come along. People were reading about what the Kennedys were eating. They just needed someone and I happened to be the right person."

3

REGULAR FISH AND SACRED COWS

WHEN I WAS A YOUNG PUP OF ABOUT TEN YEARS OLD, 'round about 1970, my younger brothers and I would start in late in the afternoon with our ritual whine, "Mommmmm . . . what's for dinner?"

If the answer were fish, we'd whine "What kind of fish?"

If she said "Regular fish," we were in luck, and we'd thank the dinner gods. Regular fish was probably something sold as sole fillets, though it would likely have been flounder, since real sole wasn't available in those parts; sometimes they were sand dabs, delicate and tender. Whatever they were, they were dipped in milk and seasoned bread crumbs, browned in butter, and served with wedges of lemon. Try it, it's not bad.

However, sometimes regular fish appeared in different clothing, and that was what we dreaded. For some reason my mother didn't want to utter the words "sole Véronique"; probably she didn't want to give away that it wouldn't be *regular* regular fish. The other kind of regular fish was also white fish fillets, but these were baked in the oven in the big rectangular Pyrex dish in some insipid liquid (water? milk? a pale white wine? I'm sure she wasn't making a fumet.), with canned green grapes scattered throughout. I think sometimes she added slivered almonds, bought in little cellophane packages, that tasted like they'd spent a couple years on the shelf.

My mom, always a natural cook with good instincts (though she had only learned to boil water in 1959), had turned "gourmet." Youch. Yet sole Véronique was considered very sophisticated in the 1960s.

Who inspired my mother to add an attempt at sole Véronique to her regular fish repertoire? Julia Child. Although *Mastering the Art of French Cooking* offered no recipe for sole Véronique (which was too bad, since if it had, we probably wouldn't have dreaded it), Julia was largely responsible for hundreds of thousands of people like my mother becoming interested in such a thing.

The sole Véronique incident—and others like it—simply represents a temporary period of experimentation and transition in our house. Until then my mom hadn't been exposed to much serious food, other than a few visits to cozy little inexpensive French restaurants in New York City when she was in college and dating my dad in 1958. But through the 1960s and early 1970s, she really began to discover food, and her "discovery" of Julia Child played a major role in that. And like many other women, with Julia as teacher, she was a fast learner.

Never in the history of American cooking has there ever been anyone like Julia Child. Through her cookbooks and her television programs, Julia inspired two generations of Americans to cook—that is, my mother's generation and mine. And not only did Julia spawn a wave of serious home cooks, she also inspired more than a few cooks to become professionals.

At century's end, all of America is on a first-name basis with Julia. Her birthdays are occasions for elaborate gala celebrations, attended by the Who's Who of gastronomy and chefs galore; symposia convene at Harvard University to discuss her life and times; she's a beloved personality. Apocryphal tales about Julia have circulated for decades—stories of her dropping chickens on the set and serving them anyway, for example—and many more. In the early 1980s, Dan Ackroyd imitated Julia on *Saturday Night Live*—and in fact, most people I know can even do a creditable Julia impression. Let's face it: Julia's an icon.

By now, much of Julia Child's biography is well-known, especially since the publication of Nöel Riley Fitch's excellent 1997 book *Appetite for Life: The Biography of Julia Child,* so brevity will prevail here.

In the late 1940s, the thirty-four-year-old woman from Pasadena, California, had moved to Washington, D.C., with her husband, Paul Child, who was in the diplomatic service. The couple met while both worked for the Office of Strategic Services during the war; they were stationed in Ceylon and then China. Since her husband Paul was a gourmand (and since his mother was a wonderful cook), this young woman thought it would be nice to learn the art herself. To that end, she had enrolled in a cooking school in Los Angeles just before her marriage.

Her stint as a culinary student was less than auspicious, however. Her most dramatic misstep occurred when her roast duck exploded in the oven because she forgot to pierce it to let the fat drip out. But if at first you don't succeed, the saying goes, try try again. And try she did: she subscribed to the newly founded *Gourmet* magazine, and following the well-explained recipes, tried her hand at some dishes.

Child looked to *Gourmet* "to get presumably the French touch," she told me. "My nieces and I had been up in Maine, and we decided to make a bouillabaisse. They were about ten and twelve, and we made a lovely soup. My husband had been to France, and he said, 'Well, it's very good, but it's not bouillabaisse.' "

Half a century later, three generations of cooks refer to Julia's recipe for bouillabaisse in her 1961 tome, *Mastering the Art of French Cooking,* or as it's more fondly known, Volume I.

Julia Child worked on the book (or "The Book," as she referred to it) for almost ten years, along with Simone "Simca" Beck and Louisette Bertholle—although Bertholle's participation was limited, and Beck and Child later bought out her participation in royalties.

The road to publication for *Mastering the Art* was rocky, however. Simone Beck and Louisette Bertholle had already written a much smaller book—under contract to Ives Washburn—that they called *French Home Cooking,* but the New York publisher insisted that they find an American to adapt the recipes for American kitchens.

The two met Julia in Paris when the Childs were living there in 1949. Julia had enrolled in courses at the Cordon Bleu cooking school; there she studied for six months with Max Bugnard, a disciple of Escoffier. Julia was studying privately with Bugnard when she met Simone Beck, and Beck, seeing in Julia a kindred spirit, brought her into the Cercle des Gourmettes, a women's gastronomic group of which Bertholle was also a member. By now Julia had picked up a thing or two in the kitchen, and the three started running cooking classes out of Julia's apartment. They called their operation "L'Ecole des Trois Gourmandes." Beck and Bertholle found in Julia the ideal partner for their American cookbook venture.

At this point, they had already made another pass at their manuscript and sent it along to Ives Washburn, but in the meantime, Julia took a stab at completely redoing a chapter on sauces. So they followed up the new draft with a package containing Julia's sauce chapter, as well as a letter informing him they'd reconceived the project. Nevertheless, Washburn and Les Trois Gourmandes parted ways, the publisher finding the book too unconventional. Julia's friend Avis DeVoto got the book to Boston publisher Houghton Mifflin, who sent them a contract along with a $200 advance.

The Childs had to pick up and move twice in the intervening four years, once to Bonn, where Paul had a new post, and then to Washington, D.C. Meanwhile, Julia worked away on her manuscript, which by the end of 1957 consisted of over 700 pages just on poultry and sauces. In the meantime, Louisette Bertholle realized she was in over her head and curtailed her participation in the project, and although all three would be listed as authors, according to their contract with Houghton Mifflin, the three cut a deal for distribution of royalties, in which Bertholle would receive 18 percent and Child and Beck would take larger shares of 41 percent each.

Houghton Mifflin, upon receiving the manuscript, replied, "We are not going to publish an encyclopedia," requiring Julia and Simca to edit the mammoth book. This they did over the next two years, and finally turned in *French Recipes for American Cooks* in September 1959. Houghton Mifflin rejected it, explaining that the still voluminous book would be too costly to publish in relation to its projected sales. Avis DeVoto urged the women not to fret and sent the manuscript to a connection at Knopf.

In 1961, Knopf published *Mastering the Art of French*

Cooking to much hoopla. According to Evan Jones's biography of James Beard, Beard was instrumental in getting the book recognized. "As nobody else could do as well," Jones wrote, "he made it his role to see that the fledgling American food establishment did what was necessary to put *Mastering the Art of French Cooking* on the map." Jones was in a position to know this first-hand: His wife, Judith B. Jones, was *Mastering the Art*'s editor at Knopf.

Interestingly, the single mention of the book in Beard's letters to Helen Evans Brown was equivocal. "I think the Knopf book is wonderful," Beard wrote, "until they get into the chicken and meat department. The idea of cooking a piece of American boiling beef for four hours is insane. . . . And I think all the chicken recipes are overcooked. Otherwise, it is a great book. Nothing new or startling, but a good basic French cookery book." That Beard would reserve his criticisms for his friend while publicly lauding the book is understandable, yet the fact that neither Beard's nor Julia Child's biographers saw fit to mention his initial ambivalence indicates that both Beard and Child have since become culinary sacred cows.

In any case, Craig Claiborne raved about *Mastering the Art of French Cooking* in *The Saturday Evening Post;* reviewers all across the country soon followed suit.

In the first five years it sold 300,000 copies; the first hardcover edition would eventually go on to sell 650,000 copies. Through *Mastering the Art,* Julia Child taught legions of Americans to cook. One of those she taught was Susan Stamberg, who today is a special correspondent for National Public Radio.

Stamberg didn't know her way around a kitchen in 1961, the year she was married and *Mastering the Art* was published. "I didn't grow up with good food," Stamberg told me. "My mother would buy a can of peas, dump it in a saucepan, and retrieve each of them with a slotted spoon.

She couldn't miss one." The year she married and moved from New York City to Washington, D.C., Stamberg's idea of haute cuisine was string bean casserole—the kind made with canned cream of mushroom soup and canned fried onions. That was, as she refers to it, "food B.C.—Before Child."

But Stamberg taught herself to cook by studying *Mastering the Art* soon thereafter. "Front to back," she said. "I read it from page one." Soon she was tackling recipes, jotting marginal notes as she tried out Boeuf Bourguignon, Suprêmes de Volaille à Brun, Tranches de Jambon en Pipérade ("good, not great" reads her note), and Quiche aux Champignons—which she happened to be preparing when she went into labor with her son Josh. "We ate this," Stamberg had later gone back and noted in the margin, "the night Josh was born."

With the advent of the jet plane and easier, less expensive transatlantic travel, the world became a smaller place. President Kennedy founded The Peace Corps in 1961. On July 23, 1962, the world became smaller still, when Telstar, the first major telecommunications satellite, was launched.

America's love affair with France heated up even more; if Julia Child had had misgivings that her book was too long in the making and that she might have missed the boat where America's Francophilia was concerned, her worries must have evaporated quickly. In fact, it's entirely possible that if she'd made shorter work of the project, she would have been ahead of her time, and not become the phenomenon we know her as today. Barbara Pascal, who became interested in food in the early sixties, remembers her Los Angeles crowd: "People were real Francophiles in that era. People would go to France, cook from Julia Child, only drink French wines."

Francophilia extended even to the press, which didn't

hurt *Mastering the Art*'s reception. "When you talk about Julia," Barbara Kafka pointed out to me, alluding to Craig Claiborne's *Saturday Evening Post* review, "I think you have to see her in the context of Craig's French bias." After all, she said, Claiborne had attended the Ecole Hôtelière cooking school in Lausanne, Switzerland, known for its concentration on French cuisine; he'd also worked with Pierre Franey—hence Claiborne was inclined to be predisposed to anyone espousing the cause of French cuisine. In any case, rave he did.

The New York Times Cookbook, by Craig Claiborne, was also published in 1961. The *Times* book, a compilation of some 1,500 recipes that appeared in the paper between 1950 and 1960, appealed to a slightly different, if overlapping, audience. With its minimal headnotes, it reads more like a catalogue of recipes; many home cooks found it less intimidating than the perfectionist and conceptual *Mastering the Art.* A recipe for Coq au Vin, to pick a random example, runs two pages in *Mastering the Art,* half a page in *The New York Times Cookbook.*

Jo Brans, author of a charming 1993 book, *Feast Here Awhile,* never felt as comfortable with *Mastering the Art* as she did with *The New York Times Cookbook.* As she put it in her book, "Under Julia's tutelage, I learned not to use canned soup for sauces, or at least to lie about it if I did. But I never really mastered *Mastering the Art of French Cooking.* . . . Julia Child had opened the world of good cooking to me, but I felt a lot more at home with Craig." In a later conversation, Brans elaborated. "I did think her recipes were unduly complicated."

It seemed to be the moment for definitive, comprehensive cookbooks. In the preface to *The New York Times Cookbook,* Claiborne wrote "There probably never has been such an absorbing interest in fine cuisine in the home as there is in this decade." This was the age when housewives did their best to make themselves into connoisseurs, and since exposure to fine restaurant cooking was impossible for those who didn't travel to France—which is to say most, since outside of New York City, San Francisco, and a few other metropolises, excellent restaurants were still scarce—the cookbook became their Baedekker of dining.

But if *The New York Times Cookbook* took its place on bookshelves all over America right alongside *Mastering the Art,* Claiborne represented a wholly different type of food personality: more journalist and critic than cook. *The New York Times Cookbook,* whose opening pages serve as a primer on serving caviar and foie gras, smoked salmon and oysters, is filled with recipes for dishes like Steak Diane and Beef Stroganoff, Veal Scaloppine alla Marsala and Shrimp Fondue. Next to Julia's technique-oriented recipes, the *Times Cookbook*'s instructions were more mechanical, work-aday, showing readers how to open jars and make things look appealing. Julia asked readers to really understand a dish; her disciples were then able to apply the given techniques to other dishes (and they were thrilled to follow such a charming instructor). So *Mastering the Art* functioned more as a cooking course from which students could take as much or as little as they chose, while the *Times* book really was more of a standard cookbook.

Claiborne's peers have leveled a few quiet criticisms against him over the years. Julia Child, according to Noël Riley Fitch, believed Claiborne to be "really in the 'business' of food." (At the same time, Julia managed to excuse James Beard's penchant for business, choosing to believe that he was manipulated by others.) Barbara Kafka points out that *The New York Times Cookbook* wasn't exactly Claiborne's book; he just happened into it, benefiting in terms of royalties. "When he came to the *Times,*" she says, "it was all done and assembled and tested, and it was part of the lagniappe that he got the royalties on it. And it really, in some ways, helped make his reputation. But it was not his book." Kafka's assertion makes perfect sense, since most of the recipes predated his tenure there. However, Kafka also points out that Claiborne was the first to champion the idea of the cook as personality, an idea that would gradually come to the fore over the years. "He was also interviewing lots of people who were cooking," she says. "He was discovering *people*."

Culinary historians John L. Hess and Karen Hess came down rather hard on Claiborne in *The Taste of America,* criticizing him for plugging Pepperidge Farm and other branded products, as well as "gourmet" frozen foods in the late 1950s; publishing thinly disguised pilfered, inauthentic, inaccurate, or cartoonishly mundane recipes; using flour to excess in sauce recipes ("The same old library paste, *ad nauseam*"); giving bad advice about cooking with wine. They also slammed him for his slavish dedication to expensive ingredients, as symptomatic of what they called "the gourmet plague" and for his writing partnership with Pierre Franey, whom they never let the reader forget was Executive Chef of Howard Johnson's.

One must note that the Hesses also criticized Julia Child, for crimes ranging from her fondness for Golden Delicious apples, aspics made with gelatin, dishes encased in pastry crusts, and McDonald's French fries, to calling for canned broth in recipes. They objected to her calling herself "The French Chef" when she was "neither French nor chef." But they can't refute that with Julia Child, many Americans' tastes in food and skills in cooking took a quantum leap forward.

In 1963 Boston's public television station, WGBH, began taping Julia's cooking show, *The French Chef,* and her celebrity increased one hundred fold.

Now Julia was making serious cooking accessible to a

wide range of people for the first time. "The Hindi word for 'kitchen' is 'science laboratory,' " points out home cook Susan Stamberg. Julia led Stamberg to realize that "it wasn't some magic somebody did in the back room, but there were chemical connections that made things tasty." And Julia, especially with her television program, made the challenge fun.

Although Stamberg was too busy working at her first job at Washington, D.C., public radio station, WAMU-FM, to watch much TV, she remembers not only being bowled over by Julia, but at the same time identifying with her. "I was too tall, too big-boned and too outspoken to be the sort of stay-at-home mom in the Donna Reed model," explains Stamberg. Since Julia was ". . . ungainly, big, kind of loud, thoroughly professional, really smart" she served as a role model. "She taught us about more than food, really. . . . I think she taught us how to be a woman, how to be professional and an odd duck, and [she was] wonderfully successful at it."

By 1965, WBGH was receiving 350 letters a week: Julia was captivating the audience. Ingredients for the dishes she prepared each week sold out anywhere the show was picked up on local public television. That year, Julia made the cover of *Time* magazine. "Everyone's in the Kitchen," declared the cover line, and to prove it, *Time* presented captioned photographs of Vice President Hubert Humphrey, author Barbara Tuchman, M.I.T. Provost and former presidential adviser Jerome Wiesner, Mrs. William Pereira ("wife of the Los Angeles architect"), and August Busch III of Anheuser-Busch—among others—all in their respective kitchens, heads bent in attitudes of chopping, slicing, stirring, and tasting.

Despite these shifts in the culture, it would be misleading to say that most Americans suddenly started eating and cooking well in the span of a few short years in the early

1960s. At that time, the would-be American cook didn't readily find many essential ingredients—leeks, for instance—at the supermarket. Shallots were considered a specialty item, available mail order from an ad in the back of *Gourmet* from a company called "Les Eschalottes." ("*The real thing in its natural state indispensable for béarnaise* and many other sauces," read the ad; it hastened to add "*Used in many French recipes.") Equipment was a problem, too. "You couldn't find the good knives," recalls Susan Stamberg. "You just went on looking." When Stamberg and her husband traveled to France, they'd look for kitchen equipment in hardware stores, bringing back food mills that they picked up "for nothing" for Christmas presents.

This was less of a problem for ardent home cooks who lived in a few major cities; Judy Marcus, for instance, frequented the Farmers Market in Los Angeles for provisions for her elaborate dinners. Though it was no longer a farmers' market in the strict sense of the word, the Los Angeles Farmers Market, in the early 1960s, was a covered marketplace with permanent stalls selling seasonal offerings such as string beans, peppers, tomatoes, and avocados, but also out-of-season vegetables and tropical fruits, international prepared foods, bakery items and kitchen gadgets. Marcus shopped there in the late fifties because, "they had a wider range of things available than they did at a regular market—butchers, and a wide range of fruits and vegetables; you just had the feeling it was high quality and a larger selection."

As a young child, I happen to have lived in West Hollywood near the Farmers Market, and I can remember going there when I was three years old. One of my earliest memories involves visiting the market with our next-door neighbor, an optometrist named Louie Lenchner, who bought an entire fresh strawberry pie, lavishly garnished with whipped cream, and proceeded to polish it off. My strongest memory is the peculiar, wonderful smell of the place, a combination, perhaps, of smoke, fruit, baked goods, and the fresh horseradish that one food stand grated for customers. As an adult in my early twenties—once again living in West Hollywood—I often returned, and found, much to my delight, that the odd smell persisted.

Even within major urban centers, the food revolution was happening in fits and starts. By the time my family moved over the hill from Hollywood to the San Fernando Valley in September 1964, some of the most compelling moments of my childhood would involve Reddi-Wip, that pseudo-cream-in-a-can with its essential decorative spout. What came out of it had little to do with real whipped cream, but my brothers and I loved its airiness and even its vaguely chemical aftertaste. Shake-a-Pudding, Whip 'n' Chill, and Jell-O also loomed large; as did Shake 'n Bake (even I, a child, thought it was fun to put chicken drumsticks in a lunchbag and shake), Lucky Charms (they were disgusting even then, but at least in those days, they weren't blue), M&M's (ditto), and Incredible Edibles (toy insects we made by cooking some terrible powder in bug molds). My next door neighbor Patti Roberts owned an Easy Bake Oven, powered by a lightbulb, which we both loved. We soon ran out of the cake mixes it came with, and took to using the Easy Bake Oven to roast Meyer lemons from the Roberts' prolific tree (verdict: yecch). Even though this stuff was introduced after Julia's book was published, that was the backdrop against which our mothers were discovering French cooking.

To set the record straight: *My* mother was discovering cooking. Patti's mother—a straight-ahead Betty Crocker type (in fact Polly Roberts sort of *looked* like Betty Crocker) with seven children to raise—was not. Nor, to my knowledge, was anyone else on our not particularly upwardly mobile middle-class block interested in the pleasures of the table. I do remember that Andy, the youngest Roberts child, enjoyed ketchup in his corn flakes, a vaguely Nixonian concept. And down the block, Tom Sorby's father worked for the Creamettes noodle company, which seemed sort of glamorous to me at the time.

My Mom, married in 1959, didn't discover Julia until later, around 1970, when Volume II was published. I'll dwell on Mom's cooking for a moment, since in many ways, my mother was typical of the segment of her generation that fell in love with food. Like so many brides, she received the cliché fondue set as a wedding gift, though when she and my father got married, she didn't know how to cook. At all. "After we were married," she told me recently, "I learned how to make Jell-O." Aunt Ruth, who had raised my mother since she was orphaned as a child, copied out her own five soup recipes—vegetable-beef, chicken, beet borscht, cabbage, and Manhattan clam chowder—and slid the pages into my mom's first cookbook, *Joy of Cooking.* Those soup recipes served her well (and now serve me well), especially the two stock-based soups, since they taught her important basic techniques that she'd later apply elsewhere.

At first, my mother had a number of standard dinners, which she'd rotate with depressing predictability. I don't remember ever seeing wine at home before about 1968; after that, it was reserved for special occasions. If it was a spaghetti night—no one called it "pasta" yet—the wine my parents served was sure to be "Famiglia Cribari" red (we called it "Family Crybaby"). Otherwise, it was Almadén "white Burgundy," or Mateus rosé. My parents always had a cocktail after my father came home from work, usually scotch or what my mom called a "dry rye Manhattan on the rocks," to which she added two maraschino cherries, even though it was dry. (Cocktails, of course, are notorious palate numb-ers. That didn't stop Julia and Paul Child from enjoying them before dinner, either, though. . . .) Bread was absent from our table, except for the occasional frozen Sara Lee Parker House dinner rolls (delightfully mushy) or Pillsbury Poppin' Fresh biscuits my mom would inevitably serve with beef stew. We'd often have a salad to start, as was the custom in California—iceberg or occasionally romaine lettuce with supermarket tomatoes and sliced cucumbers and Good Seasons salad dressing from a mix. Good Seasons was so omnipresent in our house that my brothers and I made up a chant about it, to which we used to samba around the kitchen (much to my mom's irritation): "Pour in vin-e-gar to vin-e-gar line. Add wa-ter to wa-ter line. Add Good Seasons salad dressing mix. And shake! Add oil to oil line, and shake!" Packaged foods retained their place of importance in our house long after my mother became interested in more serious cooking.

In any case, here was the rotation:

1. Spaghetti (always with meat sauce), served with romaine salad with garbanzo beans, quartered tomatoes, cucumber slices, and Good Seasons garlic dressing
2. Roast beef (delicious) with mashed potatoes
3. Pineapple chicken (baked, with Lawry's teriyaki sauce and canned pineapple), served with Uncle Ben's Converted rice and Green Giant frozen peas in butter sauce
4. Beef stew, accompanied by wide egg noodles and Pillsbury Poppin' Fresh biscuits
5. Lamb chops with spinach and admirable mashed potatoes
6. Steak with baked potato
7. Hamburgers (on the barbecue, warm weather only)
8. Barbecued chicken
9. Regular fish
10. Ham steaks with slices of canned pineapple, maraschino cherry in center of pineapple slice

11. One of Aunt Ruth's five soups
12. Salmon salad (warm weather only), accompanied by noodles 'n' cottage cheese, tomato wedges, cucumber slices

If my parents were going out, it would be minute steaks, salmon patties made with canned salmon, TV dinners, McDonald's, Lido pizza, or Kentucky Fried Chicken.

At some point in the late 1960s, my mother bought *McCall's Cookbook*; she read *McCall's* magazine and *Redbook,* clipping recipes and taping them into a big orange vinyl binder. *Sunset,* a popular West Coast magazine, published single-subject cookbooks; she owned and cooked from several of these—*Food with a Gourmet Touch, Sunset Seafood Cookbook.* New dinners were now added into the rotation: sweet-and-sour ribs (only in summer), always with "fried rice" (raw bean sprouts were an avant-garde touch); pepper steak (sautéed beef cubes with green pepper) with Uncle Ben's Converted rice; meatballs, which was the same preparation as pepper steak, simply substituting meatballs for chunks, with the same rice.

Although my mother managed to avoid it, by the mid-1960s, the competitive dinner party scene was really heating up. In 1965 Joyce Goldstein started teaching cooking in San Francisco to would-be hostesses. Goldstein, who today is well-known as the former chef/owner of San Francisco's Square One restaurant (which she closed in 1996), as well as a cookbook author and journalist, had moved to San Francisco from New York City in 1960. "When I started teaching," Goldstein told me at an interview in her Pacific Heights Victorian house, "the only thing people wanted was gourmet French. If you wanted to learn to cook, that's what you had to do." Most of her students had, by that time, some basic cooking skills, she said. "That was the era of the competitive dinner, and so everybody was looking to impress everybody with a dazzling dinner party. Of course if I taught my students a few fancy dishes and some basic good desserts and things that they could make ahead, they were stars." When her students dined out, they went to Ernie's (which also closed in 1996), Fleur de Lys (still open), and a couple of other classic French restaurants. "And when they entertained," Goldstein said, "there were these drop-dead fancy French dinner parties. Other cuisines were considered . . . of lesser interest." When interviewed, Goldstein downplayed Julia Child's influence, focusing instead on the "powerful" *Gourmet* magazine, to which she had subscribed since sometime in the 1950s. "It was *the* food magazine," she said. "There were no other renegade publications coming in. There were the ladies' magazines, where you opened a can of cream of mushroom soup to make a sauce, but *Gourmet* was excitement, romance, drama, fine dining. That's what people aspired to."

Goldstein also used the cookbooks that *Gourmet* published in 1950 and 1965. She liked them because "there was a little room for interpretation. They weren't totally anal, but they were elegant. It was the kind of food that people wanted to eat. People bought into it. And all of a sudden [things] started to change."

Gloria Burg, an interior designer in Columbia, South Carolina, got married and began cooking in 1961, the year *Mastering the Art* was published. Though she came from a family of good home cooks of Greek and Mediterranean ancestry, she herself "couldn't boil water." Burg started with *Gourmet* and still keeps bound volumes from 1966 through 1977; she didn't buy a copy of *Mastering the Art* until "probably the late sixties." As for *Gourmet,* "I just thought it was wonderful," she says. "I tried to cook something out of it every month. I would take the color centerfold meal and try to duplicate it. A lot of people felt it was too intricate, but I would have the color center page on the little Lucite cookbook holder."

Like many a sixties housewife, Burg had to be prepared for the inevitable unexpected dinner guest. "My husband used to call at five-thirty or six and say so-and-so is here from out of town, and I'm bringing him home to dinner. I'd fly to McDonald's for the kids, throw 'em into bed, and by eight have everything ready." Burg, whose husband was in the wine business, had traveled widely; she was a natural candidate for the dinner party scene, and in fact belonged to a "dinner club" of five couples whom she describes as "wonderful and extravagant." Three out of the five men cooked, which was quite unusual at the time, and as Burg puts it, "They would really put on the dog when it was their turn—from roasted pig to escargots." The three men began to offer classes to other men who wanted to learn to cook.

Coquilles Saint-Jacques was one of Burg's favorite dishes to prepare; she served it in the traditional scallop shells. She'd pour a white wine with the coquilles, and usually they'd have a red wine with the main course, and then a cheese course. "I'd serve Reblochon and the French chèvres way back then before goat cheese became [mainstream]. We were eating goat cheeses in the sixties." These she sometimes found, surprisingly, in a local gourmet shop, or she'd buy them when she visited New York. "I was copying the French," she explains, "and they'd just roll out the cheese cart, so I would do the same at home. We would have a wine with the cheese course," she recalls, "and very often a Sauternes or something to go with dessert. Sometimes there'd be five or six glasses on the table. There weren't a lot of friends our age doing that." Burg even kept a "hostess book" listing all the dishes and wines served so she wouldn't duplicate a meal for the same guest at a subsequent dinner party.

Like my mother, Barbara Pascal cooked from *Sunset* magazine's cookbooks, especially for her family. Her husband Tony, at the time an economist with Hughes Research, also cooked, favoring *The New York Times Cookbook*. Pascal was a willy-nilly participant in the competitive dinner game. "Doing a dinner party," she remembers, "you were really nervous; you were shaky. Tony and I would look over recipes and decide two weeks in advance and talk about it for days and days. And I know it was all competitive. I was really nervous and anxious about it because we had no help and babies! Doing a dinner party was an enormous undertaking, especially if you had gourmets or people from work—Tony's bosses—it was like a comic strip."

All her friends were in the same boat. "Everyone cooked," she says. "These were educated people, middle income. Everyone was doing it. Not necessarily expensive food, but really hard food, and it was ninety percent French."

By 1968 the cutting edge of the American food landscape had changed quite a lot, though for much of middle America, many things had stayed the same. A 1968 cookbook called *Simple Cooking for Sophisticates* still found it necessary to counsel readers: "By all means buy fish fresh from a dealer rather than from the freezer of a chain store." However the authors of this book were pushing their audience well ahead of the curve when it came to an understanding of products and produce. Under the heading "Homemade Butter," they wrote: "Load a blender with heavy cream and let it run. It won't be the best butter in the world because the cream itself is not that good, but it will be infinitely superior to the packaged material." They bemoaned "the poor quality of so much of our fruit. Not that it is ugly, wormy or overripe. Quite the contrary. All of it is just lovely, bright, shiny and flawless. What much of it lacks is flavor. The reason for this is that to the industry, storage and appearance, which helps it sell, are more important than flavor and juiciness. The tastiest varieties have been replaced by those which have been bred for the mass market."

A 1969 cartoon in *Gourmet* provides a snapshot of the state of restaurant cooking. It pictured two chefs. The caption: "Henri, what went wrong? The broccoli tastes just like broccoli." Chefs, at this point, were still assumed to be French (he's Henri, not Henry . . .). And the governing idea is that one had to transform food—an idea that Julia certainly helped perpetuate—in order to make it seem more sophisticated. Ingredients that tasted like themselves were seen as undistinguished; anyone, it was supposed, could make broccoli that tasted like broccoli. Twenty-five years later, the best cooks would be striving to make food that tasted like what it was, prettily calling it "showcasing ingredients."

Williams-Sonoma, which had started out in the late 1950s doing a big wedding gift business and had been supported through the mid-sixties by upper-middle-class homemakers who cooked elaborate French meals, now found its business fueled by the most unlikely source. The flower power revolution in the Haight-Ashbury saw the formation of communes, and communal living required large restaurant-quality equipment.

Though Williams-Sonoma was a boon to the West Coast, professional equipment had long been available in New York City. A store called Bazaar Français had been offering professional quality equipment from its downtown Manhattan location since 1877. Though it closed its doors in 1975—much to the chagrin of New York gourmets who saw it as "another sign of the deterioration of the city,"*—at least New Yorkers still had Lamalle Kitchenware, which

*New York was in the grip of a crippling fiscal crisis at the time.

had been in business since the early 1930s, and continues today. But Chip Fisher, who bought Lamalle in 1994, sees it this way: "Williams really led the way; we have a lot of respect for what he's done. He was the pioneer in a certain way because before he came into the business, people were using less illustrious forms of cookware. He really developed the copperware." Although Lamalle has been in business much longer than Williams-Sonoma, Lamalle has always been geared more toward chefs and wholesale to retail stores; outside of New York, most Americans have never heard of it; even within New York it wasn't known by all. "From here on in," said one New Yorker when Bazaar closed, "I guess it's Bloomingdale's." It really took Williams-Sonoma to bring professional-quality cookware to the masses.

Julia Child, for her part, recognizes Williams's contribution as well. "He was tremendously helpful to me when I started on the television in 1963," she said when I interviewed her in 1995, "because I was doing French cooking, and a lot of the implements weren't around. But he had them, or he got them. He did a tremendous amount to introduce really workable kitchen equipment to people. And they seemed to have people in the stores who knew the subject. I'm very grateful to him."

By 1971—still long before he expanded beyond his original store in San Francisco—Chuck Williams started his highly successful catalog, mailing out 10,000 copies; quality cookware became available for the first time to cooks across the country.

Laura Furman, a fiction anthologist in Austin, graduated from college in 1968; she remembers a friend receiving *Mastering the Art* as a wedding gift. "That's the way a young bride in the sixties learned to cook for her man," she explains, adding "especially, I suppose, a young intellectual Jewish bride with a Ph.D. from Harvard." Furman remembers her friend making a *chaude-froide* of chicken breast for a luncheon, something that greatly impressed her. "It never occurred to me you'd go to that much trouble for your girlfriends," she muses. "Roz poached the chicken breasts and made the sauce—it was really delicious, with whipping cream, chicken stock, tarragon, and you add gelatin and white vermouth. Which now sounds ridiculous. You could put on top fresh tarragon leaves or finely diced truffle. Roz did put either watercress or parsley as a garnish, as Julia suggests."

As for her own cooking, Furman also began with *Mastering the Art.* "I think the thing that broke my back with Julia Child was Veal Orloff—actually veal that was baked in its own sauce. It sounds sort of loathsome now, but it was the height of my elegance."

By the time Volume II of *Mastering the Art of French Cooking* was published in 1970, a cooking mania had seized the popular imagination. A cartoon in the January 1971 issue of *Gourmet* depicted a guy swimming in the ocean who was being attacked by an octopus. A woman on the beach exclaims, "Get him for my bouillabaisse!"

It was at about this time that my mother came into possession of her boxed set of *Mastering the Art of French Cooking Volumes I and II,* and as a result, more changes took place around our dinner table. (Incidentally, it bears mentioning that we almost always all sat down together for dinner, which my mom prepared every night, and this did not by any means seem odd. This remained true even after she started working a full-time job in 1973.)

The first dish my mom attempted from Julia? Hamburgers. Okay, Julia called it Bifteck Haché à la Lyonnaise, but in our house they were called Julia Child burgers; in any case, since the main ingredient was ground beef (gussied up with onions and herbs, sautéed, and served with a reduction sauce), they didn't intimidate my mom. I still occasionally rely on these when my culinary imagination runs dry.

Post-Julia, my mom became even more scissors-happy with her women's magazine recipes.

Chicken curry, clipped from *McCall's* magazine, was the most notable newcomer to our table; it was accompanied by saffron rice and a dozen condiments, and we always greeted it joyfully. It always had to be served in a particular way: One made a circle of rice, spooned the ochre-colored curry into the middle, and added condiments—peanuts, sweetened coconut, dried unsweetened coconut, mango chutney, diced green pepper, sliced scallions, sliced bananas with lime juice—around the outside of the circle. To depart from this procedure would have meant ejection from the family. We still ask for chicken curry on visits home, though Mom has since updated the recipe.

Julia's leg of lamb became a standard *chez nous,* along with her suggested accompaniments. But the most important contribution Julia made to our household was her roast chicken recipe—the recipe that involved basting the chicken every eight minutes and flipping it this way and that—which my mom and I both still use. In fact, it's such a standard that I once called my mom, only to have her say, "I'll call you back in two minutes." When she did, saying, "Sorry. I had to turn-baste-salt-and-strew," I knew exactly what she was talking about. Julia's roast chicken is served with a simple sauce made by deglazing the roasting pan. In fact, that was probably the biggest change in my mother's cooking post-Julia, when she began to deglaze *everything* to "make a little sauce."

Julia's influence, it's commonly said, was really limited to home cooking. But the interest in and understanding of food that Julia engendered in so many people made them hungry for a different kind of restaurant dining experience, and that was an extremely important prerequisite for what would follow in the coming years. In the meantime, people's perception of cooking began to evolve; it began to seem like less of a chore, and acquired a patina of glamour. To be a good cook was sophisticated, urbane. An Al Kaufman cartoon in the March 1974 issue of *Gourmet* showed a woman on the couch at her shrink's office ("seeing a shrink" had recently become very hip). She's saying, ". . . then I add a half cup of diced celery and salt and pepper to taste." The shrink is taking notes and managing to look interested.

Once Americans were able to latch on to food personalities such as Julia, making them into celebrities, the rest was history. For we love our stars the way the Brits love their royalty (and, ahem, the way *we* love their royalty). For the first time, we saw character as it was reflected in a personal cuisine. Julia was generous—lots of good butter, cream, meats, and so forth, just as her television persona is generous—big, warm, plump, good-humored, and Francophile. Beard was a jolly all-American type who made us love jolly all-American food. Another TV cook, Graham Kerr, *The Galloping Gourmet,* was a dandy, and his food was dandy bachelor food.

The performing cook trend that Julia started on her show in 1963 has mushroomed enormously in the three decades since. Today Julia hosts other chefs on her "Baking with Julia" series; the show is a spin-off of other "Cooking with Julia" shows of the past. Cooking on TV has become ultra-specialized—not only do we have a pastry chef on public television with his *Dessert Circus* (a sign of the times—today even a pastry chef can be a celebrity!), but we have radio shows about food, TV travel shows about food, and even an entire TV Food Network, offering not only cooking shows, but beverage shows, news programs about food, and a couple of cooking game shows. On *Ready, Set, Cook!,* for instance, three chefs are given a certain limited number of ingredients, and must race to prepare a dish incorporating them in eighteen minutes flat. Regular talk shows across the country have cooking ranges as standard equipment on their sets, so common has the cooking demonstration become. And firms such as Lisa Ekus Public Relations offer "media training" to chefs and cookbook authors. It's telling that up-and-coming chefs are willing to spend thousands of dollars to learn what to wear on television, what to talk about while doing a demo, where to look (not at the camera), and so forth.

The chef-as-celebrity phenomenon that began with Julia on TV and Craig Claiborne actually naming chefs in restaurant reviews finally reached peak silliness in 1997, when *The New York Times's* newly redesigned food section featured an article about where various chefs buy the shoes they wear to work.

How broad was Julia Child's reach? Though it may have been a bit of an exaggeration, the headline for the cover story of *U.S. News and World Report* on September 22, 1997, speaks volumes: "How Julia Invented Modern Life."

4

XENOPHOBES NO MORE: THE FOREIGN INFLUENCE

VAVY VILAICHAND, A TWENTY-TWO-YEAR-OLD WOMAN from Bangkok, had learned to cook—like many Thai girls—from her mother back home in Thailand. She came to the United States in 1972 to study in Southern California at California Polytechnic University at Pomona, and there she earned a degree in education, receiving her teaching credential. Two years later she met her husband-to-be, Ken Kittivech. Ken had studied engineering in Bangkok and had just moved to Los Angeles from Berkeley. One thing she and Ken had in common was their passion for cooking; they loved to cook for friends, and did so often. In the heat of such a passion, they decided to jettison their intended careers and in 1976 they donned aprons, grabbed knives, and opened a restaurant, Chan Dara, in Hollywood. Although since then the Kittiveches have divorced, they're still business partners. Business is—to put it mildly—thriving.

Chan Dara, which started with twelve tables in a tiny North Cahuenga Boulevard storefront and the Kittiveches behind the range, introduced slews of Angelenos to the joys of Thai food. But twelve tables wouldn't suffice for long; soon the Kittiveches took over the storefront next door, and a few years later added another location in nearby Larchmont Village. By this time, Vavy was working the front of the house. When I worked in Hollywood in the summer of 1979 (by that time Chan Dara had doubled in size), I lunched there frequently. I remember being struck by it because it was the first ethnic restaurant I had eaten in that felt really fashionable. The waitresses, all gorgeous Thai women, were dressed impeccably in the New Wave miniskirts of the day; the stylish work of young photographers hung on the wall, and the dishes incorporated an unusual variety of fresh ingredients.

"When we first started," recalls Vavy Kittivech, "we toned [the food] down a little bit because real Thai food is very spicy and has a strong aroma." Finding essential ingredients such as fresh Thai basil and chilis was a problem when they first opened, and the Kittiveches had to make do with dried herbs and spices. But five years or so after they opened, Laotian and Cambodian immigrants had established themselves in farming communities in Fresno and San Diego, and provided the Kitteveches with a source for fresh ingredients, even fresh Thai basil in the winter. "After many years in the business," says Vavy, "the customers have gotten used to that strong smell and spiciness. Now I think they have the taste of real Thai food; now we can make something really tempting. . . . Now we make our food almost like in Thailand." Not only did Angelenos get used to it; they fell head over heels in love with it.

The business grew and grew, and eventually the Kittiveches opened a much larger restaurant on the West Side of Los Angeles, and a more casual Chandarette in Marina del Rey. Two years ago they finally sold the original Hollywood location because they were so busy they couldn't handle it all.

The Kittiveches' story is not at all an uncommon one. What they did, however, wouldn't have been possible if the United States hadn't changed the xenophobic immigration laws that had ruled the land for almost a hundred years before the Immigration Act of 1965. Much of the dynamism of the American gastronomic revolution came as a result of new waves of immigration that began in the mid-1960s with the passage of the Act.

Although it may be difficult to imagine today, for the first part of the twentieth century, American immigration policy had been shaped by a persistent aversion to foreigners that permeated American culture and substantially shaped the way Americans ate. At the same time, a strong desire among the immigrants of the previous big wave of immigration—and there hadn't been one since the 1880s—to assimilate into "American" culture effectively excised many foreign foodways from the American scene. So influences both new and old were blocked at every turn.

Ironically, Americans were rejecting the same immigrant foodways that we'd later come to embrace. Buying the day's bread fresh each morning, for instance, had been seen as contrary to the Domestic Science movement's notions of efficient household management. In the 1990s, many people *aspire* to buy good fresh bread every morning. For the first half of the century, buying what was fresh, seasonable (and incidentally, inexpensive) was the immigrant way. Doing the entire week's shopping in advance was seen as more efficient, the method of the more modern homemaker. With a family car in every garage, a refrigerator-freezer replacing the icebox, and a supermarket eliminating the need for separate sojourns to the butcher, the fishmonger, and the greengrocer, immigrant ways of shopping—and thus cooking—became obsolete. By the 1950s the clever homemaker saw herself navigating the wide aisles of the antiseptic supermarket, filling up the shopping cart with frozen vegetables, packaged convenience foods, and shrink-wrapped cuts of meat she could toss in the freezer. Never mind that this style of shopping made it nearly impossible to serve fresh, flavorful, inspired food.

In order to fully understand the effect of the Immigration Act of 1965, one needs to look at the immigrant influences that were already in place before World War II.

Naturally, in a country founded by immigrants, the basis for all cookery was foreign. With the notable exception of the contribution of African slaves, from the founding of the union through the mid-1960s, the foreign influence on our country's cooking was almost wholly European. Since the early settlers were English, French, German and Dutch, it was the gastronomy of those countries that formed the basis of our national cookery.

Thus many dishes we consider all-American actually have their roots in Europe. Chicken pot pie has a heritage that can be traced back to Europe in the Middle Ages. In the sixteenth century, anything that fluttered was popped into a pie—quails, partridges, waterfowl, and even crows. Remember the four and twenty blackbirds? Chicken pie eventually made its way from England to the American colonies. Martha Washington made chicken pie for George—at least the dish appears in her *Booke of Cookery,* the handwritten manuscript of recipes handed down through generations of her family, which had British roots.

Cole slaw was a Dutch import (*cool sla*), as was the cookie (*koekje*); frankfurters were German *wienerwurst* (Vienna sausage), though the habit of plunking them into buns, adding trimmings, and calling them "hot dogs" was American. Hamburgers also came by way of Germany, according to culinary historian Jean Anderson. "The forerunner is believed to be Steak Tartare," she wrote in *The American Century Cookbook,* "which German sailors discovered while on leave in Russian ports in centuries past. They liked this Tartar raw beef specialty and carried the idea home to Hamburg where some enterprising chef shaped the minced beef into patties and grilled them. They soon became known as 'Hamburg steak.' " But again, it took Americans to plop them onto buns and dress them up.

Even apple pie—the dish we think of as quintessentially American—has its roots in Europe. Its pedigree may be as ancient as the Roman empire, and it's at least as old as England, according to Karen Hess, who has found recipes for apple pie in late fourteenth-century English manuscripts.

Yet besides the various influences that America's original settlers brought with them from Europe, the influence of African-Americans in the antebellum South was also considerable. The half a million slaves who had been forced to immigrate from Africa contributed mightily to American cooking, especially in the South, beginning before the Pilgrims even landed at Plymouth Rock.* In her illuminating 1995 book *The Welcome Table: African-American Heritage Cooking,* Jessica B. Harris pointed out a number of "culinary tendencies" brought by the Africans, giving us composed rice dishes, fritters, smoked ingredients used for flavoring, okra, nuts and seeds as thickeners, leafy greens, and peppery hot sauces. The Africans brought not only slow-cooked, exotically spiced stews that would later appear as dishes such as gumbo (from *tchingombo,* Umbundu for "okra"), but also a taste for a number of ingredients that would become

---

*According to Jessica B. Harris, in 1619, the year before the Pilgrims landed, a Dutch vessel on the James River in Virginia sought to trade twenty-three Negroes in exchange for provisions, and presumably they would have brought some culinary traditions with them from Africa.

mainstays of the Southern culinary repertoire—black-eyed peas, yams, okra, sesame seeds, and wild greens, for example.

Once the African-Americans arrived, extreme adversity became the mother of new culinary invention for them. "The Africans brought techniques from the Motherland that helped them use food their owners had thrown away—" explained Joe Randall and Toni Tipton-Martin in their 1998 book *A Taste of Heritage: The New African-American Cuisine,* "internal organs, hooves, ears, and tails of hogs, and bottom-feeding garbage fish (catfish)." They continued:

> They overcame adversity by transforming unwanted foods—wild game and vegetables, which were plentiful—into savory dishes. Meat played only a supporting role in the theater of African-American cooking; vegetables and grains were the stars.
>
> Simultaneously, the Africans created delicacies: They pickled pigs' feet and ears; adopted the French way of serving brains and scrambled eggs for breakfast; and found use for chitterlings just as the French had crafted andouillettes from pork entrails in France.

African-Americans influenced what the plantation owners ate as well. "Wherever African-Americans did the cooking," wrote Karen Hess in *The Carolina Rice Kitchen: The African Connection,* "there were subtle African influences even when they followed the [recipes] read aloud by their English mistresses as conscientiously as they were able. . . . such cooks had known other products, other fragrances, and because of a phenomenon known to the Chinese as *wok presence,* they insensibly changed the English palate into the Virginia palate, which came to expect headier sauces. It was this African presence that accounted for the near mythic reputation of Southern cookery."

When Julia Child took hold of our imaginations, mainstream American culture was fairly white-bread, in more ways than just gastronomically. Throughout the 1950s, more than half of all immigrants to the United States had come from Europe. And although African-Americans made up a significant part of our population, one didn't see them on television or in movies; blacks weren't even allowed to play major league baseball until Jackie Robinson broke the color barrier when he joined the Dodgers in 1947. With the notable exception of its influence on Southern cooking, through the 1950s, black culture's imprint on white America was pretty much limited to that of jazz musicians. Nor were Americans of other ethnic backgrounds visible in our culture. The image of America as portrayed on the small and large screen was suburban, white, and middle class.

It took the Civil Rights Movement of the 1960s to bring black culture, including "soul food" to the attention of white America. Even today most white Americans are unaware of the gastronomic contributions of the African-American slaves.

Besides the northern European and French influences that were in place and the foodways brought over by Africans, the only other foreign influence that made any significant mark was that of Italy. Italian-American families tended to take great pride in the wonderful dishes they brought from their homes in Italy. They withstood the pressure to assimilate and the influence of Domestic Science. Non–Italian-Americans took to Italian dishes much more willingly, and much earlier in the twentieth century, than other cookery of foreign origin. Spaghetti and macaroni made it into the American lexicon early in the twentieth century, some seventy-five years before "pasta" would become a household word.

There was, however, one city in which ethnic cuisine

and dining were more readily possible, visible, and embraced even before the mid-1960s. For most of this century, New York City provided the exception to the rule that ethnic eating was not popular. According to Michael and Ariane Batterberry, ". . . the most distinctive culinary aspect of the twenties and early thirties was an outbreak of small foreign restaurants all over Anglo-Saxon New York." Besides Italian, German, Chinese, and French food, the intrepid diner could find Russian, Jewish, Turkish, Armenian, Greek, Spanish, Swedish, Egyptian, and Indian food.

But for the rest of America, the types of immigrant food that would most strongly come to influence the way we eat today had not yet arrived.

With the Immigration Act of 1924, America went from an attitude of "Give me your tired, your poor . . ." to "Give me your well-heeled, your white." The Act severely curtailed immigration from Asia, Latin America, and Africa, as well as Eastern Europe, instituting a system of quotas, whereby each country was allowed only a certain number of immigrants; the quotas for western and northern Europe were much higher than any other countries. The law also made it illegal for anyone to immigrate from a country from which it was illegal to become naturalized, and this was aimed, most notably, at the Japanese this time.

By the time the 1960s rolled around, Americans were so resistant to new immigrant cuisines in general that besides spaghetti, macaroni, French cuisine, and a few other well-entrenched adoptive American dishes, Domestic Science's influence over American cookery was more evident than anything else.

Before 1965, bagels were exotic in most of the United States. In fact they were produced outside of New York City for the first time only in 1927, when Henry Lender brought the recipe from his native Poland and opened a bagel bakery in Connecticut. (According to James Trager, the first recorded mention of a bagel in history was in 1610, when community regulations in Cracow, Poland, stipulated that *beygls* should be offered as gifts to women during childbirth.) When I was a child in Los Angeles, we used to go to Western Bagel, not too far from where we lived in the San Fernando Valley, once in a while for a baker's dozen. Otherwise one would only see them in Jewish delis. Bagels only appeared in the mountain states as recently as 1976.

And though America was more receptive to Italian food, it was only the most basic dishes that were widely adopted in the New World. Italian food meant spaghetti with meatballs and red sauce. Or macaroni and cheese. The word *pasta* was never used. Pizza was popular, though 1960s pies were never adorned with today's "gourmet" toppings, such as smoked duck or golden caviar, but rather were only offered with pepperoni, sausage, meatballs, anchovies, olives, peppers, and mushrooms. And, in giddy California, pineapple and ham.

Just as Scandinavian design became popular in the early 1960s, its food also made a splash. There had long been a large Scandinavian population in the northern Midwest; there were also small pockets elsewhere, in Solvang, a Danish community halfway up the California coast, for example. In Los Angeles, Scandia, widely considered to be one of the best restaurants in the country, was for many *the* place to eat.

Similarly, German cuisine had enjoyed an enduring popularity in places with large German populations, such as New York City and San Francisco, but two world wars put quite a damper on our enjoyment of sauerbraten. One saw a parallel in spoken language: The German-American population was sizable, but just as German had been widely taught in primary and secondary schools before World War I, it was phased out during the war, since it was the enemy tongue.

Japanese food couldn't become popular until quite a long time after the end of World War II, so prejudiced were we against the Japanese. San Francisco had boasted a Japanese neighborhood, Little Osaka, as early as the turn of the twentieth century, in the same location the Japanese Cultural Center occupies today. By World War II there were 6,000 Japanese residents in San Francisco, but that was before they were sent to so-called relocation camps. In the meantime, there weren't any Japanese restaurants to speak of, except Yamato, which opened in the 1930s, primarily to serve Japanese visitors to San Francisco.

The xenophobia from which Americans had long been suffering began to soften somewhat during World War II, ironically at the same time we were guilty of outrageous crimes against Japanese-Americans, putting them in internment camps and confiscating their property. And our attitudes toward German-Americans weren't exactly kind. But with the wholesale slaughter of millions on ethnic grounds during the war, many Americans now became somewhat less accepting of ethnic and cultural intolerance in their own country. (Exceptions abounded, of course; for instance, in the segregated South.)

The war was also responsible for exposing servicemen to cuisines they had never seen before—not only in Europe and Asia, but also in North Africa and the South Pacific. And the GIs brought their newfound likes (and dislikes) home after the war ended.

After the war, Senator Joseph McCarthy's ultraxenophobic communist witch hunts had an unintended backlash. Many Americans, particularly those on the political left, came to abhor xenophobia. People became much more open to outside influences, and certainly their food horizons opened up. (It's interesting to note that Julia Child's husband Paul was investigated and questioned by the Office of Security for the U.S. Intelligence Agency regarding his connections with alleged communists, and that Julia and Paul detested McCarthy and his aims.) Yet fear and suspicion still ruled the lives of many.

By 1952, even though America was nowhere close to being ready for Japanese food, Helen Evans Brown, in her *West Coast Cook Book,* offered a recipe for *Mukozuki,* "a Japanese dish resembling eggs foo yung." Made with canned tuna, bean sprouts, onion, eggs, and soy sauce, cooked like an omelet, this dish hardly sounds Japanese. This gives one an idea of the depth of our knowledge of things Japanese at the time.

Elsewhere in that book, she wrote, rather presciently:

> *Japanese Cookery* is becoming more popular, but so far it really hasn't contributed very much to our regional cuisine. We like sukiyaki and tempura and the crispness of their vegetables, and those of us who know it are quite mad about the way they charcoal broil their fish. . . . Still, Occidental palates balk at raw fish and dipping meat into raw egg at table, though both dishes are really excellent. The Japanese have two other culinary customs that we would do well to adopt and adapt: the little charcoal brazier which sits on the table and is used for sukiyaki and other last-minute cooking should lend charm to any cocktail party; and their presentation of food—the exquisite way in which they serve even the humblest meal.

Brown couldn't have suspected that Japanese presentation of food would one day inform everything Americans would eat, since it so strongly influenced *nouvelle cuisine,* and consequently all of American restaurant cooking.

By the early 1960s, Japanese food was a *little* less esoteric in California. "In San Francisco today there are many Japanese restaurants and bars," wrote Doris Muscatine in her 1963 book *A Cook's Tour of San Francisco.* "We no longer boggle at fish cakes or bean sprouts, although some of us still retain a certain reserve in the face of raw fish." Yet a 1968 book that collected the menus of the Golden State's most interesting restaurants, *101 Nights in California,* includes only three Japanese restaurants. Sukiyaki, teriyaki, tempura, and sha-bu sha-bu were typical dishes at all three (one each in San Francisco, Monterey, and Los Angeles), with a big deal made about the kimono-clad waitresses, sliding screens, and traditional floor seating. San Francisco's Mingei-Ya and Monterey's Ginza each listed sashimi inconspicuously at the bottom of their respective menus. Each described the dish as "filet" of tuna or sea bass; neither happened to mention that it was served raw.

Outside of California, Japanese restaurants were rare. Jean Anderson's *American Century Cookbook* puts America's first sushi bar in New York in 1957, though she doesn't offer a source. According to James Trager, the first sushi bar opened in Manhattan in 1963, Restaurant Nippon; the chef, Eigiro Tanaka, had previously worked for Japanese prime minister Shigeru Yoshida. Benihana of Tokyo opened, also in New York City, in 1964, predating the Immigration Act by a year and bringing teppanyaki and sukiyaki to the Big Apple. Hiroaki "Rocky" Aoki, a Japanese American member of Japan's Olympic wrestling team, had stopped in New York en route to the 1960 Olympics in Rome and decided New York could use a Japanese restaurant; soon he went nationwide with his central grill-kitchens and theatrical knife-wielding chefs. But this food had nothing to do with the type of Japanese fare that would captivate America later.

In the second half of the nineteenth century, anti-immigrant sentiment in the United States had been particularly strong against the Chinese, especially on the West Coast. In California, where the Chinese community made up the largest non-European immigrant group, racism ran rampant and was even violent at times, particularly among laborers who thought of Chinese immigrants as "coolies" who wanted to snatch their jobs. Largely as a result of political pressure, Congress passed the Chinese Exclusion Act of 1882, suspending immigration of Chinese workers for a period of ten years, deporting Chinese already in the United States illegally, and barring Chinese immigrants from becoming American citizens. Far from being deplored, this law was so popular that the immigration ban was extended an additional ten years; in 1902 it was extended indefinitely, and in fact remained in effect until the Chinese Exclusion Act was repealed in 1946.

Not surprisingly, this long history of exclusion severely limited Chinese influence until the Immigration Act of 1965. Before then, Chinese food meant chop suey and chow mein, wonton soup, gooey sweet-and-sour sauces, and white sauces thick with cornstarch. It was all Cantonese, but a sad rendition of the real cuisine of Canton, which unbeknownst to much of America, is actually among the best in China. Because immigration from China was cut off for so long, there was no infusion of new blood and fresh culinary ideas from the east, and Chinese cooks were left executing the same dishes over and over again that harkened back to the original dishes of the Gold Rush days—chop suey, for instance. To make matters culinarily worse, before the Exclusion Act was even passed, most of the Chinese immigrants in the United States were men who had obtained work visas and came to build the railroads. Few had been professional cooks, and few lived in families. The Chinese immigrants in New York at the end of the nineteenth century formed a bachelor society; many lived in boardinghouses in shared rooms. The Exclusion Act removed any hope of their families joining them, and in any case, rarely would there have been a woman in the kitchen to show them how things were done. Historically, throughout the world, it generally has been women who not only do the family cooking, but who are responsible for passing traditional foodways along from generation to generation.

Of course we ate Cantonese when I was growing up in the 1960s; I learned late in life that Chinese food on Sunday night has long been a Jewish-American tradition. We'd usually eat at a restaurant in Sherman Oaks, near where we lived. Ho Toy's, like many of the "fancier" Chinese restaurants at the time, was dark, with red walls, plush banquettes, lantern lighting, and many Oriental touches that were not lost on a seven-year-old. I thought it wonderfully glamorous. If my parents were in the mood to really do it right, we'd go downtown to L.A.'s Chinatown, to Man Fook Low—not as fancy as Ho Toy's, but it seemed more authentic, even to a pip-squeak. It never failed to amaze me that my father seemed to know all the waiters, even though we hadn't been there in what seemed like forever to me. Perhaps it was my dad's habit of treating everyone like his best friend, a trait that must have gone back to his days slicing lox at Abrams' Delicatessen, Minneapolis's only Jewish deli in the 1950s. Dining out once, he watched someone eat something delicious-looking at another table. Finally he said, "Excuse me—that looks good. Can I have a bite?" embarrassing me to no end. I think perhaps he would have felt more at home in Portugal, where it's customary for diners in casual restaurants to invite strangers entering the establishment to stop at their table and have some of their dinner.

There *were* a few good Chinese restaurants before 1965. Johnny Kan opened Kan's in San Francisco in 1953, serving serious Cantonese food such as sliced abalone over Chinese ravioli, wintermelon soup (advance notice required), squab

Chung Kwong ("first steamed, then deep fried"), and Peking duck. Imperial Palace, also in San Francisco, offered ginseng root soup, bird's nest soup, five willows rock cod, and roast squab stuffed with sweet rice. At special banquets, it presented smoked tongue, 1,000-year-old eggs, mushrooms costing $300 per pound "found sprouting up just as the snow melts," "the marrow of young bamboo," abalone imported from China (which was odd, since California had indigenous abalone), sautéed shark fin that had been first steamed for two days (*bon chee*). Or "You might have crab leg prepared with Chinese cabbage," wrote Doris Muscatine in *A Cook's Tour of San Francisco:* "the heart of the cabbage hangs for a week to age like a steak; then the cook deep fries it whole, lays it on a plate, covers it with steaming chicken broth which it soaks up until tender; creamed crab legs go over the top, and the dish is finished off with a sprinkling of Chinese ham."

Needless to say, this level of authentic cooking was rare; most Americans had never tasted of such delights.

In 1958, Boston saw a different kind of Chinese restaurant—New England's first Mandarin restaurant, owned by Joyce Chen; her cookbook followed in 1962. Otherwise, Cantonese was the rule. And just about every place had similar offerings: barbecue spare ribs, egg rolls (with hot mustard and either duck sauce on the East Coast or ketchup on the West Coast for dipping), fried shrimp, wonton soup, egg drop soup, sweet-and-sour pork, fried rice, moo goo gai pan, egg foo young, chow mein, lo mein, litchi chicken. Litchis again for dessert, accompanied by the obligatory fortune cookie.

As for Mexico, for obvious reasons, its influences were felt mainly in the border states. There were a number of restaurants in Southern California, but not many serious Mexican restaurants before 1970. Mexican ingredients and styles of cooking seemed to reach into our culture in other ways, however. Mexican-Americans enjoyed good Mexican food at home, for example, and to a limited degree the influence spread outward from there. "Today our people most recently from Mexico, and we have many," wrote Helen Evans Brown in *Helen Brown's West Coast Cook Book,* "still eat largely in the Mexican manner, but the rest of us have it just occasionally, and enjoy it when we do. Those of us who know Mexican cuisine usually have pretty definite opinions about what we like best. For those of you to whom it is new, the so-called Mexican plate, usually consisting of a taco, an enchilada, a tostado, sometimes a tamale, and always some beans, is a good sampler. . . ." El Cholo, a restaurant that's still going strong in Los Angeles, with new branches in La Habra and Santa Monica, opened on Vermont Avenue in 1927.

Mexican food was not unknown on the East Coast. Michael and Ariane Batterberry tell us in their 1973 book *On the Town in New York* that before 1940 "an authentic Mexican restaurant was conducted by two spinsters from New England who didn't know a word of Spanish between them." (One wonders how authentic it could have been!) James Beard made carnitas for twenty people in 1953 at the Connecticut home of Cheryl Crawford, one of the founders of the Group Theater. He roasted the pork, though, instead of frying it, which might have made for sorry little carnitas.

Sadly, Mexican food wasn't much a part of my Southern California childhood, except that when we moved to the San Fernando Valley in 1964, we had a cleaning lady, beloved by my family, named Anita "Norma" Toremaru. (She was married to a Japanese man named Ken Toremaru.) Norma occasionally baby-sat for us. She would make us tacos, frying the tortillas rather than using store-bought "shells"; they were a wonderful combination of crisp and chewy. Occasionally she'd make us enchiladas.

Despite our enjoyment of her tacos, authentic Mexican cooking wasn't Norma's forte: The native Oaxacan used ground beef, grated cheddar cheese (instead of *queso blanco*), diced tomatoes (instead of *salsa* or *pico de gallo*), and iceberg lettuce to fill the shells. Since we lived adjacent to a Mexican-American neighborhood, Chicano children made up about half of the population of my grade school, and the school cafeteria served enchiladas on Wednesdays. These were practically inedible, and I wasn't exactly a finicky eater. Just remembering the day of the week they were served attests to their awfulness. So when my mom made such proclamations as "Good Mexican food is an oxymoron," I had no reason not to believe her.

Others in my hometown were luckier when it came to Mexican food. Judy Marcus recalls, "It was so ubiquitous, somehow." When she married for the second time in 1968, she had a Mexican maid named Amparo, who was a wonderful cook. "I learned a lot from her," says Marcus. By then Mexican food had become a part of mainstream culture in California, even at the corporate level. Marcus, for instance, learned how to make *enchiladas suissas* from a recipe booklet put out by a cheese company.

New York boasted a few Indian restaurants. In March 1965, Alvin Kerr reviewed Taj Majal in *Gourmet,* portraying it as exotic. For all intents and purposes, Thai food didn't exist, nor did Vietnamese.

The Immigration Act of 1965 brought with it a sea of change. When the act took effect in 1968, the portals of the United States were unlocked to immigrants from around the globe, and since then millions have come from China, Hong Kong, Taiwan, Japan, Korea, Thailand, Eastern Europe, the Philippines, India, Pakistan, the Middle East, Africa, Mexico, the Caribbean, and Central and South America, bringing their foodways along with them. These new immigrants would forever change American culture—and more particularly for our purposes, our gastronomy.

At that time, the country was in the throes of the antiwar movement. Those active in it tended to be young, anti-establishment, politically liberal or leftist, and in any case, vehemently opposed to close-mindedness. It bothered the young people in the Movement that the Johnson (and later Nixon) administration viewed Vietnamese lives as worth less than American lives. These politically active types were not the same as hippies, who tended to be politically apathetic.* But in terms of culture, those in the antiwar crowd jettisoned their business suits and Jackie Kennedy pillbox hats in favor of jeans, often topped with African dashikis, Mexican-embroidered blouses or Indian cotton-print tops, and other ethnic fashions.

Not surprisingly, it was also very chic among this outward-looking set to eat ethnic. Besides appealing to their expansive ethos, ethnic restaurants tended to be inexpensive and unpretentious, appealing to this set's disgust with conspicuous consumption and other bourgeois values.

Suddenly, it seemed that xenophobia was waning in many pockets of our culture, if not among the Establishment.

The presence of the ethnic communities that had entered when the immigration laws changed didn't really make itself felt until the tail end of the 1960s and into the 1970s, since it took some time for communities to establish themselves.

---

*The relationship between hippies and the politically active proponents of the New Left was a complicated one. In his authoritative book *The Sixties,* Todd Gitlin wrote that in 1966 "Berkeley seemed to be building sturdier bridges between freaks and politicoes." But he also pointed out: ". . . the Haight-Ashbury merchants, rock impresarios, and dope dealers who financed the *Oracle* [San Francisco's hippie newspaper], and the hip influentials who starred in the media, were antipolitical purists," as was Timothy Leary.

Though we were still in love with France, and to a lesser degree with Italy, those countries now had rivals for our culinary affection. By February 1969, in a column on grilling in the previously Francocentric *Gourmet* magazine, James Beard was offering readers, along with Shish Kebabs, Shashlyk, and Shrimp and Bacon Kebabs, a recipe for *Kabayaki*—Japanese Eel Kebabs. Americans were certainly becoming more open-minded, yet one can imagine the reaction to his instructions: "Skin 1 or 2 eels and cut them into 3-inch lengths . . ." (The *New Yorker* could well have run this one under its signature headline of those times, "Recipes We Never Finished Reading.")

That same year, one year after the Act took effect, *Gourmet*'s pages were filled with paeans and references to exotic foreign foods. In New York City, Argentine, Danish, Italian, Polynesian, and Indian restaurants were reviewed; features ran on Indonesian Rijsttafel and Turkish cooking and travel pieces appeared on such far-flung destinations as Bengal, and Colombia, Ecuador, and Peru, which Elisabeth Lambert Ortiz covered. Such intense interest in South America coincided with huge increases in immigration to the United States from that continent. Latin America was hot; suddenly ethnic in general was most definitely *in*.

At family dining room tables across America, foreign influences were also steadily creeping in. Again in the pages of *Gourmet,* along with Quenelles with Shrimp Sauce and Veal Chops on Toast, a "Sunday Luncheons" menu column suggested Chinese Cabbage Salad with Watercress Dressing, Sukiyaki, and Baked Tomatoes with Sesame Seeds.

Alongside the straight-ahead establishment, the "eclectic" restaurant began to emerge, with elements from different cultures appearing on the same menu. In New York City, Restaurant Associates (Joseph Baum's company, once again on the cutting edge) opened Promenade Café in Rockefeller Center. *Gourmet*'s reviewer, Donald Aspinwall Allan, wrote, "I doubt there is another restaurant in America where *taramosalata* and terrine of duckling appear on the same menu." How commonplace such juxtapositions are today!

Though the coasts were in the throes of a food revolution, the heartland followed much more slowly. *The New York Times* reported in 1976 that the owner of a restaurant in Montana was having trouble getting her customers to accept dishes they perceived as exotic, though she said she "occasionally gets away with escargot and caesar salad." At the time there was only one well-stocked wine shop in the whole state, located in Great Falls.

In 1972, Richard M. Nixon made history by visiting mainland China; it was the first time an American President had done so in two decades. Nixon's perplexed-looking, droopy-dog face appeared on newspapers throughout the land as he watched Chou En-Lai demonstrate how to use chopsticks. (My brothers and I already knew how, as my father felt that being a cultured person included possessing facility with the eating utensils preferred by a quarter of the world's population.) After Nixon feasted in the Great Hall of the People (along with 700 of Chou En-Lai's closest friends) on small carp and bacon in vinegar sauce, spongy bamboo shoots, shark's fin in three shreds, and other delicacies, his historic visit paved the way for an opening up of relations between the two superpowers. For the first time since the revolution in 1949, Americans began to visit the People's Republic of China. This exchange sparked an interest in regional Chinese foods in the United States, and for the first time we learned of an alternative to workaday Cantonese.

In the five years or so that followed, the kind of Chinese food one ate said more about a person than the clothes he wore. All across the country, the red chili pepper came to symbolize what one sought, and Szechuan and Hunan were it. Red-hot was the idea, like the new communist-chic. It was daring to embrace a cuisine from behind the Iron curtain. Those who fancied themselves to be aficionados—and the country was crawling with them—now looked down on Cantonese food.

New York's cutting-edge entry in the mid-seventies was Shun Lee Palace, the sister restaurant to Shun Lee Dynasty, which had opened in 1965 with fairly predictable fare. But Shun Lee Palace offered something new to New Yorkers: Jay Jacobs wrote about mandarin* cuisine in a review of Shun Lee Palace in his 1978 book *New York à la Carte*. "It is China's *haute cuisine,*" he wrote,

> and its foremost exponent in this country may well be Tsung Ting Wang, who, in a nomenclatural inversion, is known to New Yorkers as T. T. Wang. Trained in Peking, Chef Wang also has been one of the prime movers in a gastronomic upheaval that during the past decade has toppled Cantonese cooking from its traditional position of preeminence and won thousands of New York Chinese food lovers hands over to the fiery cooking of Hunan and Szechwan provinces.

By the 1980s, regional Chinese cooking in most restaurants across the country would become as predictable and boring as Cantonese restaurants had been fifteen years before. Ruth Reichl, the *New York Times*'s erstwhile restau-

---

*Mandarin cuisine does not come from a particular region. In China, a mandarin was a high-ranking public official; the word came to mean "aristocrat," and consequently it is used to describe any *haute cuisine* from China.

rant critic, recently bemoaned the failure of Chinese *haute cuisine* to take off in the United States; she quoted Michael Tong, who today owns Shun Lee Palace, as saying, by way of explanation, "In the seventies we invented all these dishes: orange beef and crispy sea bass. There's no such thing in classic Chinese cooking."

In Los Angeles in the eighties, the most interesting Chinese food was now to be found in Chinatown at a number of restaurants specializing in seafood—Mon Kee, ABC Seafood, and Hop Li, to name a few. The food here was quite authentic, this time from Hong Kong; specials listed in Chinese characters taped to the walls promised an advantage in ordering to Chinese customers, who were many. The menus at all three were similar, with a few must-haves, at least for the non-character-reading public: whole Dungeness crab in black bean sauce with scallions or ginger sauce; steamed or fried whole catfish with a choice of sauces; salt shrimp, served whole in the shell and sautéed. All of it was messy but fabulous, served family-style at large round tables with lazy susans, in no particular order, on tiny plates that looked better suited for a donut in a coffee shop.

Since then the Chinese community in Monterey Park, a suburb of Los Angeles, has exploded, and in the late 1990s the best Hong Kong seafood is to be had there, at restaurants such as 888, NYC Seafood, and Harbor Village.

Beginning in the late 1970s, Italian food began to change in status. As the old standby marinara sauce and checkered tablecloth type of southern Italian establishment gave way to the graceful new expensive northern Italian restaurants, lasagne and veal parmigiana gave way to *parpardelle con la lepre* (papardelle with hare sauce), *osso bucco, tortelli di zucca* (pumpkin tortelli), and *risotto alla milanese.*

During the 1980s, the trattoria-style Italian restaurant came into ascendance—casual restaurants such as Chianti

Cucina and Angeli in Los Angeles, and Trattoria dell' Arte in New York. At these trattorias, authentic touches were the order of the day: Small dishes of olives appeared on the table, as well as bottles of fruity extra-virgin olive oil for bread dunking; Parmigiano Reggiano cheese was shaved onto salads. Simultaneously the quality of Italian wines coming into the United States began to improve dramatically. No longer did we drink cheap Chianti from the straw-covered *fiasco*; now we ordered Chianti Classico and paid attention to the vintage.

Most important, we saw the rise of the antipasto table. The focal point of these trattorias was a long rectangular or large round table covered with various room-temperature first courses—luscious slices of *bufala* mozzarella layered with tomato and basil; succulent shrimp with white beans and parsley; squiggly purple and white calamari salad; perfectly cooked string beans tossed with olive oil, lemon juice, and shallots. Who could resist? Primi, a Los Angeles restaurant, flew with the concept, offering entire meals of *primi,* or first courses. In any case, what distinguished these antipasti from anything we had been accustomed to eating was their utter simplicity, the clarity and vibrancy of their flavors, and the freshness of their ingredients—especially vegetables and seafood. American diners so enthusiastically embraced these dishes that gradually this new (to us) style of Italian food stopped seeming like a foreign cuisine and started to feel American.

In fact this style of cooking would become a bridge between the French cuisine of transformation and the lighter, fresher, bolder style of American cooking that has evolved in the late 1980s and into the 1990s.

By the time I left Los Angeles for college in Northern California in 1977, Mexican food had become so popular it seemed there was a Mexican restaurant every two blocks in L.A. In Northern California, burritos were very big, whether sold out of a Mexican grocery in Menlo Park, a storefront diner in Redwood City, or a muralled burrito stand in San Francisco. By 1982 burritos had become so mainstream that in my college circle, a machacas burrito was the most popular hangover cure the morning after.

As things evolved, if San Francisco and the rest of Northern California distinguished itself with burritos (really more Cal-Mex than Mexican), Los Angeles's Mexican cooks made their statement with tacos.

Beginning with the opening of Antonio's, a small, fairly authentic restaurant on Melrose Avenue, in 1970, the trend in Los Angeles has been toward Mexican food with fresher and fresher flavors, food that tastes and looks more like home cooking. Standards in the 1970s—such as chicken enchiladas, tacos with deep-fried shells, and chile rellenos—always served with rice and refritos (long mistranslated as "refried beans"; Diana Kennedy suggests in her definitive book *The Cuisines of Mexico* that "well-fried beans" is a better translation) have given way to homey preparations such as carnitas; soft tacos of *carne asada,* goat, fish, or shrimp; tamales (the green corn tamales, served seasonally at El Cholo, are among my favorites); and *mariscos,* Mexican seafood. Cilantro, limes, *salsa verde* (made with tomatillos), and *salsas crudas* have become more predominant; cooked red salsa and hard taco shells have faded into the background. In the more serious restaurant, regional specialties prevail: The marvelous La Serenata de Garibaldi in East Los Angeles, for instance, excels in regional seafood dishes.

At the same time, Mexican ingredients and preparations have found their way into mainstream American cuisine. Salsa, something most Americans had never heard of thirty years ago, is now America's top-selling condiment.

One knew that Mexican food hit the culinary big time once Mary Sue Milliken and Susan Feniger, two Anglo women, put it in an upscale West Hollywood setting, opening Border Grill in 1985. That same year they opened another restaurant, City, achieving some local fame with their stylish—and sensible—fusion cuisine. They've since closed the first two and opened Border Grill in Santa Monica, and have become national celebrities, starring in "Too Hot Tamales," their show on the national TV Food Network as well as a local Los Angeles radio show.

In New York City, two more Anglos, Debra Ponzek and Bobby Flay, began doing creditable nouveau takes on Mexican food when they were chefs at Miracle Grill in the East Village in the late 1980s. Flay later opened Mesa Grill, with even more dramatic food and a trendy, high-decibel setting. But it's no longer really Mexican, more Southwestern-inspired.

Rick Bayless has been wowing Chicagoans with his take on regional Mexican food at Frontera Grill and Topolobampo.

Curiously, in general it has not been Mexican-Americans who have made a name cooking Mexican or Mexican-inspired food in the United States, with the notable exception of Zarela Martinez, of New York City's Zarela restaurant. Josefina Howard, owner of Manhattan's excellent Rosa Mexicano, is Spanish, though she did spend a number of years in Mexico. I would guess that Mexican-American chef-owners such as Jose Rodriguez of L.A.'s La Serenata de Garibaldi are less well-known than their Anglo counterparts in part because they tend not to hire slick public relations firms, and in part because the food press tends not to take Latinos seriously. The attitude seems to be "perhaps they can cook, but we don't want to make stars out of them."

Outside of California, Texas, and perhaps Chicago, Mexican food has a long way to come, largely resembling what it did in the 1970s in California or Texas: the enchilada combination plate–type of dining experience from California, or the fajitas on a sizzling platter/chimichanga Texas take.

Although New York City has gained a notable Mexican population since 1990, good Mexican restaurants have not proliferated there. Aside from a handful of taquerías and expensive restaurants such as Rosa Mexicano, Zarela, Maya, and Mi Cocina, New York City Mexican food is woefully inauthentic, usually prepared by cooks who aren't Mexican.

If nothing else, a shift in décor was a dead giveaway that ethnic food had become trendy. At one time, ethnic restaurants tended to run the gamut from bare-bones to shabby to kitschy. At about the point ethnic cuisine began to grow in popularity, stylish upscale restaurants began to flourish. After Chan Dara, L.A.'s Border Cafe was one of the first. But many Los Angeles restaurants were quick to catch on.

Next to Japanese, Thai food was probably the biggest thing, gastronomically, to hit Los Angeles in my lifetime. In *101 Nights in California,* published in 1968, not one Thai restaurant is included. Today there are an estimated 200 to 300 Thai restaurants in the Los Angeles area alone.

The boom in Thai food in Los Angeles had a lot to do with a technicality in immigration law. Just because the Immigration Act of 1965 opened the doors to millions of new immigrants, it didn't mean that admission to the United States would be automatic for those who wanted to come. The quotas set up by the Act were simply maximums that would be allowed in each year; immigrants still had to qualify for work permits and green cards. There were, however, generous allowances made for immigrants who would start businesses that would employ U.S. citizens. From 1976 through 1978, anyone who invested at least $40,000 in a business that would hire at least one full-time U.S. citizen would be granted a green card. (For several years before that, only a $10,000 investment was required. Today the requirement is $500,000 and at least ten full time U.S. citizen employees.) In any case, it was known in 1976 that the requirements would soon toughen, so immigrants scrambled to scrape together the money to start businesses that would allow them to stay in the United States. Naturally, the majority of immigrants couldn't come up with that kind of money, but as it happened, many Thais were able to, and restaurants were the businesses they chose to start.

Tepparod Thai, opened a few years before Chan Dara, was L.A.'s first well-known Thai restaurant. The decor was not as "hip" as Chan Dara's; it was more elegant, but the food every bit as good. Today Thai restaurants are everywhere. Some of the best—the most authentic, anyway—are in strip-mall storefronts, with little in the way of décor. A favorite among aficionados, Vim, packs them in at its small, nondescript Vermont Avenue location in Koreatown. Since I left Los Angeles in 1986, I've noticed that West Coast palates have continued to change. At a recent trip to Vim I was astounded at how spicy the food was: I could hardly eat it, while my friends didn't even seem to notice. Vavy Kittivech must have been right.

Thai food has strongly influenced American cooking all over the country, especially up and down the West Coast. Away from the larger concentrations of Thai immigrants, the restaurants aren't nearly as good.

By 1978, ethnic dining was so "in" that Caroline Bates wrote, in reviewing Sushi Shibucho, a Los Angeles sushi bar,

> We have all met the type at one time or another, the self-proclaimed gastronomic cosmopolite with a seemingly inexhaustible enthusiasm for the offbeat eating experience. Suggest that he try a smashing new

> French restaurant, and he responds, with an air of condescension, that French food bores him now and he eats only in ethnic places.

Yet inevitably there was still a limit to the food adventurism of such a character, and Bates reveals how "challenging" sushi still was to many people:

> One way to blow his cover is to invite him to be your guest at a *sushi* bar and then sit back and enjoy the creative excuses he gives for being unable to share the pleasure. There is no faking an appreciation of raw fish and vinegared rice. One either likes it or leaves it alone, and the Japanese, who invented *sushi,* have an insatiable appetite for it. Now, there are Westerners who have acquired a taste for *sushi* as keen as any Japanese . . .

Bates went on to define sushi, since its presence in popular culture still hadn't been established (nota bene that *Gourmet* still italicized it). She then described what happens at a sushi bar (that the fish is kept in a glass-covered case, that one points to it to make one's order known, and how a sushi chef works). Clearly, this was *news* to her readers.

For the gastronomic thrill seeker, fugu—blowfish, which is deadly poisonous unless prepared properly—was already being served in 1977 in New York City, at a restaurant called Hyo-Tan Nippon.

Today Japanese food has become so important in California that in *Zagat Survey 1998 Los Angeles* the top three restaurants in the food ranking are Japanese; a total of forty-five Japanese restaurants are covered in the book (compared with thirty-eight French, some of which are not even French).*

By the mid-1980s, many of us flocked to our new ethnic restaurants whenever we could. The craving for Mexican carnitas with fresh tomatillo salsa or Thai tom yung kung soup with shrimp, straw mushrooms, and lemongrass or Indian saag paneer curry, naan, and coriander sauce never seemed to subside; on the contrary, we got hungrier and hungrier.

Likewise, American chefs, even French-trained American chefs, rushed to embrace these extracultural influences.

Is Asian fusion cuisine new? There was some precedent for it in Vietnam under colonial French rule, where Asian adaptations of French dishes such as ragouts of beef and rabbit cooked in red wine sauce appeared, along with bread, coffee, croissants, crème caramel and Ga-To, decorated pastries. But according to An-My Lê, a photographer and expert on Vietnamese cuisine, "these were more appropriations and adaptations rather than fusion because most Vietnamese dishes were a hundred percent Vietnamese."

I'd put the beginnings of Asian-French fusion cuisine in the United States at some time around 1980. It was then that I happened into a tiny former sushi bar in a marginal neighborhood in Los Angeles, where the Japanese chef had studied at the Cordon Bleu.

Nearby, Tomi Haresi opened his Café Blanc on Beverly Boulevard and Virgil in 1988; today he's become something of a cult chef in L.A., where he cooks at his Nouveau Café Blanc in Beverly Hills.

*Among the "French" restaurants listed that aren't really French are Chinois-on-Main, Diaghilev, L.A. Farm, Patina, and Shiro. There is also a listing for "French Bistro," but at least a third of those are not French either.

Then there was La Petite Chaya, owned by Yuji Tsunoda, who also owned La Marée de Chaya, just outside of Tokyo. Tsunoda's family had been in the restaurant business since the seventeenth century; "Chaya" means "teahouse." It was at La Marée that Franco-Japanese fusion was considered to have been originated, with its chef Kihachi Kumagai. In the late 1970s Tsunoda began working on plans to open a Chaya in California. In 1982 he finally brought Susumu Fukui over to be chef of his new restaurant, and Fukui came to be known as the first chef in America to do Franco-Japanese fusion.

In the early 1970s, France and Japan had shared mutual admiration, gastronomically speaking, and quite a bit of exchange. Paul Bocuse had traveled widely in Japan; Alain Senderens had studied Japanese cooking. And when Michael McCarty studied at the Cordon Bleu, he said there were half a dozen Japanese men and women in his class who won all the aspic competitions. Caroline Bates pointed out that the two cuisines share notable similarities: "There's a sense of order, a sense of codification," she said.

New York City actually had Japanese–New York hybrid restaurants called Hisei as early as the 1970s. The first opened on Grove Street in Greenwich Village; eventually there would be four locations. Hisei, also the name of the chef, broke new ground by serving seared rare fish on top of vegetables. And, remembers Rozanne Gold, "You could get a steamer basket of steamed vegetables that you would dip into ponzu [sauce]. People didn't know any of this food."

Back in Los Angeles, just a few storefronts up Hillhurst from La Petite Chaya, was the sushi bar that was widely considered in the 1980s to be Los Angeles' best, Katsu. It was terribly chic, with no sign marking it outside, just a small pile of sea salt on a leaf outside the door—since salt purifies, it is believed that such an offering cleanses the site and brings good luck. Cafe Katsu opened some years later in a strip-mall storefront in West Los Angeles, on a street called Sawtelle, which had long been home to a number of Japanese groceries and restaurants. Cafe Katsu offered Japanese fusion cuisine, but it was really more Japanese-California-French than Japanese-French. In any case, Cafe Katsu executed it quite well.

Cooks spun out of both Cafe Katsu and La Petite Chaya, which had since opened a satellite in West L.A.; another would eventually open in Venice; and soon the Franco-Japanese fusion was ubiquitous in L.A.

Caroline Bates believes that Roy Yamaguchi did some of the most original and important work when it came to L.A.'s fusion movement. Born and raised in Japan, Yamaguchi spent summers growing up in Hawaii, his father's birthplace. Back in the 1940s, his grandfather had an informal restaurant in Hawaii, the Vineyard Tavern, where he cooked for the plantation workers. As a youth in Japan, Yamaguchi, studying at an American high school, enrolled in a home economics class "with the girls," and fell in love with cooking. In 1974 he set off for New York's Hudson Valley to study at the Culinary Institute of America, and got a job in Los Angeles, working at L'Ermitage from 1979 to 1981. By early 1981 he wound up at a restaurant in the San Fernando Valley called La Serene, and it was there he started cooking what he called "Euro-Asian" cuisine, "French with an Asian overtone." His signature dishes were sea urchin rolled in oysters, then in Napa cabbage, and served with a seaweed cream sauce; also a scallop mousse with sea urchin sauce. After stints at Michael's in Santa Monica and later, briefly, at Les Gourmets at the L.A. Airport Sheraton, Yamaguchi opened, with a partner, 385 North in 1984 on La Cienega, restaurant row.

Yamaguchi didn't limit his influences as much as some of the other Franco-Japanese fusion chefs in L.A. did. "As

I progressed in life," Yamaguchi explained, "my style of cooking [incorporated] a lot more Asian ingredients, not only from Japan." Flavors from Korea, China, Malaysia, and Thailand also figured in to Yamaguchi's vision. Here Angelenos were treated to grilled soy-marinated duck leg salad with raspberry vinaigrette, lobster potsticker with basil sauce, or shu mai salad with mango vinaigrette and roasted hazelnuts.

Wolfgang Puck opened Chinois-on-Main, Southern California's first Chinese-French fusion in 1983. Although many Americans may think Puck invented Franco-Asian cuisine, obviously he didn't.

Indian, North African, and Middle Eastern foods also became popular as a result of the Act of 1965.

By the late 1970s, falafel stands began to open in Los Angeles, bringing hummus, tahini, and baba ganoush into our gastronomic vocabulary; Middle Eastern restaurants were already ubiquitous along Brooklyn's Atlantic Avenue. But the first time I saw pita bread must have been 1973. My parents had just divorced, and my father, who didn't yet know how to cook (he would later become an excellent cook), made us dinner for the first time at his new bachelor pad. "Pita pizzas," he called them: store-bought spaghetti sauce spooned onto the top of pita breads, topped with the rubbery stuff that passed, in those days, for mozzarella cheese, and run under the broiler. We weren't anxious to repeat dinner at Dad's. Besides its presence at falafel stands and Middle Eastern groceries, pita bread was adopted by the health food movement—in a whole wheat version, of course—as its sandwich bread of choice. Today pita, as well as the Middle Eastern spreads baba ganoush (made from eggplant) and hummus (made from chick-peas) in a dozen different varieties, is available in supermarkets throughout the country.

Indian restaurants proliferated in New York: By the early 1980s, one block of East Sixth Street in Manhattan's East Village housed dozens of inexpensive Indian restaurants—a paradise for my underfunded, spice-starved friends and me when we were in graduate school—and locals would joke that they all shared the same kitchen. A few had sitar players performing in the front windows, and several had clay tandoor ovens inside turning out puffy, delicious naan bread and tandoori chicken. In the meantime, the Jackson Heights neighborhood in Queens had become home to a sizable population of new immigrants from India, and in that neighborhood one found not only some of the best Indian restaurants, but also groceries chock full of masalas and lentils, green mangoes and jars of ghee.

In Los Angeles, however, the two or three good Indian restaurants were expensive, until the mid-1980s, when a strip-mall storefront called India's Oven opened on Pico Boulevard, serving fabulous vindaloos, tandoori, and naan on paper plates for next to nothing. Before India's Oven, Angelenos had to be satisfied with buying spices and chutneys in one of the small Indian groceries in Culver City and making their own curries. By the late 1980s, a number of other inexpensive Indian restaurants opened, and by the nineties, Indian food had become another popular ethnic option in that land of fabulous exotic dining.

California did excel when it came to North African restaurants, which, according to Caroline Bates, came about because a very good Moroccan one, Mamounia, opened in San Francisco in the early 1970s, achieving extraordinary popularity. In Los Angeles, Dar Maghreb was the chic place to eat b'stilla and couscous with one's hands in a mosquelike setting with a dreamy skylight, while nearby Moun of Tunis had bellydancers and wonderful tagines.

★ ★ ★

While all this was going on in California, a different type of fusion was being invented in Miami, Florida. Yet this had nothing to do with the Immigration Act of 1965, and in fact it preceded it. In 1960 a huge influx of Cuban immigrants began arriving in Miami, and these immigrants would eventually become a major influence on chefs such as Norman Van Aken and Allen Susser, who would create what they'd call "New World Cuisine." When Juanita Plana, a caterer, arrived in Miami in 1960, she says, "There was only one grocery where they sold mangoes and yucca. And from there it started." The Cuban immigrants opened restaurants serving *lechon asado* (roast pork), *camarones al ajillo* (garlic shrimp), yucca and boniato (two Caribbean root vegetables), and other specialties. Bakeries opened as well, where one could get high-octane Cuban coffee in tiny plastic cups. According to Plana, Norman Van Aken and many other chefs were in Key West at the time, where there was a very large Cuban community. "[The Cubans] started showing them how to use all those fruits," says Plana. "They started using what the locals were using."

Otherwise, Caribbean food made its appearance in restaurants in cities that had large populations from the islands—New York City, for instance. When I moved from Los Angeles to New York in 1986, Los Angeles had just seen the opening of a tiny restaurant called Cha Cha Cha in a marginal neighborhood. Manhattan had hundreds—from Jamaican meat patty stands and West Indian jerk restaurants to the brightly lit Dominican seafood palaces with plastic lobsters in the windows, where one feasted on asopao, or soupy rice. There were also a good number of "crossover" Caribbean places—trendy eateries on the Upper West Side (Bahama Mama's), the East Village (Sugar Reef), and West Village (Caribe, Day-O). Since then, Caribbean has gone upscale on both coasts, with Tropica,

Bambou, and Palmetta Plantation House in New York, and Babalu, Calypso, and so forth, in Los Angeles.

Other waves of refugees outside of the purview of the Act of 1965 would also make their mark on American dining. Refugees from Vietnam started coming in the early 1970s. It's taken some time, but today Vietnamese restaurants are much more common than they were even in 1990. The Westminster district of Southern California boasts an entire neighborhood where Vietnamese phô (beef noodle soup) restaurants line both sides of several streets; Houston has a thriving Vietnamese community as well, with a good concentration of restaurants. In the foreword to *The Tummy Trilogy,* a collection of three of his books, Calvin Trillin pointed out "The change in the number and composition of the immigrant population was accelerated by the end of the war in Vietnam, and . . . when helicopters were snatching people from the grounds of the American embassy compound during the panic of the final Vietcong push into Saigon, I was sitting in front of the television set shouting, 'Get the chefs! Get the chefs!' " Apparently, they got at least a few.

The breakup of the Soviet Union in 1989 unleashed a flood of immigration from its former republics; relatively few refugees had been allowed out of the USSR before that, and suddenly the United States was seeing huge numbers of immigrants from former Eastern Bloc countries. Now communist chic became either communist kitsch or Tsarist elegant, and a flurry of new Russian restaurants opened in the 1990s: Pravda and Firebird in New York; Diaghelev had opened in Los Angeles in 1984.

By the early 1990s, fusion cuisine would make its appearance in the hautiest of haute kitchens. Lespinasse opened, in 1991, in a gold-leaf-encrusted Louis XV room in New York's swanky St. Regis Hotel; there Executive Chef Gray Kunz, a Swiss-born chef trained in Singapore, brilliantly brought the flavors of southeast Asia into the most elegant of French settings. Jean-Georges Vongerichten, the Alsace-born chef who had hitherto headed up the kitchen at New York City's Lafayette and gone on to open a bistro, Jo-Jo, opened Vong, featuring a bold French-Thai fusion. A meal at Vong was certainly the first time I sampled Asian-spiced foie gras.

By the late 1980s it was clear that foreign influences had made their indelible mark on American cuisine. Diners to whom Thai and Mexican, Italian and Cuban were old hat could now light out for Ecuadorian or Brazilian, Tibetan or Malaysian. Today New York City's *Zagat Survey* lists three times as many Afghan restaurants as Scandinavian. New York also boasts Chilean, Colombian, Cambodian, Laotian, Sri Lankan, and Lebanese restaurants, while Los Angeles has Persian, Ethiopian, Indonesian, Salvadoran, and Peruvian. By the 1990s, exotic foreign restaurants would even make their way to small cities and towns across America. In 1994, for example, an Indian, a Thai, and a Greek restaurant all opened in Lancaster, Pennsylvania, a town more accustomed to chicken-corn soup and shoofly pie than mee krob and pooris.

But it wasn't only in ethnic restaurants and the new up-scale fusion restaurants that the foreign influences showed up. In the thirty years after the Immigration Act of 1965, one saw its effects more and more often on the plates of American restaurants. For example, at New York's Monkey Bar one finds squid stuffed with merguez sausage and cous-cous in a spicy tomato-cumin broth on a menu that also features a salad of smoked trout and Belgian endive with pea shoots, radish, shiso, and wasabi. At San Francisco's Aqua, a single dish—steamed littleneck clams and shiitake tortellini with spicy Thai coconut broth and basil chif-fonade—shows influences from Japan (shiitake), Italy (tortellini), Thailand (coconut broth), France (chiffonade), and America (steamed littleneck clams).

By the end of the 1990s, influences from the foodways of the new immigrants would be seamlessly integrated into what we consider American food. Today, when we sear tuna and cut it into rare slices, we don't necessarily think of that as Japanese, nor do we necessarily think of the pasta we're tossing with olive oil, sun-dried tomatoes, and parsley as Italian. When it comes to food, anyway, we're xenophobes no more.

5

THE CALIFORNIA VISION

"ALICE WATERS SINGLE-HANDEDLY CHANGED THE WAY Americans eat." A magazine food editor actually said that to me recently, and no doubt she believed it.

Of course it's ludicrous.

But if Julia Child and foreign influences including France significantly affected American eating habits in the 1960s and 1970s, what happened in California beginning in the 1970s would not only radically change California gastronomy, but eventually that of the entire country.

Conventional wisdom holds that Waters began the revolution in California when she opened her Berkeley restaurant, Chez Panisse, in 1971. It's true that what Waters did was extremely important for a lot of people—for instance, she was probably the first to forge relationships between chefs and farmers and other food producers. This method of procuring the finest ingredients became essential to what was to happen in American restaurants over the next twenty-five years. But Waters was by no means the first to introduce the main precepts that would come to form the basis of so-called California cuisine. Nor was she the only one practicing them in California at the time.

To be sure, the term "California cuisine" is a hazy one; not everyone agrees on what it really means, and some people, especially in California, deplore its very use.

In general, however, certain dishes, cooking techniques, and elements of dining exemplify what most people consider California cuisine: Field green salads topped with grilled meat or goat cheese; simple grilled foods; roasted garlic; grilled pizza with nontraditional toppings; fresh local ingredients; attractive yet unostentatious presentation; casual service. Asian and Mediterranean influences work upon local products to create something fresh, with unmuddled flavors, truly showcasing the best qualities of the ingredients. The cooking of Provence strongly informs California cuisine: Rosemary, which grows wild in California, is very important, as it is in Provence; wild fennel grows and is used in both places as well. And so does Italian cookery—roasted red peppers, roasted garlic, and olive oil feel very much at home in California.

Rozanne Gold calls California cuisine the "grill it and garnish it school of cooking."

"Maybe California cuisine is nothing more than Sonoma County goat cheese, fresh basil, Santa Barbara shrimp, California caviar, mesquite, and that's it," said Michael McCarty in 1983; McCarty's Santa Monica restaurant Michael's was seminal in the creation of California cuisine when it opened in 1979. "Composed salads," offered McCarty in 1996 when I interviewed him for this book. "My lobster salad, my lamb filet salad, chicken goat cheese salad. Salad is truly important, and baby vegetables. We created this whole beginning with baby vegetables."

According to Michael Whiteman, these types of salads didn't originate in California at all. Whiteman, who worked with Joseph Baum's restaurant consulting company in 1976 opening Windows on the World said, "Somewhere about 1975 or 1976 Jim Beard came back from France because he was working with us at the World Trade Center, and he said, 'Hot food with cold things.' And we said, 'What?' He said, 'Like a salad: You take a salad and then you put something hot on it.' We said, 'Get outta here. It'll make the greens warm and the food cold.' And he said 'That's it. Hot food on cold things.' And so I asked him from where [he got this idea], and he said 'France.' " After that, it began to appear in California, says Whiteman, and along with it, "the whole notion of California cuisine, which is hot food on cold things with a vinaigrette."

What *did* make Alice Waters famous was that she sought out the freshest and very best ingredients from all over the San Francisco Bay area, using only what was at the peak of its season. What motivated her in the early days of the restaurant was that she did not have an easy time finding products that satisfied her, produce that was as good as what she had become accustomed to in France, where she had spent time as a student. But in the Bay Area in the early seventies, "There wasn't very much," she recalled when I interviewed her. "Certainly there were ethnic markets, but there weren't the big meat suppliers and poultry people that we bought things from. I had to sort through three cases of beans to get the little ones, and I thought that meant they were good." She didn't know how to discern the best quality beans, she was "just looking for what looked like what I had eaten. But not knowing really what that was. What fresh fruit was. And it was something I began to understand as I got involved in doing the restaurant."

So she'd go to Chinatown and buy ducks in the afternoon, pick wild fennel on the hillsides on the way to see friends in Amador County. She bought lettuces, arugula, and herbs from patrons who were growing them in their backyard gardens, then eventually planted her own garden in the back of her Berkeley house. "I was foraging a little bit at the beginning," she told me. "And then people understood that we wanted certain ingredients, radishes or something, and neighbors would bring that in from their backyards and say 'Well, do you want to trade a lunch for radishes?' So we'd trade a lunch for radishes and then we decided, well, we should plant salad here in Berkeley. . . . The first salad beds covered my whole backyard." The salad she planted was a mesclun mix, the seeds of which a friend in France had sent her in 1982. She says that arugula and perhaps mâche were certainly available in the United States at the time, but she doesn't believe mesclun (a mix of baby lettuces) was here yet; in any case, ". . . never that kind of mix of the first little thinnings when you're thinning the beds, or even cutting the small salad."

With the help of Sibella Krause, one of Chez Panisse's cooks at the time (today she's executive director of the San Francisco Public Market Collaborative), Waters sowed and nurtured relationships with local farmers and other producers to grow vegetables or raise lambs or make cheese to her exacting specifications. Since most people had never heard of such practices, when Alice Waters made the huge splash she did with the press, many writers trumpeted it as revolutionary.

Actually, someone beat her to the chef-farm connection a few years earlier. Okay, 129 years earlier. In 1834, fed up with the woeful quality of produce they were purchasing at New York City's Washington Market, members of the Delmonico family bought a piece of land in Brooklyn and started their own small farm to supply their famous eponymous Manhattan restaurant.

In Southern California in the early seventies, Jean Bertranou, a native of Pau, near Toulouse, was chef/co-owner of La Chaumière, an intimate French restaurant in Beverly Hills. "Jean Bertranou was extremely important in Los Angeles," *Gourmet*'s long-time California critic Caroline Bates told me. "Even though he wasn't doing wild sorts of things, he was ahead of Alice Waters. Before there was a Chez Panisse, he was trying—within the L.A. framework—to get people to pioneer locally to get a better breed of duck, like the Muscovy duck."

A look at Bates's review of La Chaumière in 1974 (though that's a few years after Chez Panisse opened) revealed that Bertranou was doing food that changed with the seasons, food with a "penchant for naturalness." Bates continued:

> His dishes are usually uncluttered, his sauces light—he doesn't believe in overpowering fish or meat with a sauce that smothers the natural flavor. It is an approach, however, that succeeds only with the finest and freshest of materials, which become increasingly difficult to locate nowadays. He buys his chickens from someone who claims to raise them organically. He roasts locally grown ducklings when he can get them. Except for shrimps, which are almost impossible to obtain here unfrozen anymore, he works with fresh fish and shellfish.

Bertranou was also a fan of the spiny lobster, native to California, a crustacean that was routinely ignored by so-called epicures, and certainly disdained by other French chefs. The spiny lobster became something of a *cause célèbre* for Caroline Bates, who believed it was a treat overlooked thanks to persistent snobbish devotion to its cousin from Maine. Bertranou had discovered what seems in retrospect to be the essence of California cuisine: The idea of focusing on an ingredient—and here it had the bonus of being an indigenous one—and making the most of it, *featuring* it. It was this concept that most impressed chefs from other regions around the country, encouraging them to feature special local ingredients and build dishes around them.

McCarty remembers his former partner Bertranou this way: "He was the only real Frenchman [who was] beginning to cook modern food at the beginning of the nouvelle cuisine revolution in France in the early seventies. He was one of the people who was beginning to showcase that philosophy—in other words, great ingredients, cook them quickly, without a lot of fanfare, and some idea of presentation; the idea of multitudes of tastes. He was beginning to do that."

Nor was Waters the first to use freshly grown herbs. Alan Hooker had been growing them in his kitchen garden at The Ranch House since 1950.

The Four Seasons, which had opened in New York in 1959, had made a point of using fresh herbs from the start, and featured farm-fresh produce, often harvested earlier the day it was served, which waiters wheeled to tables in baskets for diners' inspection. Although Four Seasons's menu didn't change daily, as did Chez Panisse's, it did change each season, along with the server's uniforms, the china, and the linens.

There was also a woman named Rosetta Clarkson who had been known in the 1950s as Connecticut's resident herbalist *par excellence.* "Saltacres," her home in Medford, attracted herb enthusiasts who visited her greenhouses, rosemary cottage, demonstration garden, and collection of fourteenth-century herbals. Though Clarkson's celebrity has slipped through the cracks of the food revolution, Clementine Paddleford, food editor of the *New York Herald Tribune* and *This Week* magazine wrote in her 1960 book *How*

America Eats: "Rosetta Clarkson was an English teacher who made herbs her hobby and started an herbal renaissance in the United States. The herbs of grandmother's time were neglected, 'yarb' cookery virtually forgotten, when Rosetta planted a city lot to herbs and savory seeds. A green enchantment grew. One amateur gardener after another fell under its spicy spell. Today, herb gardens are springing up everywhere."

Waters didn't invent using organic produce in a so-called "fine dining" restaurant. One Mrs. Cook, a Sicilian woman whose uncle Giuseppe Tomasi di Lampedusa wrote the novel *The Leopard,* opened a restaurant of the same name in a Manhattan brownstone in the 1960s. Donald Aspinwall Allan reviewed it in *Gourmet* in February 1970, a year before Waters opened her doors. The Leopard seems to have had more than a little in common with Chez Panisse. The Leopard is housed* in a brownstone, Chez Panisse in a funky Victorian house. The Leopard had no printed menu, and served mostly French dishes. "There is always a good quiche . . ." wrote Allan " or a *pissaladière.*" Caroline Bates remarked in a recent interview that when Chez Panisse opened, it was French, but it distinguished itself from other French restaurants by serving food mostly from the French countryside, especially the south. And here was The Leopard serving *pissaladière,* the onion, anchovy, and olive tart that is a specialty of Nice that frequently made appearances at Chez Panisse; it was exactly up Chez Panisse's alley. Although The Leopard's owner was Sicilian, nothing Italian was served except arugula (referred to by Mrs. Cook as "rucola") when it could be gotten; Alice Waters frequently offered salads with rocket—a.k.a. arugula. Although in 1970 the reigning fashion in duck was "à l'orange," Cook served it with cherries, peaches, or olives ("Never *à l'orange,*" she

*It still exists.

said. "Everyone has it and I won't allow it."). The night Chez Panisse opened on August 28, 1971, Alice Waters served duck with olives. About a month earlier, the August issue of *Gourmet* hit the stands; in it, in a section called "Random Notes," Allan recounted another visit to The Leopard:

> I recently enjoyed an organic *haute cuisine* dinner at The Leopard, 253 E. 50th Street. No nut cutlets: just the restaurant's excellent fare, but prepared from start to finish with organically grown or raised vegetables, fowl, and fruits. Such meals will be served daily, affording the convinced and the skeptical alike a chance to judge whether organic food *tastes* better. My dinner was excellent; but then so were the nonorganic meals I've sampled at The Leopard in the past.

Although the press fell in love with Alice Waters—helped, in large part because James Beard wrote about her early on in his nationally syndicated column—not every food writer has bought into the myth of her wholesale incitement of a revolution. A few, such as Caroline Bates, kept their gastronomic windshields wiped well enough to recognize other chefs who influenced the California cuisine movement in perhaps more quiet ways.

Unlike Alice Waters, for example, Jean Bertranou didn't become famous for his forward-looking ideas and practices. He died, tragically young, of a brain tumor in 1980. According to those who knew him, he put more of his time and energy into teaching and mentoring other cooks who would go on to become renowned chefs than he did doing what was necessary to attract publicity; he was also one of the few great French chefs in America who would take the time to teach young Americans kitchen arts.

Certainly Alice Waters also helped launch the careers of many chefs, including a number who later became stars:

Jeremiah Towers, Mark Miller, Joyce Goldstein, and others. Yet more than that, there is something about Waters that makes her a natural for publicity: She's charming, intelligent, articulate, politically sophisticated, and speaks captivatingly and convincingly about her ongoing mission. "We don't understand the difference between fueling ourselves and eating for pleasure and eating wholesome food," she told me. "We don't have the pleasure of the table that's so reflective of a quality of life and a purpose on the planet. It's just a whole misconception of what food is meant to be, and we have to turn that around." Waters is also quite media savvy and image conscious; she never appears in a photograph, for instance, without a hat.

Waters doesn't make the claims about herself that others do, nor did she intend to start a revolution. When we met one morning in September of 1996 for an interview in her just-waking restaurant, after weeks of festivities had concluded celebrating Chez Panisse's twenty-fifth anniversary, I asked her if she had any inkling that what she was doing would have such a huge impact on the way Americans would come to eat. "No," she replied. "I just wanted a little neighborhood restaurant and I wanted to eat the way that I had eaten in France."

In the beginning, the food Alice Waters served at Chez Panisse was unabashedly French. What distinguished it from the scads of other French restaurants in California (and elsewhere) at the time was that it wasn't masquerading as *haute cuisine*. On the contrary, it presented itself as simple cooking from the provinces, particularly the south.

Although Michael Whiteman believes that the California restaurant most influential on American cuisine was a French restaurant, it's neither Chez Panisse nor La Chaumière nor L'Ermitage he has in mind. "Ma Maison," he told me in an interview, with a sly smile that meant he thought I'd find his assessment surprising. I was actually more surprised that of all the people I interviewed for this book, Whiteman was the only one who pointed to Wolfgang Puck as being very influential. Opened in 1979, Ma Maison was the "in" place in Los Angeles for a number of years, so fashionable it had an unlisted phone number. As Whiteman remembers it, "It was a parking lot that had this kind of plastic building on it; it had Astroturf on the floor and lawn furniture. That was the restaurant. [Owner Patrick Terrail] didn't have any money. And he hired this unknown chef named Wolfgang Puck. Puck was an apostle at that time of nouvelle cuisine, but not in the ridiculous way that it ultimately evolved, and Wolfgang and Patrick created an enormous attention on food and technique throughout the country. They really broke new ground and made it possible for everybody else who came along. [Michael] McCarty and . . . Jeremiah [Towers] and all the rest of them followed not in Alice Waters's footsteps; they followed in Wolfgang's footsteps. What Alice Waters did was invent pizza. Not Wolfgang."

Puck and his wife, designer Barbara Lazaroff, who was and is responsible for the interiors of all her husband's restaurants, went on to establish a mammoth restaurant empire, beginning with the first they owned, Spago, the Hollywood restaurant that, from the moment it opened, was so trendy it made Ma Maison look like Howard Johnson's. By this time, Puck had become such a darling of the Hollywood set that Billy Wilder wrote the foreword to his cookbook. At Spago, Puck became known for his California-style brick oven pizza, garnished with smoked salmon and golden caviar, duck sausage, or chanterelles. Chinois-on-Main came next, bringing French-influenced Chinese cooking to Santa Monica; then Eureka, a short-lived restaurant-microbrewery, and Granita in Malibu. Eventually Puck would open restaurants in San Francisco, Chicago, Las Vegas, Seattle, and Beverly Hills (two more); together they grossed $56 million in 1996.* But perhaps more significantly, Puck brought his new wave California pizzas and other treats to the freezer sections of supermarkets across the land, making California cuisine not only mainstream, but placing it squarely back on the chilly aisles we were so happy to have escaped. By the 1990s frozen Puck fare appealed to consumers who may no longer have felt cooking was drudgery, but who were rather so harried and hassled after simultaneously working and raising children that they welcomed an alternative to Stouffer's chicken pot pie, Lean Cuisine, or McDonald's. And in Southern California, supermarkets such as Gelson's in Pacific Palisades even welcomed Wolfgang Puck Express, in-store concessions licensed by Puck that offered Chinois Chicken Salad, Tuscan Bean Soup, and pizzas with sourdough crust, spicy basil pesto, mozzarella and fontina cheeses, fresh tomatoes, and a variety of toppings. Now, not only did Southern Californians not need Spago's phone number; they didn't need Spago.

Even though Ma Maison was a French restaurant—as was Chez Panisse and La Chaumière and L'Ermitage—these young California chefs were rebelling against the French, to whom they owed everything, much as a teenager rebels against his parents. The phenomenon was not unrelated to the political revolution of the time. Alice Waters, for example, had been active in the free speech movement at UC-Berkeley, and quite politically active in general. Both her food and political rebellion followed hard on the heels of the antiwar movement; rebellion was the order of the day.

So why California cuisine? Why not Ohio cuisine or Massachusetts cuisine or Carolina cuisine? Why was it California that fomented the American food revolution?

---

*Puck and Lazaroff are majority shareholders in the company that owns them.

The main reason is California's luxuriously long growing season. I was amazed to go to the Farmers' Market in Santa Monica in the end of January 1998—weather aside, the produce suggested it was spring. At a time when my neighborhood Greenmarket in New York City had dwindled to a few leftover apples, Santa Monica's market was full of color, bustling with activity, and filled with a generous cornucopia of produce: six or seven types of exotic broccoli; juicy, flavorful strawberries; tiny, succulent mandarins that would have made M. F. K. Fisher's mouth water; Haas avocados; Chinese water spinach; an heirloom variety of watercress; fresh fenugreek; even ripe, flavorful tomatoes grown outdoors.

The rest of the country had to depend, outside of their own growing season, on produce trucked in from California, which was a week old by the time it arrived on the East Coast. Of course this presumes that what begged to be created was a new cuisine based on fresh ingredients. Perhaps something else could have been invented in its place—a cuisine based on spices, perhaps? Or one based on slow cooking? But as in France, Italy, England, Australia, and other countries, the focus on fresh ingredients was the direction that caught America's fancy.

And another factor prevented something like California cuisine from springing up in New York, the other likely locale, in the 1970s: a mammoth fiscal crisis that caused major stagnation in the city.

Finally, the general open-mindedness associated with Californians also goes a long way to explain why the revolution started in that state. Californians have always been adventurous, willing to try new sensations, and they (okay, we) readily embraced a new way of eating.

One might say that the California cuisine that we have come to know was created largely out of a collision between home cooking and restaurant cooking. Alice Waters opened Chez Panisse having had no prior restaurant experience; nor did her original chef, Victoria Wise, nor did pastry chef Lindsey Shere. Since they didn't know about buying wholesale, Waters and her crew purchased their ingredients willy-nilly from sources ranging from Chinatown across the bay in San Francisco, to a friend's farm, to a Japanese greengrocer in Berkeley, and the local co-op. Unfettered by the usual notions of what was supposed to go on in a professional kitchen, Waters, her chefs, and her cooks allowed themselves a latitude that engendered creativity.

Michael McCarty also operated much like a home cook when he developed his style while working in France. Before he opened Michael's, he'd owned a tiny Paris restaurant on Ile St. Louis. McCarty had no storage space there, so like a home cook, he bought not wholesale, but rather according to what happened to look good that day at the local purveyors' shops in the neighborhood. As a result, his style of cooking focused on ingredients, and it was a style he would bring with him to California.

California cuisine developed simultaneously in the San Francisco Bay Area and Los Angeles, which is curious, since San Francisco had a great restaurant tradition and Los Angeles did not.

Historically, San Francisco had long been considered a great dining town, dating all the way back to the days of the Gold Rush in 1849. Elsewhere in the country that year, Henry David Thoreau was lamenting that East Coast shad were being decimated by the building of dams. Meanwhile a French restaurant called the Poule d'Or opened in San Francisco, founded by a French chef from New Orleans; in fact, scores of French chefs came to San Francisco to feed the newly gold-rich. The still extant and long-famous Tadich Grill also opened that year as the New World Coffee Stand (curiously, a name with a fin-de-cette-siècle ring*); it became Tadich Grill in 1887. Chinese immigrant Norman Asing opened the first documented Chinese restaurant in American history, in San Francisco in 1849—Macao and Woosung—making the year also auspicious for ethnic food. When the Poule d'Or changed its location in 1868, its name changed officially to Poodle Dog, as its gold-mining customers had fondly anglicized it when it opened. Probably the most famous and influential restaurant for many decades, the Poodle Dog was renown for its rendition of frogs' legs, called à la Poulette, and other *délices*.

In 1906 many great restaurants, including the Poodle Dog, were destroyed either by the earthquake or the fires that immediately followed. The Poodle Dog was rebuilt, as was Jack's (founded in 1864 by French-American Georges Voges). So was, eventually, the resplendent Palace Hotel, which made a mission of championing local products; even though the Eastern oyster (Ostrea virginica) was the most popular variety of oyster in San Francisco at the time, the Palace featured the far superior tiny, succulent Western oyster known as the Olympia.

By the end of World War II, San Francisco remained a venerable eating town. Jack's and Tadich Grill still flourished, as did Ernie's (opened in 1935) and The Blue Fox (1993). In the early sixties, gourmands could choose among La Bourgogne (opened in 1961), Tadich Grill, Sam's, Fleur de Lys, Ernie's, Alexis, and The Blue Fox, to name a few.

San Francisco's culinary reputation didn't exempt that city from harsh criticism at the time. However, by our standards today, much of the criticism would translate to praise. Legendary gadabout Lucius Beebe wrote disparagingly about San Francisco dining in 1965:

---

*In fact, there is a chain today called New World Coffee Bar.

> It's all very well for chauvinists and local boosters to claim that San Francisco is a mecca of transcendental gastronomy despite the gruesome circumstance that only at a single restaurant, the ageless and ineffable Jack's, is it possible to get a real mutton chop.

Amusingly, for Beebe, the presence of mutton defined an epicurean experience. The New York–based chronicler and critic failed to take into account delicacies that might be indigenous to the West Coast—Dungeness crab and Olympia oysters, for instance. One wonders whether he sought out either of these treats from the sea, neither of which have equals on the East Coast. Yet this was how many epicures thought about food in those days: There were certain comestibles that were considered *de rigueur* on any serious menu or in any gourmand's pantry: caviar, foie gras, smoked salmon, and so forth. Continental cuisine was it.

Beebe continued, pleased with finding shad roe—not something to seek in California, but one of his favorite dishes—at Jack's, a San Francisco institution since possibly as far back as 1867, and châteaubriand at a restaurant in Carmel. He didn't miss the opportunity to poke fun at California's habitual casual " 'come as you are' slogan of hospitality." Beebe's only fair criticism, it seems, was that another San Francisco restaurant, City of Paris, kept its caviar frozen before thawing to serve.

Los Angeles, on the other hand, had only one or two *great* restaurants. Perino's was considered the best; in fact, Perino's was reputed to be the best restaurant west of the Mississippi, or as one reviewer wrote, "maybe even west of the Hudson." When national magazines wrote about Los Angeles restaurants in the 1950s and early 1960s, the only other notable one was La Rue. This Hollywood restaurant was founded by Orlando Figini and Bruno Petoletti, the powers behind the Italian pavilion at the 1939 World's Fair in New York, who subsequently came to L.A. and established a formidable Italian dining tradition there. La Rue's menu offered specialties of *la cucina Italiana* side by side with entrées such as Coq au Vin à la mode Du Vieux Pays, and Tournedos Strasbourgeois. Such juxtapositions may seem odd today, but in those days, French dishes were obligatory in any restaurant—even an Italian one—that aspired to greatness.

Otherwise, the Los Angeles of my youth was something of a culinary wasteland.

Since the 1970s, San Francisco and Los Angeles have enjoyed—and I use the term literally—a rivalry when it comes to their respective restaurants.

The food revolution in Northern California had a political aspect that it did not in Southern California, reflecting a general difference between the two regions. Bay Area residents have long criticized Southern Californians for—well, for a lot of things, including selfish wastefulness of water resources, political apathy, and general shallowness.

Yet the food in Los Angeles was shaping up to be anything but shallow. (Even if quite a bit of shallow food would later come out of L.A., as it did from all over the country. . . .)

In terms of home cookery, by the 1950s, California at its most sophisticated was represented by Helen Evans Brown, the California food writer and cookbook author who was a dear friend of, sometime collaborator with, and dedicated correspondent with James Beard. Brown's important *West Coast Cook Book,* published in 1952, offers some insight into the kinds of dishes Californians of a certain culinary stripe were cooking. Brown pointed out, for instance, that Californians commonly ate salads as a first course, as opposed to the rest of the country, in which salads followed the main course, as in most of Europe. The thoroughness with which this custom swept the rest of the country amounted to a minirevolution.

Artichokes, plentiful in California (the central valley town of Castroville bills itself as the "Artichoke Capital of the World"), were used often in Brown's book. As a first course, Brown offered a recipe for Artichokes Santa Anita: an artichoke bottom filled with pâté de foie gras and garnished with crab legs, served with a cream-thinned mayonnaise dressing and wedges of lemon or lime. "A rich food," Brown commented, "actually so hearty that it makes a good main dish for lunch." Despite the unhappy combination of ingredients.

Avocados were also important in *West Coast Cook Book*. "Avocados are a favored first course on the West Coast," wrote Brown. "Some like them filled with caviar, some with crab or lobster salad, and some just plain with a wedge of lemon." Guacamole, she reported, was "almost a staple with cocktails."

Seafood figured prominently. Brown gave recipes for abalone steaks (one surmises from her explanatory note that they weren't inordinately difficult to obtain); geoduck; Crab Louis; and finally Pacific Cracked Crab, of which she wrote, "In fact, so devoted are we to this West Coast treat that we usually make a meal of it, having little else but hot French bread and chilled white wine. That's West Coast eating at its best." That was certainly the way we ate Dungeness crab during my adolescence, though we were more likely to have it with San Francisco-style sourdough bread, usually sadly mushy-crusted, as real French-style bread wasn't available. Brown's recipe for cracked crab calls for plunging live crabs in boiling water, but by the time I was a child, they were usually only available precooked.

In a section called "Crab Notes," Brown remarked that

crab and avocado are a "favorite combination"; it's interesting to note that this became the basis for the highly popular California rolls now served in sushi bars even in Japan. A bevy of oyster recipes included Hangtown Fry, Barbecued Oysters, Oysters Poulette (from San Francisco restaurant Maison Dorée: oysters in a white sauce with sliced mushrooms); Pickled Oysters; Portland Oyster Rarebit; Prescott's Olympia Pan Roast; Oysters Kirkpatrick from the Palace Hotel, baked with bacon and—yecch—ketchup.

Sand dabs were also big in California: They were sometimes the "regular fish" of my childhood. Brown called them "one of the prizes of the Pacific." One rarely sees them anymore, though James Beach, a restaurant in Venice, California, has been featuring them lately.

Cioppino, a hearty tomatoey seafood stew invented by Portuguese fishermen, was "one of California's most famous dishes."

Such was the culinary background inherited by Alice Waters, Wolfgang Puck, Jean Bertanou, Jeremiah Towers, Jonathan Waxman, Deborah Madison, Michael McCarty, and the other authors of California cuisine.

In 1973, as President Nixon (a native Californian) was mulling over his Watergate problems, California began to seem important enough for the East Coast to sit up and take notice. At any rate, the editors of *Gourmet* decided after thirty-two years of publication and covering the restaurants of New York, Paris, and London, that it was time to admit that California was significant. Caroline Bates had been an editor at "The Magazine of Good Living" since 1958; ten years later, she and her husband Ken moved to California. They settled in Santa Barbara (where Julia Child has long maintained a residence) so her husband, formerly managing editor at *American Builder,* a trade magazine in New York, could attend the well-known Brooks Institute of Photography, with the idea that he would provide the photographs for the travel pieces the couple had started writing together. Bates herself continued to work freelance for *Gourmet*, writing articles—mostly unsigned as staff-written pieces were—and testing recipes. The two produced a guidebook on Baja, California, that was brought out by the company that also published *Sunset* magazine and cookbooks. In the meantime, Bates fell in love with the West Coast.

When *Gourmet*'s publisher and editor decided to add a second "Spécialités de la Maison" column covering San Francisco and Los Angeles—to debut January 1974—Caroline Bates was the natural choice. How lucky for *Gourmet*'s editors—and even more so, for the food-loving population of California and visitors there—that Bates happened to be in the right place at the right time! We've been able to enjoy her column and benefit from her infallible palate ever since.

But Bates also points out that part of the reason for the decision to add the California column was that a large part of *Gourmet*'s readership resided in the Golden State. Californians have long been interested in food.

Michael McCarty started a duck farm in partnership with Jean Bertranou in Southern California in 1975, the same year that Bertranou, having left La Chaumière, opened L'Ermitage. In doing so, this team was ahead of Alice Waters when it came to raising its own ingredients.

McCarty had been introduced to Bertranou by Lois Dwan—at the time the food critic for the *Los Angeles Times*—when McCarty asked her whom in L.A. he should meet who was "tops in food." McCarty's problem was essentially the same as the one that would lead Waters to plant gardens and barter for ingredients: He couldn't get the products he needed to make the food he wanted to.

In both Southern and Northern California, the networks

of small farmers, other purveyors, and chefs grew and grew. In 1983, Alice Waters and Sibella Krause organized a Tasting of Summer Produce in San Francisco, which would become an annual event for the next six years, one that brought together more than a hundred of the top producers to meet potential buyers. "That very much helped expand the networks of farmer contacts into the urban community," says Sibella Krause. "It was very encouraging to farmers."

At some point, Alice Waters stopped printing her menus in French. "There was a point when we had to stop in French because we were saying 'huîtres de Bodega Bay.' And it seemed so foolish—why don't we just say 'Bodega Bay oysters'?"

Waters also had to face the fact that "the foodstuffs are different from what they are in Europe. The lobster's different." So no matter how much she wanted to make a bouillabaisse that tasted like one in Marseilles, she would turn out something else. "And I think it's very tasty, but it's different from a French bouillabaisse." Putting the menu in English and understanding that it was folly to try to exactly duplicate French food in California marked a definite turning point: California cuisine was on its way.

At the same time chefs were going gaga over rapidly improving regional products, duck farms, organic greens locally farmed, and so forth, another aspect of supplying restaurants was changing. This revolution, unfortunately, wasn't as politically correct as Alice Waters would have liked, but on the contrary, owed a great debt to the gasguzzling jet-age state of transportation. "If we had really been smart," Michael McCarty told me, "we would have been the founders of FedEx." Long growing season or no, winter did eventually come to California. And when it did, says McCarty, "I could get state-of-the-art berries from Australia or New Zealand. Fresh John Dory red snapper." People who thought McCarty used only California ingredients became confused. "I said, 'No!' " recalled McCarty. "I serve more goddamn white truffles than any Italian restaurant in this city does. And the same with the French ones. And if it turns out that the only place *haricots verts* grow during August is Senegal, then that's where we're going to get 'em from!"

The irony is that this countertrend exists in many of the same restaurants that toot the horn of political rectitude, boasting of their attachment to local products in season. And not just in California. On a trip to Miami in 1997, after listening to a rah-rah-local-products speech from one of the proponents of Florida's New World cuisine, I was amused to find that a dish he'd served me included asparagus—in January.*

France was as important to McCarty as it had been to Alice Waters. In 1972, just as Chez Panisse was getting off its feet, McCarty, who had finished stints at the Ecole Hôtelière and the Cordon Bleu, was wielding a knife at his Paris restaurant, treating twenty-two Parisians per seating to his modified interpretation of American food. "I was extremely lucky in terms of the timing," McCarty recalled, "in being there when Michel Guérard was just starting *nouvelle cuisine* and *cuisine minceur.* All this stuff was happening. The revolution was going on and chefs were becoming important, versus restaurant owners. Which was the same thing historically in America: [Before then] nobody knew who the chef was in any of these restaurants." More important was "the guy at the front desk. The man who was the maître d', the owner of the restaurant that ran the joint, and the chefs

*For those who are too young to remember, asparagus season is in the spring. These spears came from South America.

were slaves who were working in the background toiling away."

Interestingly, Alice Waters didn't fit the model of chef-proprietor that largely came to define modern restaurants in the seventies and eighties. Although she occasionally served as chef over the years, she has generally hired a chef to run the kitchen, running the front of the house herself, much as the old-fashioned kind of owner had.

By 1979 or 1980, things were really beginning to gel in Los Angeles, which is where Michael McCarty believes the real revolution happened. "You have to understand," he told me, "it couldn't happen in San Francisco. It couldn't happen in New York. It couldn't happen in Chicago." All the clichés about Los Angeles were true, he explained: "laid-back, where's the beach, I don't get up until twelve. All those clichés worked in our favor because people were so open. We were an open society here. We probably had one of the wildest gay communities here, way before San Francisco. There's just an openness about it here, with the entertainment business and the relationship between the press and the stars and the people, and the fact that you'd walk down the street and movie stars were all over the place. It was a very open blossom." The experimentation level was high, he said. "The petri dish was just ripe for growing things. It was time for a change. The generation of people who were running those French restaurants were retiring or dying, the door was open for something new, and it doesn't happen often."

What was happening, exactly, that was so different from what came before?

Most important, it began to *feel* different to eat in restaurants. Before the 1970s, so-called fine dining happened almost exclusively in French or Continental restaurants. Menus were in French, and tuxedo-sporting headwaiters (frequently with phony accents) bullied patrons who couldn't understand the menu. Food was dull; there was little creative energy.

Suddenly, food became exciting, vibrant. Things began to taste like what they were.

Or like what we didn't know. I was in college in Palo Alto in 1979 when suddenly we students became interested in cooking and food. We knew where to go for good pasta, good cheese—frequently, we shopped at a grocery store called Draeger's in nearby Menlo Park. (Since those days, Draeger's has expanded and become one of the most important sources for fine foodstuffs in the Bay Area. Gary Danko, one of the Bay Area's top chefs, presides over the range in Viognier, a restaurant located on the mezzanine of the San Mateo store.) For me and lots of people I knew, we got hooked first on Italian food.

But in professional kitchens, the revolution looked more French, and in fact, the new California cuisine owed a huge debt to France.

Beyond the food itself, Alice Waters's goal was making the pleasures of the table a part of life, the way the French do. In fact, the whole Berkeley "gourmet ghetto" that flourished around Chez Panisse was inspired by the French style of eating, shopping for food, and dining out. Waters's friend Kermit Lynch opened a retail shop near Chez Panisse and began importing interesting wines from small French producers. In the intervening years, Kermit Lynch has become Northern California's premier source for French wines. The Cheese Board was already in business on Sutter when Chez Panisse opened just across the street. Piet's Coffee and Acme Bread opened, providing high-quality European-style alternatives to Berkeley's lucky residents. It felt like a slice of France in Berkeley.

Much lip service was paid to using local ingredients, but French cuisine still seemed to dictate what those ingredients would be. When Laura Chenel started making cheese in Sonoma County, it was chèvre, in the French style. McCarty and Bertranou raised ducks on their farm using the French method—and made *foie gras.* To many of these chefs, California cuisine really meant using French ingredients, grown or produced in California, and working French techniques upon them to produce something that wasn't French.

So it was with wines in California. French winemakers established the California wine industry in the nineteenth century, Beaulieu Vineyards' Georges de la Tour being the most influential. That's why American wines are almost all Chardonnay, Cabernet Sauvignon, Pinot Noir, and Merlot: French varieties. But many of the California microclimates would have been better suited to other types—Italian varieties, for instance, and even though in California Italians outnumber French in the wine industry, it was only in the 1990s that Sangiovese, Tuscany's grape, was planted there.

In any case, vintners were making wines out of these French varieties and labeling them with French place names: Hearty Burgundy, Chablis, and so on. Although in the 1970s California winemakers switched over to varietal labeling, we still use French words or models when it suits us. In California wine, for instance, Korbel still calls itself "champagne," as does the tonier Schramsberg, though Champagne refers to a region in France rather than a winemaking technique, so "Champagne" couldn't possibly exist in California. Of course these wineries know that; they're just using the cachet of the French nomenclature to help sell their wines.

Most significant to California cuisine—and to new American cuisine in general—was the *nouvelle cuisine* movement going on in France in the early 1970s. As practiced by chefs such as Paul Bocuse, Jean and Pierre Troisgros, Michel Guérard, and Alain Senderens, *nouvelle cuisine* sought to showcase the finest ingredients rather than elaborate preparations. Christian Millau and Henri Gault, two French food critics who launched a monthly magazine in France in the early 1970s, coined the term in 1973 when they announced on their cover, *"Vive la Nouvelle Cuisine Française!"* In that issue, they laid out the ten points that distinguished the *nouvelle cuisine.*

The first tenet was to reject unnecessarily complicated and pretentious dishes. "We were declaring war," explained Christian Millau nine years later, "on old, boring, degenerate classics like bouchée à la reine, which had become a bland, creamed chicken in a gluey sauce inside of soggy pastry; tournedos Rossini; Beef Wellington; flambéed dishes prepared at table; and all the other shallow tricks used to fool the naïve diner." Millau went on to enumerate the rest of his rules:

> Number two, cook what is seasonal and available in the market.
>
> Number three, reduce cooking times, especially for fish, shellfish, poultry, game, veal and vegetables.
>
> Number four, use lighter sauces with pure reductions of stock, small doses of cream, and fresh herbs.
>
> Number five, offer limited menus. No restaurant can stock all the ingredients needed all year long for an exhaustive menu.
>
> Number six, rediscover original dishes of the provinces.
>
> Number seven, use new and modern equipment.
>
> Number eight, create dishes which are light, adapted to our way of life, and still delicious.
>
> Number nine, be creative and open-minded. For instance, be free from the many traditional garnishes such as steamed potatoes with sole, green beans with lamb, or even orange with duck. It means experi-

> menting with new ingredients not only from your own country, but from all over the world. It also means experimenting with new taste combinations.
>
> And now the last point, number ten. As a chef, don't follow your clients. You are the only one who knows. People want to come to eat your cooking and experience your taste, and not the contrary.

Many Americans confused *nouvelle cuisine* with *"la cuisine minceur"* created by Michel Guérard of Les Prés d'Eugénie at Eugénie-les-Bains (a French spa) to help himself and his patrons lose weight. But they were not the same. Though *nouvelle cuisine* was lighter than the heavily sauced cooking that preceded it, it was not created with weight loss in mind. *Cuisine minceur,* on the other hand, gave rise to the "spa cuisine" craze of the 1980s. Meanwhile, Paul Bocuse focused on *la cuisine du marché,* taking journalists with him to Lyons' fabulous market to shop for dinner, anticipating chefs' dependence on farmers' markets that would develop in California and throughout the rest of the United States over the next twenty years.

"Certainly the whole *nouvelle* French movement influenced us, and we took little parts of that," said Michael McCarty, "but we are cooking here in California and we do a lot of things with the fire, like cooking in the fireplace. And we have a longer growing season than other places, but it's still a very seasonal cooking."

Rose Dosti, a longtime food columnist with the *Los Angeles Times*, pointed out that many chefs came to California from Europe at that time—among them Michel Richard, Joachim Splichal, and Wolfgang Puck. "They came to California," she said, "and tried something absolutely, totally new. Wolfgang Puck would still be in the bowels of a kitchen if he were working in France. Leaving Europe gave these guys the freedom to do things with food that no one had thought of doing. No one was around to tell them 'no.' It was the freedom of the West that allowed them to have democracy in the kitchen, and that was happening nowhere else."

In the early eighties, the Italian influence came to the fore. The relaxed, casual, Mediterranean style translated naturally to California, and the clear flavors and fresh ingredients of the trattoria lent themselves readily to a California interpretation.

The presence of Italian-Americans in San Francisco restaurants had long been quite strong, even in French restaurants such as Ernie's and The Blue Fox, both of which were owned by Italian immigrants. But a turning point was marked when Alice Waters hired Paul Bertolli as Chez Panisse's new chef in 1982. Bertolli was a native Californian of Italian descent whose grandmother had cooked from Italy's most revered cookbook, Pellegrino Artusi's *La scienza in cucina e l'arte di mangiar bene.* Bertolli, who had worked in restaurants in Florence, would bring in a more Italian flavor to Chez Panisse. Though Chez Panisse had served risottos and other Italian preparations before, Bertolli made more space on the menus for dishes such as Salmon and Scallop Carpaccio, Broccoli Roman-Style, Lamb Shanks Braised in Chianti, and Prune, Amaretto, Espresso, and Mascarpone Semifreddo.

As for Los Angeles, although there was no paucity of French restaurants, the city's strength had long been Italian restaurants, sometimes under the guise of "Continental cuisine." Curiously, although L.A. has always had a smaller Italian-American population than New York, Italian cooking has long excelled in L.A., whereas it has always been the French restaurants that distinguished themselves in New York. And even after the American gastronomic revolution was well under way in the late 1970s and early 1980s, Los

Angeles's French restaurants never quite reached the level that they did in New York.

In any case, as California cuisine developed, much of the pretentious food and service that had hitherto plagued restaurants was eliminated, and here Italy became more of a role model than France.

The new pretensions that took their place were truly American ones. We tend to embrace our latest enthusiasm to the point of losing perspective, and in culinary history we were no different. Food eventually became a religion for many Californians, and a formidable food snobbery began to creep into the culture. My mother, for instance (who as we remember, couldn't make Jell-O in 1959), became such a snob vis à vis ingredients that when she visited her family in Minneapolis in the 1980's, my dear aunt and uncle were ashamed to let her see the contents of their pantry. They knew my mother would criticize their olive oil, their vinegar, their wine (all of which were perfectly respectable), but my mom was accustomed to much fancier stuff. Luckily, the infatuation that blinded many of the best of us to sane behavior in regard to food matters eventually wore off, as infatuation matured into real love.

The presentation of food—often called plating—also became very important in California restaurants by the early 1980s. Before that, dishes were ceremoniously finished at the table by the captain, who often lit the whole thing on fire or carved a bird or sauced a meat in front of the diner. *Nouvelle cuisine* changed all that: The protein element was always "fanned out" over a pool of limpid sauce, usually garnished with slightly crunchy baby vegetables and herbs, or perhaps slices of kiwi. The whole was presented on the canvas of an oversized white plate. Squeeze bottles became popular, and chefs went wild squirting sauces of different colors in zigzags all over plates.

Jean and Pierre Troisgros wrote in the Introduction of

their book *The Nouvelle Cuisine of Jean & Pierre Troisgros* that it was their father who "did not like dishes finished by a *maître d'hôtel* in the dining room; the chef should be responsible for his cooking to the end." As incredible as it seems today, that was a revolutionary idea at the time. "He did not like complicated platters and presentations," they continued, "and from this came the custom of both presentation and service on each guest's individual plate—very large plates, which we were the first to use."

Curiously, Michael McCarty was also the first to use them when he opened his restaurant in 1979. "I brought out these Villeroy and Boch fourteen-inch plates," he told me. "No one had ever seen those before. They were white! Before that every plate in America had patterns on it. Even the French ones. And I went to [Villeroy and Boch] and I said, look, I want you to take off the basket weave—I love this plate—flat, beautiful, state-of-the-art—but lose the basket weave and all the fruit and crap like that—it gets in the way of the food."

Chef as personality also took off in California, with Alice Waters, Jeremiah Towers, Mark Miller, Wolfgang Puck, and others making headlines and giving interviews—something chefs had never done before. Of course the press and the public relations machines of the restaurants were quite important in determining who would be publicized. Alice Waters got lucky: James Beard wrote about Chez Panisse in his nationally syndicated column, bringing it to broad attention early on.

As California food began to develop its own style, California wines finally began to develop their own personalities as well. It didn't happen overnight though. When Caroline Bates started reviewing for *Gourmet* in 1974, she constantly complained that California restaurants weren't featuring California wines. Interest in wine in the United States in general was only beginning to grow; Gerald Asher had started his "Wine Journal" column for *Gourmet* a mere nineteen months earlier. At this point, the quality of American wines still hadn't bounced back after their virtual disappearance in the wake of Prohibition; California wines were only beginning to make a comeback. Therefore it should have come as no surprise that Asher's first column looked only at French wines: Burgundies and Bordeaux, the relative merits of vintages, and so forth. Two years later, when Caroline Bates reviewed La Bella Fontana, the restaurant in the Beverly Wilshire's formal dining room, she wrote, "The list of French wines is extensive and generally moderate in price. The California wines, largely nonvintage bottlings, are less exciting." In the same column, she reviewed Bertranou's La Chaumière, mentioning that they offered only half a dozen California wines.

Two months later she reviewed the Los Angeles restaurant The Tower. She was disappointed again, for though the restaurant featured American ingredients such as Missouri beef, Wisconsin milk-fed veal, Kentucky bluegrass-grazed lamb, and Delaware River shad and shad roe, "When it comes to wines, however, there is very little for the connoisseur of California bottlings. Like most French restaurants in the state, The Tower has a token selection of the *vins de pays,* but with a difference: Instead of being buried at the back of the *carte des vins,* the California wines are listed up front. Andrieux calls this 'flag-waving,' but the flag most in evidence at The Tower is the blue, white, and red tricolor." And again, in September of that year, in a very positive review of the Hollywood restaurant Le St. Germain:

> The only disappointments we've had in this very satisfying restaurant have been the wines. I wish the management would show the same discrimination

when buying California wines as they do in selecting fish or fruits at the market. The wine grape is really no different from other fruits. Each crop varies from year to year and from vineyard to vineyard, and obtaining the best means making the effort to sample the offerings of many wineries on a continuing basis. A few California wines turn up on the last page of the list, identified only by varietal names and prices—'Pinot Chardonnay $7,' for example. (Imagine a French list that named no châteaux or vintages!)

Finally, she hit paydirt at the Pasadena restaurant The Chronicle, which she also reviewed in September 1974:

California's winemakers are currently creating some excellent wines. The Chronicle, however, offers a rare opportunity to sample some of the more interesting of these. Their list is impressive for both its size and quality. There are more than 140 California vintages, only three or four of which are likely to appear on the typical *carte des vins*. Most are recent vintages priced purposely low to encourage people to drink them.

She singled out Simi Winery Cabernet Rosé 1972, Ridge Coast Range Zinfandel 1972, Freemark Abbey Chardonnay 1969, Sutter Home Deaver Vineyard Zinfandel 1970, Concannon Petite Sirah 1968, Chappellet Chenin Blanc 1971, and Spring Mountain Chardonnay 1970, and then, for twenty dollars—the upper end of the price range—"such rarefied labels as Joseph Swan Zinfandel '69 and '71 and Chalone Chardonnay '71 . . ."

By the time Michael McCarty opened his restaurant in 1979, he was making a concerted effort to be wine friendly. This started with the food. "Sauce had traditionally been something that, to use the old cliché, you [used to] bury whatever funky piece of meat [you served]," he said. "Whereas I'd use sauce as the bridge between the protein and the wine. I cook with acid in everything, whether it's a vinegar or it's a wine. I always have that; it's the fundamental theme between all my sauces. . . . Chardonnay cream sauce is now a cliché. Why? Because I took a California Chardonnay and reduced it down with shallots . . . using cream, using stock and making a Chardonnay cream sauce, whether it was for fish or for chicken or veal or whatever." McCarty's commitment to wine extended to wine service. "We had a full-time wine guy who was out there talking to people. That was unheard of then. He'd say, 'Well, you're having this? You should try that.' " Not only did the sommelier not wear the traditional tastevin, "He looked like a homeless guy," said McCarty. "It was off the wall—he still wears the same clothes. . . . The point was we were here to educate in a very nonpedantic, nonformal way." This type of casual yet educative wine service soon became the standard in California.

California's wine country, adjacent to the San Francisco Bay Area, also played a significant part in the development of California cuisine. The first really important restaurant in the Napa Valley was Domaine Chandon, opened in 1977 and headed by chef Philippe Jeanty. Soon things exploded, and the Napa Valley, and then Sonoma, eventually became home to some of California's very best dining.

Many of the wineries were quite involved with food, even if they didn't have restaurants. Margrit Biever, wife of Robert Mondavi, founded that winery's Great Chefs program in 1976, bringing in Simone Beck and Jean Troisgros to give seminars. In the first seven years of the program, all the invited chefs were either French or almost French: Julia Child, Michel Guérard, Gaston Lenôtre,

Roger Vergé, Alain Chapel, and Georges Blanc. In 1983, cooks doing American food were included for the first time.

Margrit Biever, a dedicated home cook herself, struggled to find decent ingredients. Joseph Phelps, owner of one of Napa Valley's best boutique wineries and a gourmand ("I've been known to toss an omelette," he admitted to me in an interview), purchased* Oakville Grocery, a general store in Yountville, in 1978, largely to answer his own need for ingredients. "San Francisco had a fine selection of superior ingredients," he recalled, "but you had to go all over town to find them, and they didn't exist in the Napa Valley." Anyone who wanted saffron or wild mushrooms or veal stock had to make the hour-long drive. But things have come a long way in Napa since then. Today Napa Valley is one of the best places in the country to shop for ingredients. The most amazing array of tomatoes, for instance, appears in the Valley's farmers' markets in season—some twenty-three different varieties. It's heaven to shop in such close proximity to producers of goat's and sheep's cheeses, all manner of organic farms, Marin County seafood, and much more.

Today Thomas Keller's The French Laundry, in Yountville, is arguably the best restaurant in the country. Wine is a big part of gastronomy, and it's no accident that the best restaurant is one serving people who are in the business of gastronomy, people who are used to exercising their palates.

By the time I moved to New York City in 1986, California cuisine had preceded me there. Jonathan Waxman, formerly chef at Michael's, opened Jam's on the Upper East Side in 1984. Danny Meyer opened Union Square Cafe the next year, and although it didn't bill itself as California cuisine,

*With partners, whom he later bought out.

something about the food and service made me wonder if it were named for the Union Square in San Francisco, rather than the New York City Union Square, which it overlooked.

Also in 1985, a chef named David Bouley was cooking French food at the newly founded Montrachet, owned by Drew Nieporent. In New York the California idea of chef/owner was only just taking hold, and David Bouley would have to wait a couple years before buying his own place. But by the time it was up and running at full speed in the early 1990s, Bouley was the best and most innovative restaurant in New York. For Bouley had found exactly what the artists of the French *nouvelle cuisine* and the tastemakers in California were seeking: food that tasted like what it was. Pure flavor, true gastronomy.

Residents of the San Francisco Bay Area, had, in the meantime, become dedicated epicures in multiplying numbers. Susan Jamison and Richard Sykes, for instance, close friends of mine since college, have nothing to do with food professionally, yet they keep a garden and greenhouse in which they grow much of their own produce, they forage for mushrooms with their children (their five-year-old Joe can easily spot morels since he's so short), and dive for abalone. When El Niño produced freaky meteorological disturbances in the beginning of 1998, while other Californians were complaining about the rain, Sue and Richard were chartering a fishing boat because they heard that tuna were coming closer in to shore than normal. Richard hunts for boar and deer, makes sausages, brews his own beer, and smokes the fish he catches (no, he doesn't inhale). They drink wine prodigiously and used to run a tasting group with their friends in which they'd each bring a bottle, blind taste and rate everything, and in that way look for new wines to incorporate into their cellars. Too much time on their hands? Not exactly—Sue is a partner in a high-powered law firm who works insane hours, and Richard's an engineer with Bay Area Municipal Utility District. But good food and wine are important to them; it's a quality-of-life issue. Perhaps Sue and Richard are extreme cases, but many of their friends also share the same zealous gastronomic habits.

Joyce Goldstein, however, a longtime resident of San Francisco, doesn't feel Bay Area residents are any more savvy about or dedicated to gastronomy than anyone else. "I think San Francisco is now like the rest of the world," she says. The rest of the world, or at least the rest of the country, that is.

Nevertheless, since its emergence in the early 1970s, California cooking has made a deep and lasting impression from coast to coast—so much so that twenty-five years later, a good deal of what one eats, both in restaurants and at home, throughout the United States, is informed by the precepts and philosophy of California cuisine.

6

FOOD AS CHIC

AS A CULTURE, WE ARE IN LOVE WITH FOOD. OR AT LEAST we're in love with the *idea* of being in love with food.

At the end of the twentieth century in America, food is fashion. Fashion is not deep; on the contrary, it's about surfaces, appearances. Perhaps one shouldn't read too much meaning into these things; still it's striking that the restaurant considered by many to be Los Angeles's best is called Patina.

What does it mean for food to be fashion? Certainly it means that food serves a purpose other than physical sustenance, just as fashionable clothing serves a purpose over and above covering the body. But that's also true about food in societies in which gastronomy—a real appreciation of food, its preparation, and wine—is more than mere fashion, places where food plays a defining role in terms of culture, such as Italy or France, for example, where one cannot imagine the culture separated from its cuisine.

For food to be fashion means that human interaction is a more important part of the equation than one's appreciation and enjoyment of the food. Again, such is the case with fashionable clothing: We see this season's suit by our favorite designer, and we think: Ah, how nice I'll look in this; how chic. "How nice I'll look" addresses not our sensual appreciation of the fabric, not how good we'll feel in it (though these may also play a role), but rather how others will see us.

And so it is with food in America. The sensual pleasures of eating something, truly experiencing the flavors and textures, appreciating the quality of the ingredients and the skill and creativity of the cook—these concerns may come into play, but when food is chic, their role becomes secondary to other considerations. Oh, swell, one thinks—I can tell my friends I ate at Le Cirque 2000. I can tell my boss we had foie gras in France. On New Year's Eve I'll serve caviar and everyone will know it's beluga, from the Caspian Sea, and that I can afford it.

Even as one sits in a restaurant, one is concerned (in spite of oneself) about how one appears to the server—which of course is ridiculous. But how do we feel when a waiter enumerates the ingredients of a dish we know perfectly well or explains what arugula is? Wouldn't we like to ask a halfway intelligent question about the wine list so we don't look stupid in front of the wine steward?

In our culture, an appreciation of gastronomy indicates a certain level of sophistication. We equate being knowledgeable about food and wine with being well-traveled, cosmopolitan, urbane—and as the French would say, *branché:* plugged-in. One reaches the ultimate level of sophistication in this regard if one knows restaurants in cities other than one's own. "Oh, you're going to Seattle? Be sure to eat at Rover's. New York City? You must try Jean Georges. You're going to the Napa Valley? Don't miss The

French Laundry—if you can get in." The "if you can get in" is one of the key factors in any fashion equation; if something isn't exclusive or hard to find or prohibitively expensive, it can't be *that* special, can it?

Knowing restaurants has become so very chic that it has spawned culinary name-droppers. Someone will say, with a casual air, "The first time we ate at Marc Menaud . . ." Of course the listener is supposed to know that Marc Menaud is shorthand for the Michelin three-starred restaurant called L'Espérance in Vézelay, France, where Marc Menaud is the chef. In food circles, dropping the names of Michelin three-stars is the ultimate.

But curiously, the people who engage in this sort of play rarely will tell you what they ate or drank. The point, of course, is that *they were there.* They're not real food lovers; they just love the *idea* of food and the status that these restaurants bestow upon them. They're gourmand-manqués.

Why do people go to famous restaurants—to enjoy the food, or tell about it later? Why are some attracted to the chicness of food and others not? A close friend invited me to dinner at a restaurant not long ago. "I don't know if you'll think it's very good," she said, "but it's kind of cool. I saw Spalding Grey last time I was there." The place to which she took me was a highly rated Italian restaurant. We both felt like having pasta, and the menu listed probably twenty interesting choices. I only remember the one that caught my fancy: fresh tagliatelli with a duck ragu; I started with pickled sardines. Nothing on the menu tempted my blasé friend, however; she asked the waiter if they could make her a spaghetti Bolognese, showing an amazing lack of gastronomic imagination. This friend, however, doesn't pretend to be interested in food. Unabashedly, she likes restaurants for their hipness value, their "scene." She also happens to be an avid stargazer.

On the other hand, I know people who go to restaurants

as if their lives depended on it. My mother, for example, has made restaurant going her highest priority in life. She does truly love food. In fact, she loves it almost indiscriminately. Whenever I ask her how she is, or what's new, she always gives me a restaurant report. I can't remember her ever having been disappointed in a meal. Recently I caught her sitting with her new edition of *Zagat Survey: Los Angeles,* going through the book and checking off every restaurant she's been to.

Some might argue this is better than the opposite—people whose palates are so refined, their critical faculties so finely tuned, that they're almost impossible to please. For instance, this month I flipped through *Diversion,* a lifestyle magazine for doctors, and found an article by noted food critic, author, and *Esquire* columnist John Mariani, in which he complained about having to sit through various tasting menus at restaurants throughout the United States. Keep in mind that sitting through a *menu dégustation*—as they're frequently called—would fulfill the wildest dream of many an underfunded gourmand, not to mention anyone who's ever been hungry. John Mariani is hipper than fabulous food; he's above it.

The very same month an essay appeared in a popular food magazine in which the writer bemoaned having to dine at fabulous restaurants all around the world with her restaurant columnist husband. The problem? He had to take notes, so she couldn't really enjoy the evenings. What a drag.

Perhaps food critics have too much on our plates, as it were. At a dinner at New York City's French Culinary Institute to celebrate the 150th anniversary of Escoffier's birthday, a number of members of the press were invited. Seated next to me at one of the press tables was a very likable gentleman who explained to me that his "day job" had nothing to do with food, but that in the evenings he ghost-writes for a certain well-known food columnist; that night he was there "representing" the critic. This I didn't understand at all: How could a food critic (or any other kind of critic, for that matter) have someone writing in his stead? Criticism includes opinion, which by definition is personal. Well, my dinner companion explained that he didn't write the actual reviews or columns; rather, he went to restaurants in the critic's place, and made notes for him, reporting on the food. Then the famous critic wrote it up and signed his own name.

Even if this gentleman were making the whole thing up, it's telling that someone would consider writing about food glamorous enough to lie about. And food writing is perceived as one of the most romantic things one can do, to the point where there are aspiring food writers (like actors) who hold down day jobs to support their budding careers.

Ron Bass, a Los Angeles screenwriter-producer (and, incidentally, a longtime friend, not to mention a fervent food lover), penned the screenplay for the movie *My Best Friend's Wedding.* The story involves a young woman (Julia Roberts) who realizes she's in love with her best (male) friend on the eve of his wedding. Since Bass wanted to give the glamorous star a really glamorous occupation, he made her—surprisingly, and yet not—a food critic. Throughout the movie Roberts looks pretty uninterested in food; but sadly *that's* not unrealistic. I've known more than a few food writers with eating disorders, and many who are picky eaters. I have a friend who used to review restaurants in Los Angeles who wouldn't touch vegetables or seafood.

Relatively few Americans really savor food with any kind of gusto. As a culture, we don't allow ourselves the pleasure. As we've seen, this is largely thanks to our Puritan past. It's also partly because we find it difficult to slow down long enough to relish it.

But it's also because gastronomy isn't part of our culture. We don't have the background for it. "It's a matter of education," says Philippe Boulot, executive chef at the Heathman Hotel in Portland, Oregon. "If I put sweetbreads in a salad," he told me in a recent interview, "and I put [on the menu] 'duck salad with *croustillants,*' just in French, nobody knows what *croustillants* means. They say, 'Oh, what are these crusty things in it? It's delicious.' If I go to the table and say, 'Oh, do you like my sweetbread salad?' they say, 'Ugh—sweetbreads!' "

"But surely," I said, "since they've already tasted it and liked it, surely they don't reject it after that."

Incredibly, he said, they do. "Yuck," the attitude goes. "I just ate thymus glands. Eeeuuuuu!" If they even know that sweetbreads are thymus glands, that is.

Boulot conceded that such a limited view is more likely in Portland, Oregon, than someplace like New York City, but somehow it seems just plain American to me.

We're suspicious of food. And that's because we *learn* to be suspicious of food. Last year I went to a steakhouse in Los Angeles with my brother and sister-in-law, their five-year-old daughter, and my mother. My mom had ordered a dozen oysters on the half-shell, something my niece, always an adventurous eater, had never seen before. "May I have one?" she demurely asked my mom. My sister-in-law started to say, "No, Anna. You're not going to like that." My brother covered up the comment, and encouraged Anna to try it. She ate one. We all watched her face. "Yum," she said. "Can I have another?"

I don't blame my sister-in-law; this is America, and we're raised to believe that children abhor many foods. We must unlearn that and give children a chance to form their own likes and dislikes—frequently they'll surprise us.

In France, grammar-school children are given classes in which they learn about the four different tastes and various types of foods. A number of years ago I was visiting a friend who's a cook in Dordogne; I helped her prepare dinner at a nearby château for a bicycle tour group that was coming through for the night. At lunchtime, we took a break, and my friend laid out a wonderful impromptu lunch for us and the family who lived in the château. Included in the spread was a smoked magret (duck breast) with a thick layer of fat on top. The eight-year-old boy who lived there started to peel the fat off of a slice of magret. His father scolded him: "You must learn to enjoy it *with* the fat," he explained. That's what Philippe Boulot meant when he said it was a matter of education.

Meanwhile, in the good old U.S. of A. we raise our children on McDonald's Happy Meals and Chicken McNuggets.

People who really love to eat inevitably have weird secret food loves. For M. F. K. Fisher, her private food love could be achieved only under specific meteorological conditions (winter, to be exact). To unearth her secret passion, one needs only to look in the index of her collected books, *The Art of Eating,* under "tangerine sections, radiator-dried." "My pleasure in them is subtle and voluptuous and quite inexplicable," she wrote. In brief, she peeled three or four tangerines, separated the sections, and placed them on a sheet of newspaper spread on the hot radiator. After a few hours, they grew "plumper, hot and full." She then placed them outside on the windowsill, atop the packed snow. Soon, they were ready. "The sections of tangerine are gone, and I cannot tell you why they are so magical," she wrote. "Perhaps it is that little shell, thin as one layer of enamel on a Chinese bowl, that crackles so tinily, so ultimately under your teeth. Or the rush of cold pulp after it. Or the perfume. I cannot tell."

Those, gentle reader, are the words of a woman who truly loved food. For her, food was not in the least bit chic.

"Almost every person has something secret he likes to eat," she also wrote. My mother relishes bananas with sour cream and sugar. Richard M. Nixon liked cottage cheese with ketchup, but it was no secret. Nor was it chic. It said a lot about the man. We are, after all, what we eat. In those years, our nation *was* cottage cheese with ketchup.

Our recent obsession with food in the past few decades has spawned its appearance in other art forms.

After seeing and thoroughly enjoying Stanley Tucci's film *Big Night,* I recommended it to my younger brother, who happens to be a film editor and screenwriter by trade and a wonderful cook by avocation. "Oh, I don't like films about food," he said dismissively. "I'm not going to see it." And this from someone who sees, for professional reasons, just about every movie released. I hadn't realized that films about food had become an actual genre—and one with the potential to annoy, at that. I remember in 1976 seeing *La Grande Bouffe,* a French film made in 1973 about a group of friends who, for a reason I no longer recall, decide to commit suicide by eating. It was a cult hit in Los Angeles at that time. That wasn't exactly a foodie film; in a way it was the opposite, since the reaction it inspired was not reverence for food, but disgust.

Two years later, Ted Kotcheff's *Who Is Killing the Great Chefs of Europe?* treated American audiences to sumptuous food, much of which was prepared by Paul Bocuse. In 1986, Juzo Itami's *Tampopo,* a Japanese film about slurping noodles, captured the popular imagination, but that was small potatoes next to *Babette's Feast,* a 1988 Swedish film (adapted from an Isek Dinesen story) about a French cook who moves to a small town in Sweden, wins the lottery, and treats the town to an extravagant repast. Audiences swooned. L'Ermitage, one of Los Angeles's most elegant restaurants, duplicated Babette's menu for food-loving (and well-to-do) Angelenos. (Missing the theatrical release, I tried to make it through the video twice, falling asleep within fifteen minutes each time.) In the years that followed, a whole slew of foodie films made their way onto the screen, enticing American audiences: Henry Jaglom's *Eating* (1990), in which a bunch of women sit around trying to talk about a variety of subjects, but it turns out all they can talk about is food; the Chinese *The Wedding Banquet* (1993) and *Eat Drink Man Woman* (1994), both by director Ang Lee; *Combination Platter,* American Tony Chan's 1993 film about a Chinese restaurant; and Nana Dzhordzadze's *Chef in Love,* the Georgian/French film about a French chef who travels through the Georgian Republic and winds up staying and opening a restaurant.

Our evolving relationship with food has been reflected in literature, as well. Nora Ephron seasoned her 1983 novel *Heartburn* generously with recipes, but even though the protagonist is a cookbook author, the recipes are rather pedestrian—pot roast, mashed potatoes, cheesecake, and the like. The recipes in Bob Shacochis's 1993 nonfiction book *Domesticity* demonstrate how much things changed in the intervening ten years—here we find Tarragon Duck with Mushrooms and Crushed Pumpkin Seeds, Fettuccine with Gorgonzola and Broccoli, Mango Sorbet. But at least Shacochis's book, a collection of his "Dining In" columns for the magazine GQ, was *supposed* to be about food. *Domesticity*'s cryptic subtitle, "A Gastronomic Interpretation of Love," indicates that the book isn't only about food; like M. F. K. Fisher, whom he quotes in his introduction, Shacochis knows that food and love and security are all inextricably intertwined. Somewhere in the middle falls Mexican writer Laura Esquivel's *Like Water for Chocolate* and the movie made from it. In this love story translated from the Spanish, food has mystic powers; the protagonist Tita cries into her sister's wedding cake and all the guests, upon eating it, are filled with pangs of longing; they're left crying over lost love. Here, food is actually a narrative device that drives the plot of the novel.

When I was thirteen years old, in 1974, I took a trip to San Francisco, alone, without either of my parents, to visit some friends of my mother's. These friends happened to live a couple of blocks from the then-new Japanese Cultural Center; the neighborhood was already known as Japan Town, and boasted a number of Japanese restaurants. My mother's friend's neighbor, a Japanese man, came over early one evening, very excited because he had just won a bundle at the racetrack; he invited us to dinner at a nearby restaurant to celebrate. My brothers and I were already fond of eating tempura and teriyaki, miso soup and green tea ice cream; my parents had introduced us to these dishes at Tempura Hiyama, a decent Japanese restaurant near our house in a suburb of Los Angeles. At dinner that night, my mother's friend passed me a morsel of food with his chopsticks, telling me it was tuna, and though it didn't look like any tuna with which I was acquainted (that is, out of a can), I popped it in my mouth. The luscious coolness, lovely color, and extravagant texture of that first little square pillow of *maguro* combined with the seductively alien cold heat of the Japanese horseradish *wasabi* made an indelible impression on me. I knew, even at the time, that this was a pivotal moment in my life.

"Do you like it?" he asked.

"I love it," I said.

"It's raw," he announced.

I don't know if he expected me to turn up my nose (à la Philippe Boulot's Portland customers), but I was instantly smitten. That was probably the first food I really fell head over heels in love with. I became a sashimi, and then sushi, aficionado at thirteen years old.

Two summers later, my brothers and I went to Houston to visit our uncle and aunt (again without parents); little brats that we were, we demanded Japanese food, boasting to our rube, steak-loving cousins that we liked to eat raw fish. We were young food snobs. Sashimi for us was chic; we were proud of our culinary daring, and we used it, our worldly sophistication, to lord over our country bumpkin relations. I remember how shocked I was that my aunt cooked my uncle a rib-eye (pronounced rih-baaaaah) steak every morning for breakfast.

Today, it seems we've almost run out of food adventures. Yet I was dining at a sushi bar in Los Angeles recently and came across something I had only heard about: *ankimo*—monkfish liver pâté. That sounded like something for the stout of heart, so I tried it, though I must admit to giving a little shudder when I thought about what a monkfish liver must look like. (The fish itself is so ugly—imagine the liver!) Once again, though, I was an instant convert—it tasted like a cross between foie gras and poached salmon. Upon returning to New York, I went out for sushi with my friend Janet, who took me to her neighborhood sushi bar, and I learned that Janet, who isn't particularly a "foodie," wouldn't dream of leaving the premises without her requisite order of *ankimo*. "But," she said, with a devilish gleam in her eye, "there's a sushi bar near my office that serves *bees*." She promised she'd take me there at the earliest opportunity. I realized that I had fallen behind on the sushi trends: I had blinked!

In his 1988 essay "Meat Country," writer J. M. Coetzee argued that for reasons dating back to the Old Testament, Americans only embrace food adventurism where vegetables and fruits are concerned, never with animal flesh. "The same late-twentieth-century consumers who, leaving behind the cautious eating habits of their ancestors, eagerly experiment with baby white aubergines, oyster mushrooms, pumpkin flowers," he wrote, "will not touch frogs' legs, snails, rabbit flesh, horse meat." Point well taken—but he doesn't take sushi into account. Bees! And antelope, kangaroo, emu, and ostrich—all of these game meats are showing up in the chicest restaurants on either coast.

Although in certain circles and for certain occasions, there has always been caché associated with fine restaurants, a knowledge of sophisticated cooking and dining became truly *de rigueur* for the chic set in the 1980s. If you wanted to run with the big dogs in Los Angeles, New York, or San Francisco, you had to know the restaurants. Whereas dining in certain restaurants used to signal social class, now old money and the nouveau riche mingled in the hot restaurants, and "power" meals were the order of the day. The old kinds of barriers broke down as new ones went up—the new cultural elite cared more about whether you ate in the right place than whether your blood was blue.

The 1980s also saw the emergence of the celebrity chef. One of the first was Wolfgang Puck, who made his name at the time when Ma Maison was as famous for its unlisted phone number as for its brave new food. In contrast, back in July 1967 Alvin Kerr had reviewed The Four Seasons in New York City, which had opened in 1959. In his *Gourmet* magazine review he noted the table linens, waiters' uniforms, flowers, shrubberies, and art, and of course the food, but he didn't mention the chef. In fact, the word *chef* is never used in the entire review. Today chefs have *agents*.

Chef as chic reached its logical conclusion in the early 1990s. In 1991, a number of top restaurants in New York placed a table in the kitchen so that diners-in-the-know could eat *right next to the chef.* I suffered through such a dinner at the Edwardian Room in the Plaza Hotel. The atmosphere in most restaurant kitchens is anything but relaxed; I finished the dinner feeling I needed an air conditioner and a vacation. One of New York's best restaurants, Le Bernadin, built a glassed-in private dining room adjacent to the kitchen: This way one was privy to the goings-on, but insulated from the noise, heat, and tension. In 1998 one of the most exclusive restaurant experiences in Los Angeles is Table One, the in-kitchen experience in the elegant Bel Air Hotel.

In 1993 Barry Wine, who, with his wife Susan, had owned New York's toniest restaurant in the mid-1980s, The Quilted Giraffe, was hired by the Sony corporation to create their executive dining room in New York. The result was a sushi bar with a stream running through it and only five seats. To dine here was (and still is) the ultimate in exclusivity: One has to be a studio head or movie star to gain entry.

Okay, so knowing food and restaurants in general is now chic. But what of the history of chic ingredients and preparations? Even when knowing a lot about food wasn't particularly a status symbol, certain dishes, or even ingredients, were.

Celery graced the hippest tables in the 1860s. Chic because it was difficult to grow, celery had to be blanched by mounding up soil around it to keep the stalks white—an unnecessary procedure with modern strains. Those who could afford it displayed it in silver or glass celery vases. Oranges became fashionable in the 1870s, thanks to the developing transportation system that brought the juicy and very perishable fruits north for the first time; a newly introduced exotic fruit called the banana was chic the following decade. Eggs Benedict, Oysters Rockefeller, and sardines were chic as the nineteenth century came to a close. Russian dressing contained caviar when it was created in

1917—no doubt that was chic. Vichyssoise and Caesar Salad were fashionable in the 1920s. Diners in the 1930s who wanted to impress ordered Boula Boula (green pea and green turtle soup) or cooked Chicken Divan at home. French Onion Soup, Saltimbocca, and Scampi all came into vogue after World War II, as the returning GIs brought back a taste for them. Then it was Vitello Tonnato, Steak Diane, Quiche Lorraine, Rock Cornish Game Hens, and Chocolate Mousse in the fifties, the decade when the avocado became terribly fashionable. The early 1960s brought the fondue craze, and in came Beef Wellington, Pheasant Under Glass, Ratatouille, and cheese as dessert.

In the late 1970s Chinese food was very chic, but it had to be regional Chinese—Szechwan or Hunan; none of the Cantonese stuff that was popular in the 1950s and 1960s. Few of us knew what Szechwan or Hunan meant, exactly, nor did we know whether what we were eating resembled anything one would actually find in those regions. (According to Ching Yun Pu, a master chef who worked in prerevolutionary China and wound up in San Francisco in the seventies, "What is often called Hunanese food is something made up to please the American palate. Once the pattern of spiciness and the overuse of garlic was established, nothing could change it.") But never mind; it was chic to eat spicy. Spicy food acquired a kind of machismo, even in those years. In 1979 when I was a student at Stanford, my friends and I frequented a restaurant in San Francisco called Hunan. We all went crazy over the incredibly hot food, and for some reason the thing to do was to wash it down with Coke in the small green bottles. That was chic.

Italian food also became chic in those years. Anyplace where you could find lots of roughly chopped garlic swimming in olive oil was in. And homemade pasta became very big. In 1980, a friend of mine who was advanced in these matters invited me and some other friends over to make pasta with him—he had just bought a pasta machine. (By the next year, everybody I knew had one, including me.) But it wasn't just any pasta; it had chocolate in the dough. Thinking back, I can't remember what on earth possessed him to make that; perhaps it was some spin on Mexican mole.

For the haughtier haute set, it was Northern Italian. That was very important—to distinguish it from any kind of marinara-based cuisine, which was considered passé or déclassé or both. In Italian food, red was out. In those days we ate Fettuccine Alfredo and got away with it. Since then, we've had flings with a succession of ingredients from northern Italy. Sun-dried tomatoes became so chic in the 1980s that I used to wake up in the morning with them on my breath, even though I had brushed my teeth. Proscuitto di Parma made us swoon; then it was Parmigiano Reggiano cheese. Both ingredients hail from Parma, the cheese producers of which have retained a New York public relations firm to recruit food writers to visit the region; and as if the paid trip itself weren't enough incentive to help in making the cheese chic, the Parma producers offer a cash prize every year for the best work written about Parmigiano Reggiano.* But today the chic Northern Italian ingredient of the moment is the white truffle. Winter of 1997 saw Wednesday food sections across the country singing their praises, and restaurants offering special truffle dinners. The chicest kitchen utensil? Why, the truffle shaver, of course.

In the late 1970s, sushi became very chic. For me, the culmination of this trend came in 1979, when I received sushi cooking lessons as a birthday gift. At nineteen, I was

---

*This is not to imply that Parmigiano Reggiano doesn't deserve its exalted reputation; personally, it's one of the few things I'm sure to always have in the refrigerator. Okay? Do I win the prize?

the youngest in my class of seven or eight people who gathered around the sushi chef of a Los Angeles Japanese restaurant. How disappointed I was to learn that the slightly higher body temperature of women makes them less adept than men at forming the little mounds of rice under the fish (I didn't think to question this piece of information). I did come away, however, with a store of interesting sushi knowledge that was to forever enhance my sushi appreciation—for instance, that two of the most reliable tests for the skill of a sushi chef are tamago (a sweetened omelette made in a square pan) and Spanish mackerel, something one rarely sees non-Japanese people ordering. I must confess that I felt proud to have such a connoisseur's edge over my fellow sushi lovers in those days.

The ultimate in sushi chic happens also to be the ultimate in food adventurism: fugu, or blowfish. If not prepared properly, it's deadly. Kobe beef, from cows that do nothing but drink beer and enjoy sake massages, was chic in the early 1980s.

Sake has recently attained chic. It used to be that one ordered sake, plain and simple, and it arrived hot in a little pitcher with a tiny cup. Then came cold sake, served in pretty wooden boxes. I used to frequent a sushi bar in Los Angeles's Little Tokyo district that would give these boxes to regular customers. The customer wrote his name on it and drew a little picture with a felt pen, and the sushi chef ceremoniously put it up on a shelf, confirming the customer's status as not only a regular, but a regular who was hip enough to drink sake cold rather than hot. By the fall of 1997 *The New York Times* ran an article on how to become a sake expert. "A fine sake is a complex drink slightly higher in alcohol than wine and can range from a bright, crisp, perfumed refresher with hints of citrus to something mellower, aged in wood with a whisper of mushrooms and spice," wrote Florence Fabricant. By the following year,

Manhattan would boast a number of rarefied sake bars: Denial, a SoHo lounge that serves junmai, a pure rice sake, and Nigori-zake; Decibel, a sake bar in the East Village that offers seventy types of sake; and Sakagura, in midtown, owned by the same proprietor as Decibel, and serving a whopping 200 choices.

Yesterday evening I stopped at my neighborhood greengrocer's, the same greengrocer's in which I recently saw a young mother identifying different vegetables for her toddler ("This is asparagus, this is an eggplant . . ."). The cashier is right next to the salad greens, and as I waited in line, a woman caught my eye, looking a little sheepish, and said, "Excuse me, do you know what arugula looks like?" "Yes," I said, pointing it out to her, "it looks like this." I was a bit shocked: Here it was 1997, and arugula, the chic green of the early nineties, wasn't recognizable to someone.

When I moved to New York in 1986, I might not have recognized the arugula either, though not because I wasn't familiar with the green. In the California garden I had just left I had planted arugula, but I harvested it when it was very young and tender, pale green. New York City's arugula is grown up, very dark green, and thick as mistletoe. Its flavor is much more assertive, too.

In an Italian restaurant here in New York City recently, I asked about the arugula salad on the menu. "Oh, it's baby arugula," the waiter informed me, proudly. "Much less bitter than the regular kind."

Arugula's chic began in the 1970s. Alice Waters called it "rocket," in the French manner, on her menus. The *Silver Palate Cookbook,* which used it prodigiously, kept it chic through the 1980s; its fashionableness didn't really start to fade until the early nineties—a time of arugula backlash, when it was eradicated from many menus.

Radicchio was the arugula of the eighties. It was so beautiful, the violet-red streaked with white; it looked like parrot tulips in a Flemish still life. So we all thought it was dandy. In *Why We Eat What We Eat,* published in 1991, Raymond Sokolov waxed rhapsodic about it. I don't remember when I stopped liking radicchio, but it was probably sometime around the time when I realized it had become a culinary cliché. Today I find it waxy and flavorless, and surreptitiously try to fish it out of my mesclun with the tongs at the greengrocer's. Could it actually have tasted better fifteen years ago?

Now I'm beginning to fear frisée might be tomorrow's radicchio. I have a friend who hates frisée. ("It falls in the category of stupid food," she says. "It's like a shrubbery on the plate.") I love frisée—real frisée. But there's something that passes for frisée in many mesclun mixes, only it's harvested much more mature than frisée is supposed to be, broken off at the ends to look younger, and the broken ends are inevitably brown, casting a pall over the entire salad.

Today one finds both "greens" in most mesclun, which is the trendiest salad material of the moment. Twenty years ago, almost no one had even heard of mesclun. Alice Waters claims to have had the first mesclun seeds sent to her from France in 1982, but this seems unlikely. In fact, mesclun is simply an assortment of baby lettuces. I once saw it listed on a menu in New York City as "mescaline," and it wasn't intended as a joke.

When it first appeared, which was only in the best restaurants, mesclun seemed precious, but not in a bad way. It was a little like eating flowers, which used to be mixed in with it occasionally (edible pansies, nasturtiums, and the like). Strangely enough, in France, mesclun appears mainly in top restaurants, and has only recently became available in markets. Probably one of the first times we Americans have been ahead of the French food curve!

It was certainly chic in the late seventies and early eighties to eat flowers, not only purely ornamental flowers, but also zucchini and other squash blossoms. Edible ornamental flowers are still offered for sale at Gelson's, a well-stocked supermarket in Pacific Palisades, California. I grew my roses pesticide-free in 1985 so I could use them for cooking; I particularly remember candying them, a trick I learned from Lindsey Shere's cookbook *Chez Panisse Desserts* (though I recently saw a recipe for them in an early twentieth-century San Francisco community cookbook).

Wild mushrooms became chic in the late 1970s; at least that's when I had friends in Northern California who would hunt for them in the woods—specifically, chanterelles in the fall and morels in the spring. On one occasion in, I believe, 1980, a friend who lived in West Marin and I found an enormous, chunky-looking mushroom we thought might have been a cèpe (porcini, or *Boletus edulis*). Though this mushroom later became chic, at that time, my friend and I were only familiar with the sight of them dried. Unfortunately, by the time we were able to make spore prints and get a positive identification, it had desiccated. Today any self-respecting gourmand would recognize it. How times *have* changed!

Chanterelles became very chic by the mid-1980s—so chic that David and Karen Waltuck named their New York City restaurant—one of the city's very best at the time (and very chicest) Chanterelle.

For some reason, many chic ingredients tend to belong to salads. Raspberry vinegar was so chic it eventually became a cliché. Balsamic vinegar followed a similar path. One began hearing a lot about it in the mid-1980s, and soon it became so ubiquitous one began to dread salads. But most of what was around, of course, was not the *true* balsamic vinegar, which is made from white Trebbiano grape juice and aged for years in an elaborate succession of barrels of varying sizes and different types of wood. With balsamic vinegar the search for the authentic ingredient became a kind of game, a type of food snobbery. The real stuff is much too expensive for most people to use in salad; one teaspoon is all that's used to give a dish exquisite flavor. How chic it was in the late 1980s to have a small bottle of this in one's possession!

But as it would turn out, balsamic was not the ultimate in vinegar chic; in fact, it wasn't even close. In 1994 a German named Georg-Heinrich Weidmann introduced Americans to his ultra-recherché apéritif vinegars in varieties such as eucalyptus-honey and robinia-honey Riesling. They sold for about $120 per quarter-liter bottle at the Santa Monica, California, restaurant Röckenwagner, where they were also on the menu, not only as apéritifs in glasses Weidmann designed himself (also sold at Röckenwagner, $43), but spritzed onto plates of cooked food just before serving.

Olive oil carries cachet. In the late 1970s it was enough that one used extra-virgin olive oil: That was far superior to the pure olive oil we had settled for in our spaghetti sauce before that (though Wesson oil did the trick for many). Then it had to be cold-pressed extra-virgin, and then one started paying attention to where it was coming from. Most people considered Italian to be superior to Greek, but real connoisseurs sought out one particular Spanish oil, Nuñez de Prado. (One wonders, however, whether it was its outstanding flavor or the company's marketing savvy that brought it to the foodies' attention.)

Walnut oil and hazelnut oil were chic for a while in the 1980s. They're still delicious, though no longer chic.

Fiddlehead ferns were another chic salad ingredient, though they remained fairly esoteric and still carry a certain chic.

Garlic certainly became chic in the late 1970s, especially

roasted garlic, and basil was boss. In 1979 Americans were discovering pesto; people covered everything with pesto.

Back in the February 1970 issue of *Gourmet,* Daniel V. Thompson, writing about his greenhouse, stated, "We don't grow herbs and vegetables in winter for their food value. The real motive is to work a few swank miracles to astound our friends—perhaps with a freshly made *pesto* in March." *Pesto* was actually italicized since it was still considered a foreign word. But here is food at its most chic: Thompson and his wife went through the elaborate work of building and planting a greenhouse. Why? So they could impress their friends with how terribly chic they were. Not only did they know about *pesto;* they could even serve it out of season!

It wasn't, however, completely unknown in America; James Beard's mother made pesto early in the century. She learned it from her Italian truck gardener.

Risotto made its splash in the early 1980s—it was popularized by Julee Rosso's and Sheila Lukins's 1985 *The Silver Palate Good Times Cookbook* in the form of Saffron Risotto with Pistachios; this was a spin-off of the traditional accompaniment to osso buco, risotto alla Milanese. And speaking of *The Silver Palate,* when Rosso's and Lukins's first cookbook was published in 1979, it was very chic.

As I write, it's rice that's chic. Basmati and arborio are old news; jasmine's glory days are waning. Now it takes baby basmati (also known as gobindovog), Bhutanese red, Thai black, or Japonica to get rice lovers worked up. In New York City's NoHo district a new food stand called Rice offers Small Rice, Large Rice, and Special Rice on its one-page menu, as well as Thai Banana Leaf Wrap ("sweet plantains rolled in sticky rice"), Gen Mai Cha ("Japanese green tea with roasted rice") and "Rice Krispie Treats," a new-wave version of the gooey childhood snack, this time with dried cherries, cranberries, or apricots. (One of the few nonrice items on Rice's menu is something equally chic: *edamame,* but here it's adorned with very untraditional "bulgogi sauce.")

In any case, by the time this book goes to press, I'm sure rice and edamame will be supplanted, too.

Some chic foods have one person to thank for their cachet. Neat discs of kiwifruit graced the oversized white plates of so many restaurants in the early 1980s that kiwi became the shorthand for *nouvelle cuisine.* We have one person to thank for the kiwi: Frieda Caplan. Caplan, who had been selling brown mushrooms at her husband's aunt and uncle's concession at Los Angeles' Central Market for a number of years, had just started her own business at the behest of The Southern Pacific Railway, which owned the Market. They came to her and asked her if she'd go into business for herself selling fresh mushrooms on consignment, she said, because "They were desperate to develop a fresh mushroom market." She went on to explain, "About 1961 Taiwanese mushroom growers started flooding the market with canned mushrooms. Mushroom growers were devastated because it was ruining the fresh mushroom market."

The next year she introduced the Chinese gooseberry, native to New Zealand, and gambling that Americans would respond, she dubbed it the "kiwifruit." All this came purely out of a lively business urge on Caplan's part, rather than any particular fondness for food or cooking. "That's the joke of the industry," she says. "I can't cook and I'm also allergic to kiwifruit. . . . My strength apparently was marketing. Only I didn't know it and it wasn't called marketing. I just started using the techniques I would use if I were running a Red Cross campaign or a camp for student body officers." To interest food editors, Caplan sent them kiwi tarts prepared by a restaurant chef, and the rest is restaurant history.

It might seem kiwis would be a hard act to follow. But Caplan introduced Americans later that year to blood oranges, passion fruit, and pearl onions, then elephant garlic (1966), hot house cucumbers (1967), Maui onions (1970), Asian pears (1971), jicama (1972), spaghetti squash (1975), shiitake mushrooms (1977), sugar snap peas and oyster mushrooms (1979), yellow Finnish potatoes (1982), and donut peaches (1986). After a while it would seem that if Caplan decided something should be chic, she could make it so.

Cajun food was chic in the early 1980s—remember blackened fish? There was also one person responsible for that: Paul Prudhomme, the chef of K-Paul's Louisiana Kitchen in New Orleans, who invented blackened redfish. Soon chefs around the country were blackening anything that swam, and some stuff that didn't. Blackened food went out of style as quickly as it came in, though it lingered, along with Cajun popcorn, in the heartland for many years.

Tall food was chic in the 1980s; restaurant food simply had to have height on the plate. This visual concern grew out of French *nouvelle cuisine* chefs' habit of designing plates in the kitchen, using the plate as a canvas, banishing tableside service such as waiters carving birds, finishing sauces, or flamebéing desserts. By the time *nouvelle cuisine*'s influence was felt stateside, we had food that was positively architectural. The reigning champion of the trend was (and is) Alfred Portale, executive chef at New York City's Gotham Bar & Grill, a restaurant that was, in the mid-1980s, very chic.

And what of tableside service? Today, it's ultra-chic. It's the concept behind Jean-Georges Vongerichten's eponymous New York restaurant, and Executive Chef Erik Blauberg has brought it back at New York's historic The '21' Club. Elegant retro foods are suddenly chic too—crêpes

Suzette and cherries jubilee; elegant spins on retro food, such as a $30 lobster pot pie I saw on the menu of a Manhattan restaurant recently.

Baby vegetables—another legacy of nouvelle cuisine—were the *ne plus ultra* of chic in the early to mid-1980s. One doesn't see them as much anymore, though fake "baby carrots" have become ubiquitous. These are mature carrots (they usually taste overly mature, like wood) that are industrially carved into the shape of baby carrots, sort of. They're sold in small sealed plastic bags in supermarkets and greengroceries throughout the land, and Americans find them useful for so-called healthful snacking or to use as instant additions to their crudité platters. Since they're carved, one doesn't need to peel them or even wash them, though they often have something resembling carrot sawdust sticking to them.

Since the early 1990s, foie gras has been chic. In the 1970s, sautéed foie gras was all the rage in France; it took us twenty years to glom onto the trend. Today chefs plop seared, grilled, sautéed, and roasted slices of duck liver on plates like it's going out of style. (Is it?)

Bistros are chic. Cheese is chic—specifically, the cheese course once again is chic; today it's far more popular than it was in the early sixties, when only ardent gastronomes, a fairly rare breed in those days, would have sought it out. Even more specifically, nonpasteurized cheeses smuggled in from Europe are chic. Although it is legal for individuals to bring unpasteurized cheeses aged less than sixty days into the United States, it is illegal to import them. In New York City a number of cheese stewards at top restaurants have told me they have a source in the city, a person who unofficially imports these cheeses. American farmstead cheeses are also fashionable.

Five years ago, bread was chic; now, it's taken for granted. (Though curiously, while it's easy to find decent bread in Gotham, it's still relatively difficult to find excellent bread.)

What's more basic even than bread? Salt. Today the must-have is fleur de sel, the finest part of the natural sea salt from France's Brittany coast, which appears as a fragile film atop the salt marshes. It is painstakingly harvested by lifting the film off the salt beds with a skimmer. The *saunier* (salt harvester) must coordinate his efforts with the weather—for the film only forms and may be harvested under certain meteorological conditions. One is reminded of *Botrytis cinerea,* the "noble rot" that affects wine grapes only when the fog sits on the vines just so, giving certain late-harvested wines such as Sauternes their distinctive character. Fleur de sel was routinely ignored until the early 1980s, when a number of French chefs discovered its lovely flavor, vaguely reminiscent of violets. I've been using fleur de sel de Guérande since before it was chic. Which is the chicest chic of all.

Are we running out of foods to elevate to the status of chic? By the end of 1997 we were reduced to revering weeds—er, uh, foraged plants. Jean-Georges Vongerichten has been foraging for ground ivy, chickweed, miner's lettuce, mugwort, and other wild herbs for use at his Manhattan restaurant, Jean Georges, but lest the lees fail to provide a suitable bounty, he counts on Nancy McNamara, who grows a wide array of herbs normally found in the wild at her greenhouse in upstate New York. Other chefs have been known to forage in Central Park, and some "wild" herbs are also available at Union Square Greenmarket. In other parts of the United States, chefs engage the services of foragers to find herbs, as well as wild mushrooms, for use in their restaurants. Vongerichten was not the first chef in the world to transform foraged plants into haute cuisine, though: Michel Bras, the chef of an eponymous Michelin two-starred restaurant near Laguiole, France, has been doing the same thing for years, as has Marc Veyrat, chef of the three star Auberge de l'Eridan in France's Savoie region. As I write, Keats Publishing is about to bring out *The Encyclopedia of Edible Plants of North America* by François Couplan, a French botanist and herb guru to a number of chefs. Foraging was first brought to the attention of Americans by Euell Gibbons, a 1960s naturalist who wrote *Stalking the Wild Asparagus* and *Stalking the Blue-eyed Scallop.* Americans of a certain age remember him from his appearance in a TV commercial for Grape-Nuts cereal in which he said, "Cattail. Many parts are edible . . ." When we were children, that cracked us up.

Why are we so compelled to eat what's chic?

The game of culinary one-upmanship is a search for arcane knowledge that confers power. Knowledge about food has come to imply the height of culture and sophistication. To eat chic is to be chic.

At the same time, as a young gastronomic entity, the United States has been mired in a stage of discovery (or in some cases, rediscovery). As we discover unfamiliar cuisines, new ingredients, we get excited; our motors get revved up. And the attention span of our young country is as short as that of a young child.

But such gastronomic keeping-up-with-the-Joneses can become exhausting. In recent years people have started longing for home-spun dishes such as chicken pot pie, meatloaf, and mashed potatoes out of an urge to really enjoy what's known and familiar, to be "comforted" by it. At first, the desire countered the chic; it was a foil for it. But soon, comfort food itself became chic.

7

IT'S DELICIOUS, BUT IS IT *CUISINE?*

WHAT IS AMERICAN COOKING, EXACTLY, AND WHY do people around the world make fun of it? Is there such a thing as an American cuisine, or must we settle for calling what we eat by the more homely word *cookery?*

Even though many people around the world think American cooking means hamburgers, the United States does have its share of compelling traditional dishes and foodways. Part of people's lack of familiarity with them comes from our vast size—what's traditional in one corner of the United States would be quite alien in another corner.

Yet people have always moved around a lot in the United States, taking their favorite dishes with them. An eighteen-year-old from Wisconsin may go away to college in California, get a job after graduation in Chicago, meet someone from Florida, and wind up living in Miami. Those regional dishes that haven't disappeared spread themselves out all over the country, so much so that one forgets from what region they hearkened.

Since mid-century, there has been a movement dedicated to preserving traditional American cookery, which was quickly disappearing in the face of increased reliance postwar on packaged products, frozen foods, and the widening chain of national food distribution of produce, meats, and other foods.

To make matters worse, traditional American cooking has long suffered from low self-esteem. We have pooh-poohed such regional favorites as fried chicken, Carolina barbecue, grits, black-eyed peas, cioppino, planked salmon, shad roe, Brunswick stew, country ham, fresh abalone, cracked Dungeness crab, conch stew, and shoofly pie, dismissing them as hick food, not worthy of serious consideration. By the 1960s most people assumed that foreign food—specifically French food—was somehow superior, and as a nation, we turned our backs on American foods in favor of French food that was often poorly prepared. But it was French, so we assumed it was better. Such wonderfully simple, honest national favorites such as chicken pot pie, apple pie, baked potato, steak, and hamburger were not considered serious. The danger was that though the parents of the "Pepsi generation" may have remembered the regional specialties, the generation coming of age around 1960 wouldn't, raised as they would have been with the newfangled packaged and frozen foods. So when chicken pot pie made its appearance in the freezer section, there it stayed; America forgot how good the real thing was. American food? It was what rubes ate. And our regional dishes were fast becoming endangered species.

James Beard was one of the first important proponents of the movement to conceptualize and define an American cuisine, which was an effort that included preserving traditional regional specialties as well as embracing new influences on American cooking. In the Introduction to *The Fireside Cookbook* (1949), he wrote:

> More than other countries with longer histories or narrower traditions in food, America has had the opportunity, as well as the resources, to create for herself a truly national cuisine that will incorporate all that is best in the traditions of the many peoples who have crossed the seas to form our new, still-young nation. At its best American cookery is as straightforward, honest, and delicious as the fish that swim off its shores or the cornmeal dishes that were the mainstays of its earliest settlers. At its worst, it is a careless imitation, not merely of what is least good in the tradition of other countries, but, what is still worse, of its own tradition. Witness the sins that are daily committed in scores of public dining rooms—and private ones, for that matter—in the name of Southern fried chicken.

In 1949, American food indeed suffered terribly from the crime of "careless imitation" that Beard was noting.

Beard contended then that we owe a greater culinary debt to China than any other culture, since it was there that Marco Polo discovered pasta. If Beard felt that way in mid-century, when pasta was still called macaroni or spaghetti and wasn't eaten in the United States with anything like the frequency it is today, imagine if Beard, who died in 1985, could see us now.

Another early booster of American cuisine was Clementine Paddleford, who was the food editor of *This Week* magazine in January 1948 (later she also became food editor of the *New York Herald Tribune*). Paddleford began crisscrossing the United States "by train, plane, automobile, by mule back, on foot," covering more than 800,000 miles, by her own calculation, in the twelve years she spent interviewing more than 2,000 home and professional cooks in order to get a handle on America's eating habits. The fruits of her labors were published in 1960 as a book, entitled *How America Eats*.

Toward the end of those twelve years, among those she visited were Samuel Chamberlain, the author and illustrator of *Bouquet de France,* among other books, and his wife Narcissa, who translated and adapted recipes for *Bouquet* and other books. As Paddleford visited them, they were just finishing their own "check-up of what's cooking in the United States." From today's perspective, the most interesting facet of their encounter at the Chamberlains' house in Marblehead, Massachusetts, was Narcissa Chamberlain's take on American cooking at the time.

> Mrs. Chamberlain told me that she considers American cooking today under three divisions, the regional, the foreign, and the new. Heirloom recipes are the basic building blocks in our modern cuisine. It is estimated that two-thirds of all our recipes hinge back to old favorites of two types; the regional dish that grew up with the country based on products at hand; and the foreign, the international recipes which came to America with the immigrants from every corner of the world.

What Paddleford couldn't have known was how much more important the immigrant influence would come to be in the 1960s. She continued, predicting the importance of new products:

> The other third of our cooking is strictly today's, making use of the new products—the little Rock Cornish hen of recent development, the time-saving

> ready-mixes, the instants, the quick frozens. Modern meal planners want the quick and easy, but with the plus of their own distinctive touches. Women have great need, in this automatic world, to express themselves creatively.

Chamberlain was right in thinking that women needed to express themselves creatively in the kitchen, but wrong, of course, in suggesting that either women or men could do so using cake mixes, Potato Buds, or frozen broccoli.

And she was correct about the importance of regional American foods and immigrant influences, and that new products would be important. She was on the right track with the Rock Cornish hens; their development would set the stage for other innovations (including importation) in fowl, fish, and produce that would satisfy our constant cravings for new ingredients in the coming decades.

As it would happen, the California cuisine movement led the way for a much larger movement, an American cuisine movement. Today American cooking does fit into Narcissa Chamberlain's categories—"the regional, the foreign, and the new"—though one can no longer consider them separately. By century's end, the three influences have become inextricably intertwined.

After the publication of Paddleford's book, which included hundreds of recipes along with the interviews, there was a flurry of interest in the idea of American cuisine. In an article in *Gourmet* in March of 1965 a judge in New York recounted how he had long been a French chauvinist in matters of food and wine, and imparted all his considerable knowledge on the subject to his new wife, when suddenly she turned around and introduced him to American delights in their home. He quickly became a convert to the cause of American cookery, enjoying such treats as planked shad and shad roe* and maple mousse.

That June, *Gourmet* ran a review of the American Restaurant at the 1965 World's Fair. "Call the cookery American, as it actually is," wrote Alvin Kerr, "but don't expect only Brunswick stew, succotash, roast turkey, and Indian pudding. The cooking is contemporary American, presenting dishes adapted from regional specialties with great originality and imagination." Kerr noted smoked Columbia River salmon with a piquant salad of radishes; cantaloupe with Kentucky ham; a farmhouse terrine (made with duckling and veal) served with a wild berry sauce; baked shad with roe soufflé; walnut-fried Boston sole; Pennsylvania smoked pork chops. "Only fresh vegetables are served," he wrote, and this tells us more about the unhappy norm in other restaurants than it does about the American Restaurant; "the selection dependent on what of peak quality is available."

Interest in our national cookery was short-lived at that time, however, eclipsed by the French cooking mania that was gathering steam.

By 1968, the year in which the United States really began to see the gastronomic effects of the Immigration Act of 1965, James Beard had become an even more confirmed believer in the cause of American cuisine. "Now, after 350 years of inventions and borrowings adapted to please the composite American palate," he wrote, "we are on the way to establishing a cuisine that can truly be called our own." In 1972 he came out with one of his most important books, *James Beard's American Cookery.*

---

*The egg sac of the American shad, a member of the herring family native to the Atlantic, has long been a prized delicacy. Mark Bittman calls it "the foie gras of the fish world."

By 1980, the year the paperback edition of *James Beard's American Cookery* was published, Beard wrote with still more conviction and optimism:

> In the years since this book was first published in 1972, the stature of American cookery has grown tremendously. Whereas eight years ago people sneered at the notion that there was such a thing as an American cuisine, today more and more people are forced to agree that we have developed one of the more interesting cuisines of the world. It stresses the products of the soil, native traditions, and the gradual integration of many ethnic forms into what is now American cooking.

Beard didn't neglect to comment on the new direction his analysis of American cuisine had taken: Purely traditional American cookery had given way to one strongly influenced by foreign foods and traditions, and at the same time one in which California cuisine's back-to-the-land ideal was most important. Presciently, the final sentence of Beard's Foreword provided the most succinct articulation of the new direction American cuisine would take.

A new crop of preservationists soon made its presence felt. In 1981, Raymond Sokolov, editor of the Leisure & Arts page of the *Wall Street Journal,* columnist for *Natural History* magazine, and former food critic for *The New York Times,* published *Fading Feast: A Compendium of Disappearing American Regional Foods.* This book was a paean to such endangered regional specialties as Brunswick stew and burgoo (in their original incarnations, squirrel stews); aged Tillamook cheddar from Oregon; key limes; and Smithfield ham, as well as foods that have since turned out not to be threatened such as wild rice and Michigan morels.

In a folksier vein, Calvin Trillin, in his *New Yorker* articles that were later collected into three books—*American Fried: Adventures of a Happy Eater* (1974), *Alice, Let's Eat* (1978), and *Third Helpings* (1983)—immortalized, at least in prose, Kentucky barbecued mutton, Louisiana crawfish étouffé, Philadelphia cheese steak, and other delights. Far from being academic in tone, his commitment to preservation ran along the lines of "damn, if they stop making that, I won't be able to eat it anymore." Trillin was (and is) a true gourmand—without an ounce of snobbism.

Observers such as Paddleford, Sokolov, and Trillin went about the documenting of our traditional cuisines with a zeal that bespeaks the real danger we faced (and continue to face) of losing our traditional foodways.

Unlike Sokolov and Trillin, Edna Lewis was (and is) a cook; she served as chef at the Brooklyn restaurant Gage & Tollner. Born in 1916 in Freetown, Virginia, on April 13 (she shares the birthday with Thomas Jefferson, another Virginian) in a farming community that had been established by freed slaves—including her grandfather—Lewis has dedicated much of her life to preserving the traditions of Southern cooking. Her 1976 cookbook, *The Taste of Country Cooking,* showed Americans how to reproduce dishes such as pan-fried chicken with cream gravy, pork-flavored green beans, and spoonbread. In 1991 Lewis co-founded (with Scott Peacock) the Society for the Revival and Preservation of Southern Food.

In the meantime, a young chef named Larry Forgione had become fascinated with cooking he identified as just plain American.

Larry Forgione came to the idea of cooking American food and promoting American ingredients when he was cooking in, of all places, England. Having finished school at the Culinary Institute of America in 1974—two years after Chez Panisse opened, just for some perspective—Forgione was serving an apprenticeship of two years at London's Connaught Hotel under chef Michel Bourdin. Forgione was much affected by the attitude around him "that Americans didn't know very much about cooking because as a people we didn't know very much about eating." He explains further: "The world's view of American eating was hot dogs and hamburgers, and the view of fine dining was steaks and lobsters." While in Europe, Forgione was most impressed with the quality of the ingredients available. "It didn't make sense to me," he recalled in an interview, "that we didn't have these wonderful ingredients." Tasting Bresse chicken for the first time at the Connaught, he was bowled over by how flavorful it was. Yet he *had* tasted chickens that flavorful before: when he was a child at his grandmother's five-acre farm in Long Island. So as wonderful as the European ingredients were, "All of a sudden it clicked with me," he explained, "that these taste like Grandma's potatoes or Grandma's tomatoes or Grandma's corn or Grandma's chickens. That was the point for me that I realized there were great opportunities with food in America." So when Forgione came back to the United States, "I decided," he told me, "that I wanted to create a style of American cooking that used only American products," not from any anti-European chauvinism, but "purely from the point of highlighting the bounty of America."

When he came to New York City's River Cafe as executive chef in 1979, he said, the one-year-old restaurant was serving Continental cuisine; he soon turned it into an American restaurant—a rare animal in fine dining at the time—just after Michael McCarty had started Michael's in Santa Monica. Forgione explained that he began investigating products where they were grown by calling Chambers of Commerce to locate sources of ground cherries or chanterelles. "As things came in," he said, "we started putting them on the menu. We brought to a New York restaurant—for the first time in fifty years—buffalo." He also hooked up with a wild edibles forager in Petoskey, Michigan, Justin Rashin, with whom he would later start a company. "He would send me cattail shoots and morels, wild watercress, edible flowers." In 1979 or 1980, he recalled, he also asked Paul Kaiser, a farmer in Warwick, New York, to begin raising chickens for him the way his grandmother had. He asked that instead of having them stay in a coop, the chickens be allowed to roam free to make them healthier and more flavorful. As a result of this endeavor, he said, he coined the term "free-range" chicken.

People sat up and took notice of what Forgione was doing at the River Cafe. Among them was Rozanne Gold, who was just finishing a stint as then New York mayor Ed Koch's chef at Gracie Mansion. "My father was in the garment industry and used to go out to eat all the time," Gold told me in a recent interview. "We were a really eating out family. And my father discovered the River Cafe." She continued:

> I started going there a lot. . . . I really thought Larry was onto something. He wasn't yet calling it New American or anything like that, but [soon he] started to. Clearly he really did care about this, and started calling things by place names—Larry was a great researcher. . . . I started bringing people down to the River Cafe—The Fabricants*, Steven Specter†, Arthur [Schwartz]‡—and there would be a couple of round tables where there would be maybe ten foodies. And I would tell everyone about this new

---

*Florence Fabricant was and is a writer for *The New York Times*.

†Owner of Manhattan restaurant Le Plaisir. Gold said she was the first woman to work in Le Plaisir's kitchen; she did so gratis, in true "foodie" style.

‡The food critic for the *Daily News* at the time.

American cuisine and what Larry was trying to do, and they started coming, and it started catching on.

In 1983, Forgione went all-out with the idea, opening his own restaurant in Manhattan, An American Place.

As discussions about a "new" American cuisine revved up in the early 1980s, cooks, critics, journalists, and foodies of all sorts fell into two camps: the purists, who felt that we should be reaching backward into American history and resurrecting the traditional American specialties that were either forgotten or endangered, and those who saw progress in an opening up to foreign influences, especially French, but also Asian, Italian, and many others. The purist camp used James Beard to bolster their cause, ignoring the reality that Beard did not reject foreign influences.

The United States bicentennial, in 1976, got people thinking further about things American, including American food.

Barbara Kafka points out that our fascination with traditional American food in the early 1980s coincided with the election of Ronald Reagan as President, as well as a kind of rah-rah, go-U.S.A. Republican-tinged patriotic attitude that was in vogue in general.

A number of chefs around the country had begun to focus on the best ingredients of their regions, using them sometimes in traditional dishes, but more often in creating something totally new, often in a quite self-conscious attempt to construct a new American cuisine. The best of these young chefs showed remarkable inventiveness and imagination. Among them: Mark Miller at Coyote Cafe in Santa Fe, Robert Del Grande at Cafe Annie in Houston, Bradley Ogden at The American Restaurant in Kansas City, Jimmy Schmidt at London Chop House in Detroit, Paul Prudhomme at K-Paul's Louisiana Kitchen in New Orleans, and Marcel Desaulniers at The Trellis Restaurant in Williamsburg, Virginia.

In fact, the New American Cuisine took a page from recent French culinary history. During the period between World Wars I and II, the gastronomic writer Curnonsky urged French chefs, particularly Fernand Point of La Pyramide in Vienne, to take French regional cooking seriously, stressing at the same time the importance of focusing on ingredients, a real departure from the haute cuisine that preceded it.

So while these new regional American cuisines were based upon the same principals that California cuisine was based on—using the best, freshest local ingredients and applying French technique to make them into something new—the young chefs pioneering the movement owed an even larger debt to France than they probably imagined.

In the excitement of all the experimentation, a lot of awful food was prepared along with the good. Horrific combinations of ingredients abounded, as they do to this day, so important was it to do something new or "inventive" or "original" or "nouvelle" or "haute."

Certain combinations were, one hoped, good enough that one might want to eat them again; these had a chance, albeit slim, of one day becoming standard preparations.

In the summer of 1981, a restaurateur in Louisville, Kentucky, named Michael Grisante got to thinking, and casually raised a question to his friend Phillip S. Cooke, president of a food service management company then called Foodservice Associates. "Is anybody doing anything about bringing together everybody who's interested in American cuisine?" he asked. The following March, Cooke's company held a conference at a Louisville hotel, The Symposium on American Cuisine. "Frankly," wrote Cooke in the introduction to the published transcript of the Symposium, "we didn't know whether 10 people or a hundred would show up." As it turned out, they had sixty-seven. They came to discuss "this burgeoning American Cuisine movement—what it was exactly and whether it was just a passing fad or was it here to stay."

By now people had stopped calling it the new American cuisine and had started calling it New American Cuisine. Like the New Wave music that had become popular with groups such as Talking Heads, Blondie, and Elvis Costello, and also very much like French *nouvelle cuisine,* New American Cuisine was trendy, hip, spare, fresh, and highly designed, with clean lines and vibrant flavors. New Wave music reacted against the bluesier, more raggedy rock music of the 1960s and 1970s; New Wavers had short, stylish hair and wore spiffy, brightly colored or black-and-white clothes reminiscent of the Mods. New Wave music was spare rather than lush, and vocals became clear, direct, cerebral; altogether it was less romantic and atmospheric than rock vocals, and it seemed less likely to be inspired by a drug trip than a lot of 1960s and 1970s rock songs did.*

Styles in restaurant food didn't look all that different. Presentation became hugely important: The plate had to look striking. Everything was fanned out, including lots of highly styled garnishes; vegetables were perfect baby specimens, and since they were undercooked they retained their vibrant colors and perfect little shapes; the protein element sat atop a glistening pool of often brightly colored sauce. Statements were simple and direct; nothing was drowned in heavy sauce.

Suddenly there was a remarkable energy and excitement in and around restaurants. Everyone wanted to cook and

---

*Perhaps it would be more accurate to say that rather than sounding psychedelic, it seemed, if anything, cocaine-inflected. Cocaine, incidentally, was hugely popular in the early 1980s, and it made its presence felt in restaurant kitchens as much as in pop bands.

everyone wanted to eat. Cooking school enrollment soared, and cooking schools sprang up all over the country.

Needless to say, the consensus at the Symposium was that whatever was going on amounted to something more than just a passing fad, and a Second Symposium was organized for 1983, this time in New Orleans, hosted by Ella Brennan of Commander's Palace.

James Villas, who had been food editor of *Town & Country* magazine since 1973, was slated to be keynote speaker; his book *American Taste: A Celebration of Gastronomy from Coast to Coast* had made a splash the previous year. This time the Symposium's mission was to hash out what defined American cuisine and discuss where it might be heading.

Expecting the obligatory rah-rah-go-American-cuisine speech, the assembled were taken by surprise as Villas delivered his keynote address, which sharply criticized the direction American cooking had taken.

> I truly wonder if I'm really in America. I go to the West Coast, for example, salivating in anticipation of what chefs might be doing with fresh abalone, Pigeon Point oysters, cioppino, and cracked crab, but what I find instead is a veritable plethora of so-called American restaurants serving elaborate salads made with foie gras, arugula, mâche, truffles, and walnut oil, sushi, pasta with *confit de canard* and Oriental mushrooms, half-cooked monkfish floating on a lagoon of *coulis de cassis* or *beurre blanc,* baked goat cheese on a bed of radicchio, one exotic pizza after another, and tofu cheesecake.

The tenor of the rest of his speech was that we should look for inspiration closer to home—that is, in regional cookery—and forget about foreign influences. "Only then," he said, "with that solid foundation, can we justify experimenting, changing formulas, elevating menus, and trying to create dishes that may some day have that degree of sophistication and refinement so many seem to be seeking."

As it turned out, just about everyone who spoke agreed that they needed to build on what had long existed, rather than creating something utterly new out of whole cloth.

The only foreigner to speak, *Gault Millau*'s Christian Millau, laid out another challenge, after pointing out that California Cuisine, which served as the model for New American cuisine, was really French *nouvelle cuisine* in disguise. He complained that the United States at that time was becoming more and more provincial, "less and less interested in what's going on in the outside world," and such arrogance made it possible for us to imagine that we invented concepts such as using the freshest ingredients in season, reducing cooking times for vegetables, seafood, and game, and using lighter sauces.

But our real problem, as he laid it out, was that "The extraordinary diversity of this country has not been reflected in its cuisine." He cited two reasons for this. One was that the food industry had destroyed regional cuisines. The other was that we had been "trapped by the predominance of French and other cuisines." Escaping the French influence was the challenge American chefs had to take up.

Paradoxically, all these chefs soon realized that they'd absolutely have to rely on French technique as an essential foundation on which to build.

Chefs faced other problems, as well, if New American Cuisine was to survive its infancy. Even though there was a renaissance going on, it was still difficult to find good kitchen help in the early 1980s. ". . . It's very difficult for me to find people," said Jonathan Waxman, who was chef at Michael's in Santa Monica at the time. "I spent two years finding a sous chef. This is a big problem in our country."

Cooking schools were becoming hugely important. But though the number of people entering restaurant work as cooks was much greater than twenty years earlier, that didn't solve everything. It's long been my belief that many people are drawn to cooking school because they didn't grow up cooking. And if one doesn't grow up cooking, it's difficult to make up a lifetime missed in a couple of years. That's why many self-trained cooks are better cooks than their culinary school graduate counterparts; the trained chefs may have better technique, but the self-trained practitioners often have a better innate sense of a dish and how to make it work.

"There are those kids," said Waxman, "who have been trained for two years, and can perform anything that I can do, but they don't have a wide repertory. They go out and make mistakes, those culinary wrongdoings that get us all in trouble. They serve dishes that are underdone, overdone, undersauteed, overpoached, overreduced, and overjulienned."

Waxman, who came from an academic background (he graduated from the University of California at Berkeley in Political Science in 1972) had gone to cooking school, spending the better part of a year at La Varenne in Paris. But part of the problem with chefs in general in the United States—and this still holds true—is not that they don't have schooling, but that they don't put in the years of apprenticeship and assisting that is mandatory for French or Japanese cooks. A year or two in cooking school and they become saucier or sous chef, often with relatively little experience behind the stove.

Christian Millau's point about our reliance on French cooking was well-taken. As we emerged from the numbing effect of the Domestic Science movement and Prohibition, and looked toward France for culinary inspiration, we erred in looking *only* to France for our model of what good cooking should be. Even today, in any serious restaurant kitchen—with the exception of pure Asian restaurants such as Japanese, Chinese, or Thai—French technique is a given.

In the meantime, regional was big in the burgeoning New American Cuisine movement; Cajun was huge. More specifically, Paul Prudhomme, chef of K-Paul's Louisiana Kitchen in New Orleans was a sensation. Like many other regional chefs, Prudhomme took certain elements of the traditional cuisine of his region, in his case Cajun, Acadian, and Creole, and put his own personal spin on them. Prudhomme was the first to export, on a major scale, his regional food to the rest of the country. He managed to market himself (and his spice mixtures) in a way that no one else had done before. His blackened redfish became an emblem of the 1980s; eventually it became so popular that though Prudhomme had invented it, it was soon what people thought of when they thought of traditional Cajun food.

But as he told it in the Introduction to his 1984 cookbook *Chef Paul Prudhomme's Louisiana Kitchen,* his cooking was originally based on the same precepts as Alice Waters's was.

> It took me many years to understand that it was the use of local fresh products that was the single most important factor in good eating. One of my strongest memories of my mother's cooking is her use of only fresh ingredients. We had no refrigeration, so we'd go out in the fields to get what we needed. When we dug up potatoes, within two hours they'd be in the pot, cooked and eaten. *I* couldn't seem to get a potato to taste like my mother's until I realized that it wasn't anything that was done in the kitchen, it was just the freshness of the potato that made it com-

pletely different. This principle carries over to all foods.

Of course, traditionally, there was no such thing as blackened fish. Before Prudhomme popularized blackening, redfish court bouillon was the traditional preparation of redfish in Louisiana; the fish is long-simmered in a dark roux-based sauce with tomato, aromatic vegetables, bay leaves, allspice, red pepper, other spices, and red wine, served in a bowl with rice. Prudhomme's cookbook doesn't even mention this dish.

But what Prudhomme did by coating a piece of mild fish with assertive spices, then searing it in a very hot pan, perfectly captures a couple of qualities of the New American cooking. Lots of spice answered the urge for big flavors (though spices weren't used everywhere; often it was fruits or herbs, vegetable or stock reduction that provided the flavor punch) as befit a national palate that doesn't exactly appreciate the overly subtle. Searing appealed as a cooking method, giving texture to the outside and letting reduced cooking times prevail for an interior that was less cooked than in olden days and therefore also very modern. Stews and roasts were out; and overcooked vegetables represented the esthetic everyone was revolting against.

Interestingly, twenty-five years later everyone seems to be craving long-simmered foods—stews, roasts, and the like. An article by Jack Bishop in the *New York Times* in 1996 even advocated long-cooking vegetables—an idea that would have sounded like heresy in the 1980s. Barbara Kafka is working on the cutting edge of this trend, having published a 1995 book called *Roasting,* and, in 1998, *Soup: A Way of Life.* In fact, soups are this year's hot ticket, with upscale soup kitchens popping up all over New York City, inspired partly by the famous "Soup Nazi" episode of the TV sitcom *Seinfeld,* but gaining steam because of soup's high "comfort" factor. Perhaps we needed to sever our relationship with the past completely, before we could tentatively begin to reintroduce only the good parts.

Southern cooking enjoyed a renaissance in the 1980s, with chefs such as Louis Osteen, Patrick O'Connell, and Edna Lewis leading the way. Patrick O'Connell and partner Richard Lynch opened The Inn at Little Washington in 1978 in Washington, Virginia, serving local hams, wild Virginia duck, trout, fish from the Chesapeake Bay, and local apples. And Osteen was probably the first to elevate grits (stone-ground, of course) to "haute" status. Grits have finally made it into the lexicon of mainstream American cooking, as in pan-roasted quail in Pinot Noir sauce served on a bed of grits, or somesuch. Here the African-American influence was very strong.

Even outside of the South, there had been interest in "soul food" long before this. In jazz-age New York, for instance, lower Manhattanites and other New Yorkers went uptown to Harlem for ribs, grits, collard greens, hog jowl, corn pone, black-eyed peas, and other Southern favorites at Craig's on St. Nicholas Avenue.

The Black Power movement in the 1960s brought soul food into the national limelight. Sylvia's opened in 1962; today owner Sylvia Wood is going national with a new restaurant in Atlanta, and outposts planned in St. Louis, Baltimore, and Brooklyn.

African-Americans were some of the most important chefs in the United States, beginning in the eighteenth century. Besides making huge contributions to Southern cooking as slaves in plantation kitchens, they transformed humble ingredients into toothsome fare in their own kitchens. Yet oddly, they haven't made their presence felt in professional kitchens today as much as one would expect. The late Patrick Clark, who died of heart failure in 1998 at age forty-two, was at the top of the field when he was chef at the Hay-Adams Hotel in Washington, D.C., in 1992; President Clinton offered him a position as White House executive chef, but Clark refused. Instead, Clark took over the helm at New York City's Tavern on the Green in 1995, improving the quality of the food there considerably. But other than Clark and Edna Lewis, one is hard-pressed to name many other famous black chefs.

Bea Beasley, a northern California caterer who was the coordinating chef for America's Top Black Chefs Awards from 1993 through 1997, suggests that black chefs have had a difficult time attaining stature nationally because of a lack of media attention and the high expenses associated with the restaurant business. "Culinary training gets to be expensive," she explained in an interview, "and opening up your own restaurant is also very expensive." She pointed out that many of the chefs who have become well-known by the public over the years have done so with the help of publicists, who are quite expensive to retain.

Beasley added that a persistent stereotype image of what black chefs cook and are capable of cooking has gotten in the way of their success as a group. "I was trained at the California Culinary Academy," she told me. "A lot of people assume that because I'm black I do soul food."

Today the rest of the United States, outside the South, resembles a patchwork of self-conscious, though often wonderful, entirely *constructed* regional cuisines.

Some of the most interesting food in the United States is being cooked up in the Pacific Northwest, particularly Seattle, the city with the most highly charged creative energy at the moment for food. Here, the best chefs let the indigenous ingredients—fabulous salmon, Dungeness crab, Olympia oysters, Oregon truffles and morels, bounteous vegetables and fruits, and wonderful wines—do the talking.

But there's also a strong Asian accent that is so marvelously integrated in this original cuisine. Wild Ginger, for instance, a casual, inexpensive and unpretentious restaurant, offers Vietnamese rabbit satay, made with rabbits from Oregon, and Lamb Bumbu, Washington lamb wok-fried with garlic, ginger, cardamom, cinnamon, and star anise.

Pacific Rim cuisine has much in common with Pacific Northwestern and California fusion cooking; it's West Coast cooking mated with influences from Thailand, China, Japan, the Philippines, Malaysia, and Vietnam.

The food scene in Hawaii is just as vibrant as Seattle's, utilizing the best fish and some of the most interesting produce in the United States. Although the chefs of Hawaiian regional cuisine don't depend on a great number of traditional preparations, spins on a wonderful dish called poke—raw fish, usually ahi (tuna), chopped and combined with seaweed, salt, chili peppers, kukui nuts, and sesame oil—are compelling. In Hawaii ingredients really come into the forefront. Leading the way are Roy Yamaguchi of Roy's Restaurant in Honolulu; Alan Wong, Executive Chef of the Mauna Lani Bay Hotel on the Big Island; Amy Ferguson-Ota of the Ritz-Carlton Mauna Lani on the Big Island, and Philippe Padovani, formerly of Manele Bay Hotel on Lanai. Alan Wong is known for creations such as wok-fried tempura ahi with shoyu mustard-butter sauce and tomato-ginger relish, or mahimahi curry with cilantro–macadamia nut pesto and pineapple-mango salsa. Yamaguchi, whom we remember from the fusion movement in Los Angeles, moved to Hawaii in 1988 to open Roy's. He doesn't see himself as a proponent of the regional cooking movement ("One thing I've never done in my life is to be trendy," he explained), although he did belong to an organization of chefs called Hawaii Regional Cooking; rather he said he does basically what he's been doing since his days at La Serene, explaining that he came to Honolulu because it was a "cosmopolitan city where travelers come from all over the world. I felt that the foods I do would be accepted, and I would expand upon it from Hawaii."

Up in the opposite corner of the United States, New England, Jasper White tried to renew interest in New England cooking when he opened Restaurant Jasper in 1983. Its resurrection never really captured the rest of America's imagination, though. Today the most interesting cooking going on in Boston is, of all things, Mediterranean-inspired, led by Lydia Shire at Biba and Jody Adams at Rialto; Gordon Hamersley at Hamersley's Bistro presents delicious homey American-French. Of course plenty of regional dishes hearkened from New England, but it seems few really want to cook them.

In the Southwest, a number of chefs invented a new cuisine out of whole cloth, using French technique on Native American and Mexican ingredients. It's an energetic cuisine, bright, fresh, colorful, flavorful, and fun. In Santa Fe, Mark Miller's Coyote Cafe, which opened in 1987, was one of the early entries. Scottsdale and Phoenix have also become important centers for this cuisine, turned out handily by Vincent Guérithault at Vincent Guérithault on Camelback, Christopher Gross at Christopher's, Roxanne Scocos at RoxSand, and Patrick Toblete at Lon's at the Hermosa Inn at Scottsdale. Southwest cuisine is characterized by lots of grilling and the use of various types of chilies, corn, and cilantro; chipotle mayonnaise is a typical twist on a standard French preparation.

In Texas a number of chefs have done an even more tightly focused spin off of the Southwest, focusing on Texan and Mexican ingredients. Among the practitioners of New Texas Cuisine are Robert Del Grande at Cafe Annie in Houston, Dean Fearing at the Mansion on Turtle Creek, and Stephan Pyles at Star Canyon, both in Dallas. Pyles prides himself on being a fifth-generation Texan; At Star

Canyon he's turning out dishes such as coriander-cured venison with barbecued chipotles and wild mushroom chiliquias and honey spit-roasted duck with dried fruit empanada.

Florida's "New World" cuisine dates back to about 1976, when several chefs in Miami began to feel the influence of what was going on in France. According to Allen Susser, chef-owner of Chef Allen's, a number of Miami chefs came up with the name together. Norman Van Aken was self-taught as a cook, but, he told me, "I got a lot of instruction from reading. . . . I read a lot, not only cookbooks, but books on culture in general." Aken said he realized that south Florida had as much possibility of creating something worthwhile as California or the Southwest did. In about 1987 or 1988 he said he had been reading about the Columbian exchange—how Columbus's voyage changed foodways both by what he brought back to Europe from the New World but also what he brought to the New World from Europe—and he said to himself, "This *is* the new world."

The idea is that the ingredients and ideas come not only from Florida and its Gulf and ocean waters, but also from around the Caribbean, and especially Cuba—the Atlantic rim, as it were. "Grilling is very much an aspect of it," Susser told me. "And roasting and searing." Tropical ingredients such as banana leaves or yucca, he said, may be steamed; a typical dish would be "mango snapper encrusted in yucca with orange mojo." Citrus and cilantro are also used quite a bit.

Susser was inspired by a visit in 1976 to Paul Bocuse's restaurant in Lyon; he cites Bocuse and his attention to ingredients as his greatest influence. Like Hawaii regional cooking, new world cooking relies heavily on the seafood of the region, but many of the fruits and vegetables are those of the nearby Caribbean. The interest these chefs have taken in them have in turn made them more available to the general public. "Five or seven years ago," Susser told me in 1996, "very few of these ingredients were in the supermarket. Today there are three or four aisles of these ingredients." Prior to that one had to go to ethnic markets to find many of them. "Mango ketchup" is the condiment of choice at Chef Allen's; between that and the coconut, much of the food has a sweetness that complements the spiciness of habañero chilies. Contrasting textures are also important. A stone crab claw is served with stone crab cobbler with coconut milk, Scotch bonnets, lime, and coconut biscuits. Perfectly cooked, habañero-spiced pompano sits on an inky-looking, star anise-tinged sauce with coconut and cilantro. Norman Van Aken, Mark Milletelo, and Douglas Rodriguez also belong to New World chefs, who call themselves "the mango gang."

Besides cuisines taking their inspiration from the ingredients and dishes of various regions of the United States, there are also a couple of new cuisines that feel like regional cuisines, but that borrow from our foreign neighbors.

Douglas Rodriguez, whose Coral Gables, Florida, restaurant Yuca (an acronym for Young Urban Cuban-American) opened in 1989, was part of another branch of New World cuisine known as Nuevo Latino. In 1994 he picked up and brought his fanciful, imaginative cooking to New York City, opening up Patría, now Gotham's outpost of Nuevo Latino. Although some of his combinations sound overly wacky, Rodriguez really understands flavors, and his wild dishes actually work.

In another instance of a new regional cuisine moving to another region, Mark Miller brought his Southwestern cooking to Washington, D.C., opening Red Sage.

One of the most self-consciously initiated of the regional cuisines was Hudson River cuisine, which started with the New York City restaurant Hudson River Club in 1987.

Although chef Waldy Malouf is generally acknowledged to have created the movement, Rozanne Gold, a culinary consultant for the Baum & Whiteman Company, the consultants for the restaurant, was behind it. The location for the restaurant had already been chosen—at the new World Financial Center, right on the Hudson in lower Manhattan, and the owners were planning on calling it the Hudson River Club. Baum & Whiteman wondered why anybody would want to use a name that at the time brought up images of PCB-soaked fish. "Since 1977," Gold told me, "I was going up to the Hudson Valley because I have a friend who owns a winery up there. And I got to know all the local cheese people and wine people and said, 'This is going to be the next Napa Valley.' " Since then, the Hudson Valley movement has grown, though curiously, no one seems to know exactly what defines the cuisine save that it makes use of Hudson Valley ingredients.

The natural consequence of this new type of regionalism is that one winds up with chefs not native to a region doing that region's cuisine. If they're building on someone's tradition, it's not their own. Emeril Lagasse, who's making a splash on national television with his Cajun cooking, is from Massachusetts, and despite his Francophonic name, he has no Louisiana background; Norman Van Aken, cofounder of New World cuisine, is from Liberty Hill, Illinois; Robert Del Grande, who forged the way with the new Texas cooking, grew up in California; Jasper White, who made a name with his New England revival, was born in Pennsylvania. Yet there they all are, inventing someone else's cuisine.

And what happens when these regional cuisines leave their regions? When Douglas Rodriguez takes New World cuisine to New York City or David Page takes "food from America's heartland" to New York City? (New York City seems to be gastronomically for the United States as Paris is for France: the city where all regions converge.) Or when chef Jonathan Eismann opens Pacific Time, a Pacific Rim restaurant, in Miami, of all places, never even having worked on the Pacific Rim? At that point, when the cookery is removed from its native surroundings, it becomes evident which ingredients and preparations define that particular cuisine—or whether there's no there there.

And in the meantime, with the new regional cuisines having been "updated" or ditched altogether, how many of the traditional dishes in their regions will we remember? As we march forward into the twenty-first century, will we recall what crab cakes are supposed to taste like or apple pan dowdy or Brunswick stew or burgoo or a Smithfield ham? This, of course, is what has long worried the preservationists. The answer, I think, lies in how effectively these specialties can be integrated into the new cuisine—and it seems easier to incorporate ingredients than to adapt most dishes. Thus Smithfield ham and Minnesota wild rice are likely to be preserved. Larry Forgione, for example, uses Smithfield ham in places where another chef might reach for Proscuitto di Parma. While we're not likely to see a burgoo renaissance, since burgoo is a long-cooked, old-fashioned stew to which it would be difficult to impart a modern feeling, chefs across the country love to interpret soft-shell crabs, which were until recently difficult to find outside of the Chesapeake Bay area, or use Vidalia onions, or make pastries or sauces with California's Meyer lemons.

In the end, the route chosen by Prudhomme and Forgione, and Waters, Bertranou, McCarty, Waxman, David Bouley, Thomas Keller, and so many others—letting ingredients take center stage—became the salient characteristic of American cooking, no matter where the chefs stood on matters regional, national, or international. By focusing on what is the very best, and by incorporating such a wide range of ingredients onto our culinary palette, we've not only saved ourselves, but we've even distinguished ourselves. We're not just cooking French food in America anymore. The products available here in many cases have eclipsed the quality of those available in France. Not all, certainly. We don't have lentils to compete with *lentilles du Puy,* nor *cèpes.* Our cheese can't compare with French cheeses—not only do we not have the experience or tradition, but we're not making unpasteurized cheese, which even if it's potentially dangerous, is a thousand times more delicious. But we're moving forward.

At some point, it becomes impossible to distinguish between regional cookery and one that's been influenced by a foreign cuisine. What's a Michigan morel risotto with wild ramps served in a Chicago restaurant? Certainly it's an Italian preparation adapted to local ingredients—but it feels very American. The driving impulse behind it is American, as is the combination of ingredients. Eventually it becomes silly to talk about the convergence of local ingredients and foreign techniques or foreign ingredients and regional preparations, trying to pin something down; at some point, one needs to admit that American cuisine has already been born. After all, noodles were brought by Marco Polo to Italy from China, and tomatoes were brought to Italy by Columbus from the New World, but at some point *spaghetti alla marinara* became Italian. And even though the grilled Hamburg steak came from Germany, at some point hamburgers stopped being German and became American.

We're presently in the process of absorbing influences, digesting, as it were—trying things out, accepting some, rejecting others. American cuisine is here, and it's in its adolescence. Like teenagers, we may be a little confused, but we're working on defining ourselves. And one day we'll emerge with a fully formed personality.

Yet debate continues today about whether we have an

American cuisine. "I think you cannot call it a cuisine, my dear," is how Barbara Kafka weighed in on the subject when I asked her. "Cuisine is a French word that goes with French cooking, which is usually in this country about restaurants, [and doesn't include home cooking]. When the Italians talk about Italian cuisine I say the same thing to them." Yet Kafka has no objection to the idea of American cooking; she helped create the menu at Kansas City's Heartland Market (which somehow came to be known as the American Restaurant) in the 1970s when Bradley Ogden was chef. It's just the word *cuisine* with which she takes issue.

Joyce Goldstein went even further. "There is no American food," she told me.

"There is *none?*" I asked, somewhat surprised. No American cuisine, okay, but no American *food?*

"No," she said. "There are regional American dishes . . . in the south, and New England and the Southwest. That is a *kind* of American cuisine. Then we have what is known as California cuisine, which is now everywhere, [and] which is license to kill. . . . No matter where you travel, you can see the same menu, you can see the same dishes just appear on menus by people who never even ate them, but they read of them somewhere." Goldstein seems to be saying that there is no single American cuisine, but rather *many* American cuisines.

In his 1996 book *Tasting Food, Tasting Freedom: Excursions into Eating, Culture, and the Past,* anthropologist Sidney W. Mintz argued not only that Americans don't have a cuisine, but further, that we "probably will never have one." He suggested that the success of convenience foods in the United States proves that we don't care enough about how and what we eat to develop our own cuisine.

Although Mintz's argument applies to a huge segment of

the American population, the voice of the gastronomically engaged minority makes itself heard over everything else.

In his 1991 book *Why We Eat What We Eat,* Raymond Sokolov also objected to the idea of an American cuisine. "None of the standard theories for explaining the origins of cuisines in other places fits the food of this country in whole or in part," he wrote. "With the possible exception of Amerindian foods, we in this new-found land have not had time to accrete a coherent body of dishes and food customs that could properly be called a cuisine in the European or Asian sense of the word."

I do agree with Sokolov that what we have here is not coherent. But it's also true that anthropologists often define a cuisine as a group of dishes and customs that would be even more coherent than, say, what one has in France, where people from the south depend on olive oil and people in the north butter; where an Alsatian *choucroute garni* isn't at home in Bordeaux any more than *lamproies à la Bordelaise* are at home in Colmar. Or in Italy, where Arborio rice reigns in the north and no one uses it in the south, just as people veer away from tomato sauces in the north. These anthropologists would say that each of the regional cuisines of France or Italy would be its own cuisine.

A look at recent books indicates an active lively interest in American cuisine: Christopher Idone's 1985 classic *Glorious American Food* has been republished, and not even as a paperback, but as a beautiful hardcover. Sheila Lukins, half of the Silver Palate team, came out with her *U.S.A. Cookbook* in 1997; Anthony Dias Blue with *America's Kitchen* (1995); *An American Bounty; Great Contemporary Cooking from the Culinary Institute of America* appeared in 1995; Frances McCollough and Barbara Witt's *Classic American Food Without Fuss;* Merrill Shindler's *American Dish: 100 Recipes from*

Ten Delicious Decades in 1996; and Jean Anderson's *American Century Cookbook* in 1998, among many others.

Among chefs today, there are many active proponents for the idea of an American cuisine, especially in New York City. Among them: Wayne Nish (March, New York City); Anne Rosenzweig, (Arcadia, The Lobster Club, New York City); Erik Blauberg (The '21' Club, New York City); Waldy Malouf (formerly of The Rainbow Room, New York City); Michael Lomonaco (Windows on the World, New York City). Alice Waters was among those who convinced Bill Clinton to hire an American chef at the White House and use American products when he was first elected in 1992.

Although Larry Forgione certainly uses the term "American cuisine," he told me, "It's just so diverse, it's hard to pin down. I'm not sure anybody can pin it down because, like America itself, it's made up of so many different elements, so many different cultures, so many different influences." He generally refers to what he continues to do at An American Place as "American cooking." Before the American food movement began in the late 1970s and early 1980s, the better restaurants tended to be European, he said. "And I think American cooking was based not on a restaurant style of cooking but on home cooking, and many times there's great American cooking, and it's all based on home." Since his focus is historic, he said, "I look at it as food that came from homes; I look at it as cooking rather than cuisine, which most people think of in restaurant terms."

Given that he owns a number of American restaurants and that he became executive chef at The River Cafe in 1983 after Larry Forgione left, I was rather surprised by Charles Palmer's reaction when I asked him his view in a 1996 interview at his restaurant The Lenox Room. "That's a thing I've always been against, ever since I was at the

River Cafe, this whole thing about American cuisine," he told me. Palmer is also executive chef and proprietor of Aureole, one of the city's top-rated restaurants, and Alva, named for Thomas Alva Edison, and specializing in American food. He's also a partner in a cheese dairy in the Hudson Valley. "I've labeled what I do 'progressive American cooking' because . . . American cuisine is a pretty big statement. Larry Forgione and I used to always have conversations over this. I don't believe there's an American cuisine; there can't be an American cuisine yet. There might be a cuisine fifty years from now. Because it takes that long—how long did it take for French cuisine?"

"A couple hundred years," I interjected. In fact it took about 370 years between the time Catherine de Medici brought artichokes, savoy cabbage, and white beans from Italy to France and the time Escoffier codified everything in 1902. It took just over 200 years from the founding of our country in 1776 to 1982 when the first Symposium on American Cuisine was held.

"Everything happens faster in America," said Palmer, "so I think fifty years from now we'll have an American cuisine." For Palmer, the clock must have started ticking in the twentieth century.

I put the question to another New York chef, Wayne Nish, of March restaurant: Is there such a thing as American cuisine. "Yes, absolutely," came his answer. "I think in the late twentieth century in the United States, particularly in the major cities and specifically in New York, you've got something that has taken a form that has only been loosely touched on before. And I think it's getting more definable." Immigration, he pointed out, has resulted in "an evolution of the dishes, and you have to question reactionaries who insist on freezing time. It's been a hallmark of human achievement to adapt and to change, and the whole notion of fusion as a modern phenomenon is ludicrous. When

Marco Polo first brought those spices back to northern Italy, they weren't sold with recipe booklets. If people liked the smell and liked the flavor, they just started trying different applications. Eventually these things gained a foothold and *became* the cuisine. And it's happening here now. It's happening faster than in any other point in history because of the ease of travel and electronic communications." We've been compressing in the last few decades, he argued, an evolution that might have taken much longer. As for the naysayers, Nish said, "A lot of people just can't see the trees for the forest."

Tim Zagat, publisher of the hugely popular *Zagat Survey* books apparently believes in an American cuisine as well. *Zagat Survey: New York* lists three separate American food categories in the back: American (New)—An American Place and Aureole are listed herein; American (Regional), and American (Traditional). The heading for the entire section: "Types of Cuisine." The implication is that all food served in all restaurants—and Zagat includes hamburgers and pizza—is *cuisine*.

Interestingly, Zagat's Los Angeles guide lists only two categories of American cuisine: New and Traditional.

To the skeptics, I say this: *Cuisine* is simply a French word that means cooking. So the question becomes "Should we use a French word to describe American cooking?"

The answer is—equivocally—yes. Since French technique underlies everything we're doing here—certainly in restaurants, and more and more at home, I do think it's reasonable to use the French word for cooking. By the way, no one quibbles with using the French words *chef, menu, gourmet, haute,* or *sauté,* even though technically we use them incorrectly, or at least their meanings have been perverted.

In fact it's interesting that *chef* has become the American-

English word for the person who heads up the kitchen. In French, *chef* means "chief." I often forget this when I visit France, and start chatting up my French acquaintances about this or that "chef." *Chef?* they invariably ask, quizzically, and I correct myself, saying *chef de cuisine,* or "kitchen chief."

The word *menu* is a French word, and as with the words *chef* and *cuisine,* the American use of the term is slightly different from the French. In France, a *menu* is a two- or three- or four-course fixed price meal.* What we call a "menu"—that big printed list of dishes—is called *une carte.* When one orders from what we call a "menu" in France, one orders *à la carte.*

John Hess and Karen Hess, in their book *A Taste of America,* offered the French gastronome Curnonsky's definition of cuisine: "Cuisine is when food tastes of what it is." If one accepts that definition, then we certainly have chefs today who are cooking "cuisine." Not too long ago I had dinner at New York City's best seafood restaurant (and one of the best restaurants in the country, period), Le Bernadin. As part of a tasting menu, Executive Chef Eric Ripert sent out three small shrimp in some kind of light sauce that I forget. But the sauce was not the point. My husband made a joke when the plates appeared about sending out three shrimp. But we each tasted one and it was as if we had never tasted a real shrimp before. It tasted pure, essential—like what shrimp would taste like in heaven.

Neither Ripert nor owner Maguy Le Coze would tell me the secret of that shrimp. But that, no doubt, is what Curnonsky meant by food "tasting of what it is." A cook needs to have self-confidence to turn out something simple,

*Alexandra Leaf points out that the *prix fixe* menu was invented by Escoffier, when he was chef at London's Savoy Hotel in the 1890s.

and there are a number of chefs cooking today who do, and who can make ingredients sing: David Bouley (for whom Eric Ripert used to work, incidentally, at Bouley) knows how to elevate the best ingredients to astonishing heights—I still remember the exact flavor of a transparent tomato broth I had in his restaurant seven years ago; Jean-Georges Vongerichten (I'll never forget his salmon, roasted at only about 225°F and sprinkled with *fleur de sel*); and Thomas Keller at French Laundry in the Napa Valley, who thrills the palate with small concentrated tastes.

On the other side are the chefs and cooks who cook according to the "more the merrier" philosophy. The more colors on the plate, the better; the more flavors happening, the better; the more countries represented on the menu, the better. This kind of cooking is usually muddled, confused, and disorienting. It's the keep-'em-guessing-and-they'll-be-impressed school of cooking, and enrollment is up—way up. There's nothing memorable about this kind of cooking except for what one must remember: not to eat there again. Fortunately, this kind of cooking doesn't often happen in people's homes. Civilians seem to have a better intuitive understanding of what works than many chefs do, and perhaps suffer from less pressure to be cutting edge.

"Everything gets to the [lowest] common denominator in this country," Joyce Goldstein explained. "There's not a lot of points for real knowledge; it's soundbites. That's the nature of this country. And so when you ask if there's an American cuisine, yes, there is: It's called anarchy and it's everywhere, and it will continue for a while. And some of it will be good and some of it will be bad and most of it will be mediocre. Some of it *will* be good. Those are the [chefs], thank God, that will keep our palates alive."

Larry Forgione's home cooking versus restaurant cooking is an interesting paradigm. Barbara Kafka touched on this distinction as well. Part of the problem in the past century has been that one couldn't get good honest American food in restaurants; it was all pretentious and unimaginative "cuisine." Much of what was good that was being cooked in America was prepared in homes. So one might say that the American food movement of the last twenty years has sought to bring home-quality cooking into so-called "fine dining" restaurants and do away with restaurant food that is overly self-conscious. In the meantime, the revolution that Julia Child started has helped to bring serious French technique into the home, improving what we're making in our own kitchens. Even if it's American, not French, like my mother's beef stew. But Forgione's idea that it's cooking if it comes from a home and cuisine if it's done in a restaurant is a little too facile, I fear, for it implies that if one eats meatloaf in a restaurant, that's cuisine, but if one eats it at home, that's cooking. Hmm. So this paradigm is of limited use.

Of course many people continue to say that there's still no such thing as a true American cuisine, that what Americans eat today is basically an amalgam of other cuisines, foreign cuisines. If that is true, however, then neither is there a true American character. For what's always made the United States unique is that the great majority of us are immigrants, children of immigrants, or grandchildren of immigrants; our national character draws from as many foreign influences as the lands from whence we came. But something happens to us here: A certain optimism emerges, the same optimism perhaps that drew our forbears to immigrate. And we also have a willing openness, a sense of enthusiasm. Most important, we like to put our brand on things, to make them our own. So it is with our food.

Is there an American cuisine? Certainly. It's alive, it's vibrant, it's here—though it's only just starting to come into its own.

8

THE AMERICAN MENU

WHAT'S IN A MENU? IT COMMUNICATES FROM THE chef to the diner what is available to eat. But it also says a lot more. Menus have evolved into documents that reflect information about the proclivities of the chef (including his or her insecurities), the network of farmers the restaurant deals with, the practical realities of the restaurant business, and something about the patrons themselves.

The late great M. F. K. Fisher hated the part of the meal that involved consulting the menu. In *An Alphabet for Gourmets,* she wrote about "the confusion that inevitably follows the first showing of menu cards to more than two people at once." She went on:

> The waiter waits. The diners ponder, stutter, variously flaunting their ignorance or their pretensions to knowledge. They mutter and murmur into the air,

> assuming Godlike clarity of hearing on the part of the poor harried servant and disregarding entirely the fact that they are guests at a table. The men usually blurt some stock familiar order. Women hum, sip their cocktails, and change their minds at least twice after the waiter has scrawled on his pad. There is a general feeling of chaos, and nobody seems to realize that if the same human beings were invited to any normal home they would not dream of giving their orders so confusedly and arbitrarily, nor would the hostess dare leave her guests thus tenderly exposed. No, a good meal inside or outside the private circle should be ordered in advance (or at least ordered with great firmness by the host at table in a restaurant), to avoid this distressing welter of words and the resultant unrelated odors, plates, servings, when a group has gone helter-skelter through a menu.

I love restaurant dining, as much for the anticipation of culinary bedazzlement as the actuality. To me, the best part of any meal is opening the menu. At that point, anything is possible; nothing's been overcooked, underseasoned, or otherwise ruined in the kitchen. But when I pick up a menu these days, something keeps getting in the way: Chefs have been seized, since the mid-1990s, with what seems to be an uncontrollable urge to string together long lists of adjectives and ingredients and print them on menus in the places that used to be reserved for the names of dishes.

Take, for example, an appetizer from the 1995 menu of a New York City restaurant: "Windfall Farms Organic Mesculan Salad with Tomato Concasse and Watercress Oil, Grilled New York State Foie Gras with Caramelized Organic Pears in its Own Natural Juices." Spelling and grammatical errors aside, do we really need to know that much? My palate is tired from just reading the menu.

Partly this is the fault of food writing itself. Chefs mimic restaurant reviewers who string together lists of ingredients then pile on a few adjectives. This, of course, is easier than actually saying something intelligent about the food. By naming dishes the same way, the chef tells the critic what to say, if not what to think.

So what? you're probably thinking. A little florid description decorating a menu never hurt anyone. Perhaps not. Yet somehow, I feel it robs us of the pleasure of savoring food. To me, civilized dining should be fully experiencing each biteful, figuring out the different ingredients, weighing flavors against one another. With names that read like recipes, nothing is left to the imagination. All that's left is to wolf it down. It's virtual reality in dining, which robs one of the true experience, and in the bargain, demeans the work of the chef. It has also to do with the guilt associated with eating anything these days. As a culture that voraciously reads cookbooks in bed and loves to talk endlessly about food, we've become incredibly sophisticated diners, but we've forgotten how to eat.

Paragraph-long descriptions in the places where the names of dishes used to be is simply a symptom of American cuisine's immaturity: We have to have elaborate descriptions because we don't have many standard preparations that chefs like well enough to put on their menus. On the other hand, it's pretty rare to see the standards we do have presented just so. A menu rarely offers "Caesar Salad" anymore; even if it's an authentic rendition, few restaurateurs know when to leave well enough alone or are confident enough to do so. Instead we get Caesar Salad with Baby Romaine Leaves, Aged Parmesan, Extra-Virgin Olive Oil and Meyer Lemon Vinaigrette. I'm waiting for the day when I'll see Lee & Perrin's Worcestershire Sauce listed on a menu description of a Caesar Salad.

Actually, there's historical precedent for this kind of elaborately specific menu description. Although such practices soon fell out of favor, they were once employed by one of America's earliest restaurants, the Old Bank Coffee House in Manhattan, owned by one William Niblo, who treated his customers to some of New York's first truly epicurean dining experiences. According to Michael and Ariane Batterberry in *On the Town in New York,* "His agents combed the American hinterland for recherché game to extend his staggering menus, one of which included 'bald eagle shot on the Grouse Plains of Long Island,' a 'remarkably fine Hawk and Owl, shot in Turtle-Grove, Hoboken,' a raccoon, a six-foot wild swan, and 'Buffalo tongues from Russia' " Scuba-dived scallops—picked by hand by divers rather than mechanically harvested—aren't such a leap from there.

Restaurant dining as we know it, in other words where everyone chooses his or her own meal off a menu, could not have come into existence until after *service à la Russe*—the modern style of service in which food was plated in the kitchen or at a sideboard—was introduced. Before that, *service à la Française*—in which a large number of dishes were placed simultaneously in the center of the table and diners helped themselves—was the rule. With *à la Russe,* fewer dishes were served, but for the first time, they were presented in succession. Since diners couldn't see in advance what they would eat, they needed a printed menu so they could pace themselves.

It's commonly said that *service à la Russe* first came into western dining at a dinner in Paris at which Prince Alexander Borisovich Kurakin, the Czar's ambassador to France, entertained his guests with the style of service from back home. Curiously, culinary historians can't seem to agree on the date the meal took place; Michael and Ariane Batterberry place it in 1810; Margaret Visser, author of *The Rituals of Dinner: the Origins, Evolutions, Eccentricities, and Meaning of Table Manners,* asserts it was 1830; and Stephen

Mennell, Author of *All Manners of Food: Eating and Taste in England and France from the Middle Ages to the Present,* suggests "around mid-century." Alexandra Leaf, chairperson of Culinary Historians of New York, who has a particular interest in French cuisine, thinks the matter is academic; she believes this dinner probably wasn't the first occasion of *service à la Russe* in Paris, it was simply the first documented instance. Leaf says that *service à la Russe* was probably introduced around 1800, but she points out that the two services coexisted until *à la Russe* won out over *à la Française* around 1880.

Service à la Russe came into American hotel dining in the 1830s, with the opening of New York's Astor House hotel.

The American restaurant is a relatively new invention. In fact the restaurant itself was only "invented" in the late eighteenth century in Paris, just before the Revolution. Its existence presupposes the existence of a sizable enough bourgeoisie to support it, and that's something one didn't see anywhere in the world until the late eighteenth century.

Cookshops—places where one could purchase prepared food to be brought home—existed all over Europe prior to that, and certainly there were inns where a traveler could get a meal. But not restaurants per se. In France, regulations of guilds that dated back to the Middle Ages dictated what certain purveyors could and could not offer for sale. *Traiteurs* (caterers), for instance, were the only ones allowed to sell cooked meat, yet they were forbidden to serve it on their premises, and they were required to cook the whole animal, so offering individual servings was impossible. Sellers of stocks and bouillons, known as restoratives, couldn't sell *ragoûts* (stews), but in the 1760s, an upstart named Boulanger broke the rules and sold sheep's feet in white sauce, a *ragoût.* The traiteurs sued him, but Boulanger won and the law was changed, paving the way for the rise of the *restaurant,* literally, a place to take a restorative broth.

The rise of the restaurant in Paris came to pass after the Revolution partly because many chefs who had been working for aristocrats now found themselves out of a job, so they went public, as it were.

Restaurants came into being for the first time in New York in the 1820s; short-order houses appeared at the same time. Of course, there were already hotels or "bed and board" taverns that both served food. Still, that restaurants must have a menu and that all the choices on it should actually be available wouldn't become a convention until the 1890s.

Shortly after Astor House opened, Delmonico's—the Manhattan restaurant that would become an institution lasting more than 150 years—began serving hot food, *à la Russe,* to be sure. (For its first two years of operation, it served only coffee and desserts.) Delmonico's menu offered 346 entrees, which ran simply as a list of items printed in French side-by-side with often inaccurate or weird English translations.

Otherwise, menus for upscale restaurants* were generally in French. In the nineteenth century there were many more divisions of the meal than simply appetizers, main courses, and desserts. An 1838 Delmonico's menu lists *Potages* (Soups), *Hors D'oevres* [sic] (which it translated as "Side Dishes"), *Entrées de Boeuf* (which it translated simply as "Beef"), *Entrées de Veau, Entrées de Mouton* ("Mutton and Lamb"), *Entrées de Volaille* ("Poultry"), *Entrées de Gibier* ("Game"), *Rôts* ("Roasts"), *Entrées de Poisson* ("Fish"), *Entremets* ("Vegetables, Eggs, &c."), *Entremets Sucrés* ("Pastry, Cakes"), *Dessert, Liqueurs, Vins.* A selection of sherries were handwritten in at the bottom.

In a formal dinner, one might start with a cold *hors d'oeuvre,* followed by a soup, then a hot *hors d'oeuvre* (*hors*

*As opposed to short-order houses.

d'oeuvre means "outside of the work," in other words, outside of the main part of the meal), then a fish course, then a *relevé* (a word that translates to mean "highly seasoned," and indicated a dish such as a filet of beef or a vegetable such as braised lettuce intended to "awaken" the palate). Next came the *entrée,* which means "entry" in French, as it was considered the entry into the main part of the meal.* In any case, the *entrée* may have resembled something we would consider an appetizer—*quartier d'artichauts Lyonnaise,* for example, or *petits pois à l'Anglaise.* Or it could have been more substantial, such as *chaudfroid de filets de faisons* or *filet de volaille à l'Impériale.* Depending on the level of formality of the dinner, an entrée froide (cold entrée) might follow. Next came an *intermède,* usually a sorbet, to refresh the palate before the course of game and/or roasts. A cold dish such as an aspic of foie gras with salad might come next, especially if there was no cold *entrée,* or *entremêts,* usually a vegetable dish. *Entremêts sucrés* came next, and then a more elaborate dessert. No one was expected to finish every plate; at the same time, one can eat a lot more in three hours than one can in forty-five minutes.

By the middle of the twentieth century, the menu had been greatly simplified, though it was still usually in French. The French menu, in fact, served as an effective class barrier in America, since it was so intimidating to many that they preferred staying home to subjecting themselves to the humiliation of having to ask the waiter or captain, who was often hostile, for an explanation of every dish. The alternative, simply pointing to something and hoping for the best, clearly wasn't such an appealing idea either.

★ ★ ★

*In France today, in a typical two- or three-course meal, the entrée is still the entry into the meal; it's the first course. Naturally this causes confusion among many an unwitting visiting American diner.

When the Four Seasons and Forum of the Twelve Caesars opened in 1959, as I've already noted, they broke the model of the French language menu that had such a hold on serious American restaurants. They also broke the mold in terms of the menu items they offered. Continental and French restaurants all over the country could be practically depended on to offer Vichyssoise,* Onion Soup Gratinée, Green Turtle Soup with Sherry, Escargots à la Bourguignonne, Frog Legs Provençale, Sole Véronique, Canard à L'Orange, Coq au Vin, Escalope de Veau Cordon Bleu, Châteaubriand Bouquetière, Boeuf Bourguignon, Crêpes Suzette, Cherries Jubilee, Baked Alaska. As a rule, desserts were flambéed: Americans seemed to delight in seeing things set on fire.

Forum's diners, upon being seated, were instead handed a menu full of tongue-in-cheek Roman offerings. Such an entertaining menu was a new idea. Four Seasons' menu was serious, and it changed every three months. This too was new.

Both Forum of the Twelve Caesars and the Four Seasons shared the same owner, Restaurant Associates, whose dynamic Joseph Baum also broke new ground seventeen years later when The Market Bar and Grill opened in the new World Trade Center. This restaurant announced on its menu, under the heading "Market Specials," the names of the purveyors who provided the fish, meats, and produce, a practice that still feels trendy more than twenty years later.

Once the language barrier had been broken and casual restaurants proliferated, the blackboard menu became popular, as did the upscale restaurant with a long list of specials that the server had to recite. This was a low point for

---

*Though Vichyssoise was created by a French chef, Louis Diat, he created it in New York City, at the Ritz-Carlton Hotel, in 1917. Therefore it's technically an American dish.

diners, who were faced with remembering a dozen newfangled dishes with dozens of ingredients. By the time the waiter asked if everyone had decided, one inevitably had to ask three or four questions—what kind of sauce was with the scallops? What were the soups again?

By this time, the multicourse meal had gone the way of the terrapin. Although Continental restaurants, where most "fine dining" was still done, typically served a soup or salad to start, this was generally "included" with the entrée, which was served with a vegetable and potatoes or rice. Other than the stray shrimp cocktail or soup or Caesar Salad to start, Americans weren't accustomed to ordering—or paying for—more than one course, and perhaps a dessert.

When Michael McCarty opened Michael's in Santa Monica in 1978, this was a problem for him. The main courses were too small to be an entire dinner, and of course they didn't "come with" a soup or salad. Besides, some of the most interesting dishes were the starters: pasta with grilled lobster and California caviar, for instance, or wild mushroom salad. His customers didn't understand. "They'd say, wow—your portions are so small," recalled McCarty. "And I'd say, 'no, you don't get it—that's why we have the first course and the second course.' "

McCarty wrote his menu in French, but added in English translations. "Nobody had ever done that," he said. "Every restaurant you went to in town was in French. And if you didn't understand French, you were at the mercy of this waiter."

While a number of L.A.'s French and Continental restaurant menus were in French, McCarty's claim is a slight exaggeration. La Rue, for instance, offered such menu choices as "Chicken Flakes au Curry, Indienne" and "Medallions of Calf's Sweetbread, Perigourdine [sic]." This was easier to navigate than an entirely French menu, but still had pitfalls. One had to know that Périgourdine was a sauce made with truffles, although "Calf's Sweetbread" was less mystifying than "Riz de Veau" might have been. Such French-English jumbles were rather common. Ultimately, if one wanted to order without asking a million questions, one had better know what "Cordon Bleu," "sauce Béarnaise," and "à la Florentine" were—really more a matter of knowing standard preparations than of knowing French.

As California cuisine developed and distinguished itself from French food, and as New American cuisine came into the fore throughout the rest of the country, English language menus soon took over the field. By 1980 or so, menus in French (outside of classic French restaurants) were much less common.

And fairly quickly, diners became accustomed to ordering a starter (appetizer), a main course (entrée), and perhaps a dessert. The three-course dinner became the norm.

At the Second Symposium on American Cuisine in New Orleans in 1983, an audience member asked a panel on "Marketing the American Menu," "How do you feel about the trend toward tastings; that is, several small portions of menu items rather than a single entrée?" Ella Brennan of Commander's Palace jumped right in. "I don't buy that," she said. "When people go out to dine, they should select a nice menu item and let the chef do his thing. They will have a beautiful meal. I think this trying everything in one night is a trend, and I hope it goes away." Jerry Berns, at the time co-owner of New York City's The '21' Club, chimed in with "Send them to a Chinese or Japanese restaurant."

Well, fifteen years later, the trend hasn't gone away; on the contrary, it's revved up, with tasting menus sweeping the country.

In particular, the tasting menu with wines included is a boon to the restaurateur, and not bad for the diner, either. On these menus, the wine director (or other staff person) has selected a wine to accompany each course; the diner is poured one glass of each as the meal progresses. This benefits the restaurant since it assures wine sales—essential to a restaurant's economic health—throughout the meal. It benefits the diner as well, who not only will be likely to receive wines that complement the food reasonably well, but who also will probably taste wines new to his experience, and do so at a usually much lower cost than he might otherwise. Also, unless one is dining with a very large group, one doesn't normally order a different wine with each of six to nine courses.

The restaurant March, in New York City, took an interesting approach beginning in 1997, abandoning the traditional division into appetizers and entrées, offering diners instead four- or seven-course menus created by choosing among equally sized dishes.

By the beginning of 1998, the whole idea of the tasting menu had been taken a bit too far by some chefs. William Grimes wrote recently in the *New York Times:*

> Ordering from a menu used to be routine. No more. It is becoming a journey into the unknown, a junior division of the adventure-travel industry, as chefs working with new cuisines and new ideas reconfigure their menus, creating new categories, offering new combinations of dishes and befuddling the unwary. Unlike the grazing menus of yore, which merely offered scaled-down portions, the New Age menu intentionally disrupts expectations. More than a list of foods, it's a glimpse into the chef's mind, an artistic manifesto, a claim to originality and in some cases, a display of personal expression run amok.

Grimes pointed to Matthew Kenney, chef/owner of Matthew's, a New York City restaurant that now groups its dishes by their predominant ingredients, including one category called "Lemons, figs and pomegranates."

When it opened in 1996, Typhoon Brewery, a Thai restaurant in Manhattan, organized its menu around five flavors—salty, sweet, bitter, sour, and hot & spicy. However, the management abandoned this structure in favor of a traditional menu in 1997, after it realized that its patrons were too confused by the five flavors conceit.

Many diners like tasting menus because it offers them small tastes of many different dishes. No doubt this is one reason tapas have become popular and sushi continues its reign. I've long felt that appetizers tend to be where chefs do their most interesting work; for people who think like me, tasting menus are wonderful because most of the courses will resemble appetizers more than main courses in terms of their level of interest. My husband disagrees with me: He prefers to hunker down with a dish and spend some time enjoying it. He dreads the tasting menu because just as he starts really enjoying a dish, it's gone. (This, of course, falls under the category of problems that are so fancy we don't feel sorry for the person who has them.)

But menus are more than just guides for the progression of a meal. A close look at a contemporary menu is a revealing snapshot of where we are in the evolution of our cuisine at the moment.

I was struck by the 1996 summer tasting menu of Aureole, Charles Palmer's flagship restaurant in New York City. On the menu was Chilled Lobster and Avocado Salad with Lemon Sabayon and Baby Mâche, a quintessentially American concoction for a number of reasons.

The fact that it's "chilled," in itself, signals something American. Since chilling anything somewhat dims the flavors (which is why white wine shouldn't be served too cold unless you want to hide its flaws), most cultures would never think of chilling delectable seafood. In addition, the first two ingredients in chef Palmer's dish are classically American. One assumes the lobster is Maine lobster; with avocado, originally brought to us via Mexico, the combination of these two ingredients is classically American.

Now consider "lemon sabayon." Sabayon, technically, is an Italian dessert—zabaglione—made with whipped egg yolks, sugar, and Marsala; its fluffy consistency is that of a very light custard. That Palmer borrows something Italian is very American; yet he uses the French word for it—*sabayon.* Further, he puts a spin on it: lemon. Yet one assumes (hopes!) it couldn't really be zabaglione at all, since zabaglione is a sweet. (Perhaps somehow *sabayon* sounds less sweet?) So if it's not a *sabayon,* why call it one? Probably *sabayon* is meant to be understood as a preparation, as in "I've prepared this sauce using the same method one would to make a *sabayon.*" This way of using culinary terms has become very common in America, especially, for some reason, with Italian preparations. We have "carpaccio" of tuna, potato "lasagne," duck "proscuitto," and "risotto" of barley—all of which, by definition, couldn't really exist. In any case, one imagines such a sauce as Palmer's *sabayon* would include the traditional egg yolks, a dry white wine of some sort instead of Marsala, omit the sugar, and add lemon zest or lemon juice, salt, and pepper to make it appropriate as a first course. And one imagines it would be prepared, as a zabaglione, by whisking the ingredients together over boiling water to achieve the light, custardy texture.

Now "baby mâche." Mâche is a type of baby lettuce, also known as lamb lettuce, lamb's quarter, or corn salad. To qualify it as "baby" implies that there's something else out there on the market—overgrown mâche—perhaps monster mâche? The use of "baby" here seems to be an almost neurotic compulsion to use an adjective where none is necessary. If it were just "mâche," though, it would sound rather ordinary. And again, Palmer chooses the French name for it, which seems curious for someone who defines his food as "Progressive American." And yet not. For the French underpinnings to our cooking, and French chefs who have made America their home, result in some of the best American food around.

The advent of the computer has made it easier for restaurants to have menus that change daily, a trend that coincides happily with the direction our cooking has been taking.

Given that the old rules about what one ate and didn't eat in a restaurant have gone out the window, American restaurants show surprisingly little range in terms of the choices of types of meats, fish, and poultry they offer. Since we no longer have all the varieties of wild fowl, game, and turtles so bounteous in the eighteenth and nineteenth centuries, our choices are circumscribed quite a bit. Yet one wonders why frogs' legs, squab, rabbits, and snails, for instance, aren't part of our dining repertoire.

Chefs love rabbits; it's the public that doesn't want them. In a 1997 *New York Times* article "Is America Ready for Bunny Ragout?" William Grimes wrote that although ten years ago it was difficult for breeders to sell rabbits to chefs because no one would order them and the chefs wound up taking them home to their families, "The bistro boom and the rise of European-born or European-trained chefs have put rabbit back on the plate. All over town, chefs are pushing rabbit, and some of them are pushing hard."

Americans suffer from a persistent squeamishness that keeps us from enjoying rabbit, frogs, etc., not to mention offal (the South, where chitterlings are a beloved dish, and the Southwest, where menudo, or tripe, is very popular, notwithstanding).

So despite the increasingly anything-goes nature of

American cuisine, in some respects menus still look surprisingly similar. They always feature a few chicken dishes, a few fish (almost always including farmed salmon), usually a shrimp dish, and a few obligatory beef, pork, and lamb dishes. Duck is optional; venison and squid occasional. Squab is rare. One sees quail sometimes, especially in California, where our hatted friend is the state bird. One sees sweetbreads occasionally, but I wonder if it really sells? Foie gras seems to be the exception to the no-innards rule, perhaps because chefs so love dealing with it. I've rarely, if ever, seen boar on a menu in the United States.

Compared with the way American restaurant menus looked in the nineteenth century, we tend to have very few choices. A menu of Astor House from Thursday, October 11, 1849, offered the following roast game: black ducks, lake ducks, teal, widgeons, grouse, mallard ducks, plover, rail birds, meadow hens, short neck snipe, broad bills, wood ducks, gray ducks, dow-witches, and venison; if none of those struck one's fancy one could opt for broiled game—English snipe, cedar birds, robin snipe, or surf snipe. Boiled beef tongue, frog fried in butter, calf's head with brain sauce, "small birds" with Madeira sauce, and broiled pig's feet rounded out the menu. Today, however, although we may select from fewer protein sources, we may choose from a multitude of preparations made with a plethora of ingredients.

When Chez Panisse opened in 1971, Alice Waters offered one set menu, no options. The narrowing of choices becomes necessary when ingredients are fresher, assuming that waste is unacceptable. Long lists of dishes on the menu used to show a kitchen's versatility; now such excess seems foolish. But smaller menus mean fewer choices on each, and the result has been a narrowing of the repertoire, at least where meat, fish, poultry, and game are concerned.

★ ★ ★

William Grimes wrote recently that he found it odd that "cultural critics have been slow to take restaurant menus within their purview" even though a few chefs are "deconstructing the classic menu." He went on: "By dismantling old categories and creating new ones, they are, to use a fancy Marxist term, 'problematizing' the traditional categories, holding them up to criticism and questioning, revealing the arbitrary, socially constructed arrangement that most diners accept as natural."

Well, yes, okay. What chefs are doing does have the effect of such problematizing. I doubt that's the intention behind it, however. Of course, menus as we know them are arbitrary and socially constructed. But dining is a ritual, and all rituals are in a sense arbitrary and socially constructed; the very ritualistic aspect of dining is part of what makes it so valuable.

I think rather than intending to problematize anything, the chefs who are breaking the mold of the menu are doing so for a number of other reasons. One is that a differently organized menu gives them a chance to stretch, and they like the challenge. The fringe benefit—or sometimes even the main goal—is that breaking the mold attracts publicity.

In the meantime, what does the proliferation of tasting menus say about us—the diners? It represents the direction we've gone as a culture—we have short attention spans and like things in sound bites. Tasting menus give us lots of variation, lots of color, lots of different flavors. Rather than dishes, these are food bites.

In the 1990s, the American menu became a marketing tool for restaurants. Land on your favorite restaurant's mailing list, and you're sure to receive announcements for special menus—the New Year's Eve Menu, Valentine's Day Menu, Fourth of July Menu, Bastille Day Menu if it's a French restaurant, and so forth, all the way through to the special Christmas Menu. Then there's the white truffle menu, the summer tomato festival menu, the foie gras menu, the garlic menu, the Zinfandel menu. Often a publicist lurks behind the idea of the special menu—they'll seize on any excuse to send a mailing not only to regular customers, but also to local food writers, to try to stir up some interest. Chefs are only too willing to go along.

Special menus aren't the only marketing tool that chefs have popularized. There's also the chef's cookbook. Just about every important chef has one—from Jean-Georges Vongerichten (author of two books) to Charlie Trotter to Emeril Lagasse (author of four), to Stephan Pyles to Michel Richard to Wolfgang Puck. Thomas Keller doesn't have one; nor does David Bouley. (David Bouley tried to get one going some years ago, but the word around New York was that the publisher had difficulty finding a writer to work with the chef.) Occasionally chefs forego the eponymous cookbooks, instead featuring the names of their restaurants in the titles. Out of Chez Panisse has come the *Chez Panisse Menu Cookbook* by Alice Waters, *Chez Panisse Desserts* by Lindsey R. Shere, *Chez Panisse Pasta, Pizza and Calzone* by Alice Waters, *Chez Panisse Cooking* by Paul Bertolli with Alice Waters, *Chez Panisse Vegetables* by Alice Waters, and *Fanny at Chez Panisse* by Alice Waters.

Although there are certainly exceptions, chef cookbooks are notoriously difficult to cook from, since they usually assume that one has elaborately made or hard-to-find ingredients at one's fingertips. For example, to cook à la Wolfgang Puck, you'll need rich veal stock, demi-glace, or fish bones; baby leeks, whole young pigeons, and duck prosciutto; dishes created by David Burke call for tomato fondue, apple crackling, and duck-liver mousse; Larry Forgione's recipes use cuitlacoche (corn fungus) and boneless quail.

But chef books sell. Why? Because as we know, many people don't actually cook from cookbooks anyway; instead they read them like novels. The professional cookbook lets amateurs dream about elaborate constructions they'll never have time to make, featuring ingredients they may not be able to find. These books allow readers to cook vicariously, to revel in fantasy meals.

The wine list has undergone its own evolution in the last twenty-five years. Until very recently, vintages often weren't even listed on menus. This is still true in some parts of the country. But just as wine shops have begun to organize wines by variety rather than region, so have wine lists.

It used to be that wine lists in the best restaurants went on for pages and pages and pages. A good wine list was like a book. It still is in many restaurants, and these catalogs are fun to read. Older restaurants, particularly, have often had decades to build up a cellar. Newer restaurants usually don't have the luxury of buying a fully developed cellar—it's incredibly expensive, and with a restaurant failure rate of up to 50 percent in the first year in many cities, hardly sensible.

Restaurants are experimenting with wine list formats because what existed before doesn't work well. Before the appearance of American wines in American restaurants, the traditional wine list offered only French wines and was usually divided into "Red Wines" and "White Wines," and then organized by regions (Bordeaux, Burgundy, Alsace, etc.) within those divisions.

The emergence of American wines, which are varietally named rather than regionally named (Chardonnay, Pinot Noir, Cabernet Sauvignon, etc.), presented the author of the wine list with a problem. Four (or more) divisions were now necessary: Red (California), Red (France), White (California), White (France), and then organized by regions within the French categories and varietals within the California categories.

In the last ten years, wines from other states (especially Washington state, Oregon, and New York state) have begun appearing on wine lists across the country, and wines from Italy, Spain, Germany, Austria, Switzerland, Australia, New Zealand, Chile, and Argentina have also become commonplace. How to organize such a tangled web? New World and Old World is one option, then varietally or regionally within each of those. But proprietary labelings—such as Italian Super-Tuscans or a California wine such as Marietta Cellars Old Vine Red—complicate the issue, because they don't fit into normal categories.

Another problem wine stewards and waitstaff have always faced is how to help customers find a wine that will match their food order.

Creative wine directors have hit upon an interesting solution by reconfiguring their lists according to flavors rather than regions. Again, I think this is not a matter of "problematizing" on their part; I think such lists have solved a problem rather than purposefully revealing an arbitrary social construct.

Who gets the wine list? I'm amazed at how often it's still given to a man at the table, even if it was the woman who requested it. Menus used to be handed out to the ladies without prices on them. I'm too young to have seen this in the United States, but I have seen it in France quite recently. Some restaurants in France hand out menus without prices to men and women, and only give the one with the prices to the host.

It's a nice idea.

9

DINING AND THE AMERICAN PALATE

AMERICANS LOVE BIG FLAVORS. AS A GROUP, WE TEND not to have, shall we say, refined palates. We adore assertive notes, obvious tastes, and what teenagers refer to as "loud" flavors—spice. The hot tang of salsa. Garlicky, cheesy Caesar salad. Smoky-flavored grilled chicken. Shrimp with coconut, cilantro, lime. Charred, black pepper–crusted salmon. Chipotle mayonnaise. Sweet, fruity sauces with meat and poultry. We love roasted vegetables—corn or zucchini or red peppers—because roasting concentrates the flavor. We relish sun-dried tomatoes, dried porcinis, dried cherries, and dried cranberries for their intensity.

Our cuisine tends toward the vibrant rather than the subtle. It's a cookery that makes one sit up and take notice, not one likely to induce contemplative reverie.

We're also keen on texture. In an interview for the 1985 book *Cooking with the New American Chefs,* Patrick O'Connell, chef/co-owner of The Inn at Little Washington, told author Ellen Brown, "Americans are way ahead of the French in our appreciation of textures. Colors and textures have become an important part of my cooking."

We particularly like crunchy; I've even talked to more than one American chef who thinks "crunchy" is a flavor. More than anything, we like *contrast* in texture. We love seared fish for its crisp, rough, hot exterior and its cool, tender inside. We crave the gentle crackle of a spring roll wrapper, the chewy tug of foccacia. We adore foods encrusted, charred, grilled, pan-fried; smoothly puréed or chunkily mashed. Even our wines are big on "mouth-feel."

Our affinity for texture goes a long way in explaining what draws us to Thai food, Japanese food, Mexican food—even Italian food. In each of these cuisines, texture is very important. I can think of no better example than the simplest of Italian foods: spaghetti. To correctly cook spaghetti *al dente,* one boils it until the moment when a bitten strand reveals just a dot of white in the center—ensuring exactly the right resistance against the teeth.

The French, in the meantime, are notorious overcookers of both pasta and rice. In fact, lots of French food is sort of soggy, though of course *nouvelle cuisine* did away with much of the sogginess.

But in the United States, read just about any restaurant review—or even a wine review— and expect the reviewer to swoon over the "velvety" this or "silky" that.

One obvious exception to our appreciation of texture is our devotion to mushy sliced bread—which, hallelujah, we're finally getting over. Since about 1990 especially, many of us have fallen head over heels in love with the crusty, chewy, wonderful breads that are increasingly available.

Our affinity for texture, however, may be to the detriment of our careful attention to taste. We don't tend to smell our food—to notice what herbs or spices have been used—or even attend to what some of the major ingredients in a dish are. Partly it's because, as a culture, we're not in the habit of paying attention to our palates, though I think we're on our way. I do think that we, the current generation of food lovers, will teach our children to savor food more than we, ourselves, were taught to do. Still, as far as we've come since the 1950s, our lack of attention to our palates explains why most Americans still have a long way to go toward a real understanding and appreciation of food.

Historically, we've been suspicious of the palate. We're not even sure what it is. Is it an actual part of the body, as in the soft palate? Or is it an abstraction, just something that lets us understand flavor? Does it involve the nose or the tastebuds? One equates a good palate with a keen sense of smell, but what then of the "supertaster" who has more tastebuds per square inch of tongue surface than the average mortal? Whatever the answer to these questions, we shy away from talking about it at table the way we shy away from talking about sex. We're as likely to talk about our palate as we are about our penis.

It's no wonder, considering the role the palate played in America's culinary heritage in the past century. In fact, a hundred years ago, the palate was not merely ignored; it was actually vilified. At the end of the nineteenth century, Mary Abel, a food reformer, wrote cautionary tales about "King Palate," warning that allegiance to him would leave one open to the ravages of such "impish creatures" as "Indigestion, Dyspepsia, Gout, Liver Disease, Delirium Tremens, and a hundred others, big and little."

For the first part of the twentieth century, such attitudes fed into our view of food as fuel and only fuel. There was something shameful about thoroughly enjoying what we ate—said the Puritan in us—so flavor was glossed over in favor of nutrients. Consequently, if we committed the sin of enjoying it, we'd be punished—if not by God, by indigestion or some other disease.

Although much of America has taken huge leaps toward rediscovering our palates, as a culture, we have quite a lot of work ahead of us if we're to undo the ravages of the Domestic Science movement and the damage inflicted by the industrialization of our foods. By 1951 our palates were in such a sad state that Gerber Products started putting MSG in baby food to make it "taste better to mothers." Today, David Bouley—one of the top American chefs—sips orange juice as he cooks to "keep his palate sharp." But that's not something that would occur to many Americans, even devoted gastronomes, restaurant reviewers, or chefs.

Historically, foreign observers have criticized American food on, among other things, two primary culinary crimes: our overuse of sugar and our grotesquely large portions. In 1959 Craig Claiborne may have raved about the new Four Seasons restaurant in his *New York Times* review; still, he did fault it for two things: portions that were too large and overly sweet dishes. As long ago as 1880, the United States was second only to Britain in per capita sugar consumption, and many culinary historians have posited that our love for sugar comes from our British culinary heritage. Today our sweet tooth is stronger than ever, and we like our sweets more sugary than most cultures. The chocolates that Godiva produces for the American market, for example, are sweeter than those for the European market.

"It might be argued," wrote Waverly Root and Richard de Rochemont in their classic *Eating in America,* "that the sweetness maple syrup imparted to the dishes that the Pilgrims cooked under the inspiration of the Indians helped to make sweetness a dominant feature of American cooking." Sure, but the prevalence of winter squashes probably played a major role as well. Ever taste a baked sweet dumpling or acorn squash, unadorned by any maple syrup or sugar? Many of the New World's winter squashes are naturally very sweet, and no doubt were a significant part of the Pilgrims' diet, encouraging a penchant for sweetness in main course foods.

An element of sweetness in savory foods can be very appealing, when achieved organically—that is, as part of the cooking process. When caramelizing onions, for instance, one sweats them very slowly on top of the stove in a little olive oil. After hours of cooking, their natural sugars break down and become rich and sweet. Recently, I saw a recipe in a cooking magazine for caramelized shallots that called for sprinkling the shallots with sugar when the cooking was almost finished. It allowed the cooking time to be much curtailed, and obviously was a shortcut. But it's a bad choice, and does not produce the same results as those achieved the correct way.

A well-executed sweet-and-sour-type sauce, such as the *sauce gastrique* currently in vogue in France—made with reduced vinegar and a touch of sugar—can also be appetizing.

Yet Europeans are quite sensitive to our frequent use of sugar in the main part of the meal; they find it exceedingly odd. A number of years ago I attempted my first *choucroute garnie*—the traditional Alsatian dish made with long-cooked sauerkraut garnished with smoked meats and sausages. I used a recipe that called for one teaspoon of sugar, along with a few apple slices (I used tart Granny Smith apples, not wanting too much sweetness)—in an enormous pot of sauerkraut. I thought it turned out admirably well. So did one of our guests, an American citizen with an American father and German mother who was raised in Germany. His wife, however (and one of my closest friends), who's Vietnamese and grew up in France, and my husband, who is French, found one fault with it: too much sugar. Neither *knew* I had added any, and there I was, busted—for one measly teaspoon. That's the difference between the American palate and the French.

Michael Tong, owner of New York's Shun Lee Palace and Shun Lee West, pointed to the particular demands of the American palate in explaining why Chinese haute cuisine never flourished in America. "When Americans eat Chinese food . . ." he said, "they want crispness. They want sweetness. They want spicy."

We're also fond of sweet elements to accompany our savory main courses. Apple sauce with pork chops. (Show this to a Frenchman if you want to see a sick Frenchman.) Sweet relishes and chutneys—or ketchup—with any meats. Mint jelly (!) with lamb chops.

"God, the American palate is so immune to flavor that it is sinful to think of putting a good product on the market," James Beard once wrote in a letter to Helen Evans Brown. "The main flavors people want are sweetish tomato and imitation garlic. And sweet mayonnaise and sweet French dressing. Ugh."

"Immune to flavor" is, I think, a succinct description. We're so bombarded all the time by different tastes—largely because of so many wonderful foreign and regional influences—that the embarrassment of riches overwhelms our palates. Consequently, it's difficult for many of us to pay attention to nuances of flavor. If something is to make an impression in the midst of the continual symphony (in the best cases) or cacophony (in the worst cases) of flavors, it either has to be so brilliantly executed that we sit up and take notice, or else it has to hit us over the head.

It's no surprise that ketchup was the number-one-selling condiment here for most of the last hundred years. Europeans, of course, find our use of ketchup hilarious. And though he's been here twelve years, my husband still winces when he sees people drinking soft drinks with their meals.

Even good American chefs use a lot of sweet. On Larry Forgione's winter 1998 dinner menu, I counted sweet elements in a third of his first courses and half of his main courses. When I mentioned this to him, he seemed baffled at the observation. He wondered what I meant by "sweet elements." I pointed to gooseberry chutney with the Hudson Valley Camembert crisp, caramelized-gingered sweet potatoes, plum glaze and port wine jus with the foie gras, roasted beets and apples with the house-smoked pheasant salad, and so on. When I asked him to comment, he said, "I do think that in fall menus or winter menus . . . that sweet is certainly an important element of balancing flavors."

Actually, very few dishes need sweetness for balance.

Why?—you're no doubt wondering—is sweetness bad in savory food? In a way using sugar in savory dishes is akin to serving things too cold—it masks other flavors. It's also easy to use sweetness as a crutch. When I make a puréed soup out of pumpkin or other winter squash and it happens to lack flavor, I sometimes, in my desperation to make it taste like something—since it doesn't taste of itself—add something sweet—maple syrup or a teaspoon of brown sugar. I always think I'm getting away with something, but my husband inevitably rains on my parade. It's notable that few of the world's great cuisines—with the possible exception of that of Thailand—use sugar with any kind of frequency in main courses. And the Thais use sugar very carefully, balancing it against the heat of spice.

Oddly, for people who are fond of bold flavors, we not only tolerate but even seem to prefer tasteless produce. We don't routinely pay terrific attention to the taste of our produce because we've come to expect that it will have little flavor. I had some radishes for dinner recently that were very large, fresh, brilliant pink-red, very crisp, and almost tasteless—especially because they came chilled out of my fridge.

No doubt they would have been tastier if they were smaller, thinner, uglier. But in typically American fashion, I had bought them because of visual clues about their texture: and they were wonderfully crisp. One can find dozens of examples of this phenomenon in any supermarket or greengrocer. Iceberg lettuce—the biggest, crispest, most tasteless variety—is a classic example. Even those of us who love other lettuces—or string beans or zucchini or green peppers—don't often have to suffer wilted specimens. Producers have done a good job of delivering vegetables in good shape. The same is true for apples. Before the recent reemergence of wonderful heirloom varieties brought flavorful apples back to the marketplace, the salient characteristic of our apples was their lovely snap. Fortunately crisp and crunchy as textures are easy to obtain in produce—it needs only be picked early enough and shipped under refrigeration, perhaps ripened later with ethylene gas.

But for those who prefer their fruits soft and juicy, the picture isn't so rosy. Tomatoes, peaches, plums, and strawberries picked unripe can never recover their promise of flavor. And it's not as easy as blaming the giant agribusiness conglomerates that grow it or the retailing giants that proffer it: If we refused to buy it, they'd have to come up with something better to offer. And why don't we demand something different? Either because we're unwilling to forego texture for flavor or because as a culture, we've forgotten the joys of ripe fruit.

When the market does demand that new products be developed, they're usually for ease in shipping and storage. Otherwise the prime flavor characteristic the genetic engineers seek when developing a new fruit or even vegetable? Sweetness. Witness white corn and sweet corn—hybridized for prolonging the sweet flavor of freshly picked corn. Corn on the cob has classically been an American favorite because of its sweetness, but only when picked and immediately steamed. It's always said to lose its sweetness (the sugars turn to starch) if kept off the stalk any longer than that, so only those who lived on or near farms had access to this dulcet American delight. Now—hooray! Everyone can have sweet corn.

Since the 1980s, everyone can have sweet peas, too. Peas were always a huge problem for non–farm dwellers—again, after the peas were picked the sugar would turn to starch in a matter of hours. How many sad little labor-intensive wooden peas clinked around America's saucepans for how many decades? In 1979, Dr. Calvin Lamborn of the Gallatin Seed Company solved the problem that had captured his attention for the past twenty-five years by introducing the Sugar Snap pea. The produce industry awarded him the prize for the "Most Outstanding Vegetable in Fifty Years."

We do, on the other hand, look for flavor in our wines. And plenty of it. The top-selling American wines have lots of alcohol, plenty of oak, and "gobs of fruit," to use a cliché wine review expression.

Many American "dry" white wines are actually sweet. This popular style is the result of a mistake—one that paid off, big-time, for the winery that made it. In 1981 winemaker Jess Jackson, owner of Kendall-Jackson Winery, made a error in fermenting his Vintner's Reserve Chardonnay—normally a bone-dry wine—resulting in a wine that was slightly sweet. He put it on the market anyway, and Americans went crazy—they loved it. His Chardonnay become the model for hundreds of others.

Curiously, most Americans think they like dry wine. They eye the selections on a wine list with suspicion, and when the server suggests one, they say slyly, "Well, I don't *know* . . . is it dry?" What they think of as dry, however, is actually rather sweet.

And I'm not just talking about the white Zinfandel crowd. White Zinfandel, that overtly sweet, slightly fizzy blush wine, is the result of another mistake, this one made by Bob Trinchero at Sutter Home in 1975. During the fermentation process of a white wine he was making from Zinfandel grapes, Trinchero suffered a "stuck" fermentation: The sugars in the wine would not convert all the way into alcohol. Trinchero bottled it anyway, even though it had about 2 percent residual sugar, enough to make it distinctly sweet. Mistake, perhaps, but Americans loved it to the tune of 2 million cases a year; by 1987 it would become America's best-selling wine.

All this is not to say that American winemakers don't know how to make good wine. Many do. And many *are* making good wines. American winemaking has improved tremendously over the last ten years.

But aside from a very few, our wines are overly alcoholic—with percentages of 14 percent common. And keep in mind that the Bureau of Alcohol, Tobacco and Firearms, the federal agency that oversees wine labeling and marketing, allows wineries a 1.5 percent margin of error—meaning that the wine you see labeled as 14.5 percent may easily be as alcoholic as 16 percent. Even sherry, a fortified wine, has less (15.5 percent). I even tasted a zinfandel recently with an alcohol content *marked* as 16 percent.

America's favorite premium wines—Chardonnay, Merlot, and Cabernet—are also frequently overoaked. Many winemakers and consumers assume that because a little oak is good in a wine, a lot of oak must be better. Winemakers boast about their oak barrels on the label. But some of the best Chardonnays in the world—those from the Chablis region of France—are not oaked at all, and white Burgundies, generally regarded as the very best wines made from the Chardonnay grape, are much more judiciously oaked than ours are. Still, many Americans assume that Chardonnay is synonymous with oak.

American winemakers also tend to overoak one of our potentially best food wines—Sauvignon Blanc. Sauvignon Blanc has a brightness, a high enough acid content to make it ideal for complementing a wide variety of foods—especially salads, grilled foods, chicken, fish, light pastas—in other words, some of the most popular American foods. Instead of letting the lovely aromas and flavors of this grape variety make their own statement, the winemakers mask them—with lots of oak. The problem is, oak is such a heavy flavor that it doesn't go well with food. But the American public—and restaurant owners and the authors of wine lists are particularly at fault here too—doesn't seem to notice.

All this is not to say that American wines are bad; they're simply the wines of a country with a relatively short history of winemaking. In fact, a number of them are wonderful. Although winemaking goes back to the beginnings of this country, our wine industry fell apart during Prohibition, and very few wineries even survived. A large majority of the others we have were founded post-1970 and haven't had long to evolve. However, with an American public that keeps coming back for more sweet, overoaked, overalcoholic wines, there hasn't been much incentive for wineries to change their styles. Fortunately, the American wine industry slowly seems to be getting the message that we don't need wines to hit us like sledgehammers. While even the more sophisticated among us used to think a "monster" Cabernet was a good Cabernet, as the country's gastronomes have matured, we've *begun* to appreciate less exaggerated wines, and the wineries have started to respond, especially those in emerging regions such as Washington state, Oregon, Long Island, and Virginia.

In the past our inattention to our palates has contributed

mightily to the problem with wine in this country. If one is not in the habit of stopping and smelling and *really* tasting, even if one likes or dislikes something, it's virtually impossible to develop any taste memory or smell memory of it. And taste or smell memory—even if it's an artificial memory reinforced via note taking—is essential to a development of one's appreciation of wine.

The one aforementioned area, however, in which the American public has influenced winemaking in a positive way, is texture. Americans are sensitive to tannins—the substance that gives black tea its astringent quality, and which is abundant in certain red wines such as Cabernet. Tannin is perceived as texture, technically; it's certainly not a flavor. As the California wine industry began to emerge in the 1970s, the "monster" Cabernets it was producing were full of rough tannins that didn't seem to smooth out with aging. (Tannin is one of the components that preserves a wine so it can age.) Over the course of the next twenty years, it became clear that Americans preferred wines with softer tannins. Since we quickly consume a large majority of the wine we buy rather than aging it, the industry was able to respond, and as a result, the tannins in American red wines have become soft and approachable, improving the texture of wines intended for drinking young.

We haven't done so well in the area of gigantic portion sizes of food. Watch the face of anyone visiting here for the first time from another country when the plates arrive. And as a culture we're obese—what a surprise! After all the calculations about fats and carbohydrates and percentage of the total calories derived from fat and so forth, does it occur to anyone that maybe we just eat too much? This is worse in the belly of the country; it's a bit better in big, allegedly sophisticated cities (New Orleans, the national capital of obesity, notwithstanding). But order a steak in a steakhouse sometime. It could feed a family of six in much of the world. In fact, when Julia Child, Simone Beck, and Louisette Bertholle turned in their manuscript of *Mastering the Art of French Cooking* to Knopf, they were told that the portion sizes were too small for American audiences, and Julia had to go back and make them all larger.

For decades, the greatest sin an American restaurant could commit—much greater than mediocre or bad food—was that the portions wouldn't be ample. Woody Allen told a joke in *Annie Hall* about two old ladies at a Poconos resort complaining that the food was terrible—and the portions so small. The classic quibble about French restaurants was that the portions were tiny. Once *nouvelle cuisine* crossed the Atlantic (in the instances it wasn't disguised as California cuisine), people were even more aghast at all that white space on those oversized plates, and so little food!

Well, "Everything is big in America," is the way my husband puts it. We're the Texas of the Western Hemisphere.

The reason? This country was founded on the idea of abundance, and immigrants have long come here from places where there was never enough meat. That's one of the reasons—in addition to the abundance of grazing land—why the beef industry flourishes here.

Since most of us don't take the time to really taste things, we need to eat more in order to feel satisfied. Obesity is largely a result of mindless eating and a failure to derive pleasure from food.

A big part of the problem is that although we eat, most of us are not accustomed to dining. If at home we eat largely for sustenance, we generally go out to dinner as a social act. Dining out *is* a social event, or a form of entertainment. But dining has the potential to be much more than that, and in many societies around the world, it serves a much broader function than it does here.

The purpose of dining is to socialize, certainly; to relax; to engage in conversation (something else that as a culture we're not that good at); to appreciate food. And to eat. In Latin countries, for example, people gather for dinner or lunch in bistros and cafés, and it is the occasion for them to exchange ideas and debate social issues, politics, religion, philosophy, sexuality, and, as one Frenchman I interviewed said, "anything that is particularly relevant in their lives. And it must be accompanied by food and a glass of wine. In a society like America, those kinds of things are forbidden to talk about, politics especially." He went on to explain that food and debate enjoy a symbiotic relationship in French culture:

> Social ideas are understood by the American mind as something too personal and controversial: You don't talk about them. And since you don't talk about them, you can't really enjoy the dinner. That's the reason it's boring to dine in America—there's nothing going on. In France they're totally inseparable, dining and talking. Why does lunch on Sunday at my parents' house go on for three hours (or even more if people are over)? Because people are talking. You need to find topics that are controversial to make the food last that long. At the same time, in order to make the topics last, you have to have good food to go with them.

Everyone knows that politics and religion are taboo topics at the American dinner table; ironically, from the French perspective, respecting the taboo may actually inhibit civilized dining.

"In Hispanic countries," wrote Margaret Visser, "the practice of conversation after dinner—the descendant of Greek and Roman symposia but without the copious drinking—is called *hacer la sobremesa,* 'doing the tablecloth,' or 'doing dessert.' " She continued:

> Coffee is brought to the table (the sweet course itself usually counts as part of the dinner, and is removed for this ritual) and the guests linger, talking, sometimes for hours together. The Danes are similarly famous for conversation round the table. The table is felt actually to aid the conversation: moving away to the "withdrawing room" would mean a break in the togetherness achieved during dinner, and a moving apart from one another. The comfort of padded armchairs is not enough to tempt the group away. The table is something to lean on, to gesture over; it expresses what everyone has in common.

Perhaps our American custom looks more like the one favored by Chinese diners, who converse more before the actual eating begins, rather than chewing through a discussion or waiting until afterward, when according to Margaret Visser, "everyone is too replete to start discussing business or the meaning of life."

These days, we as a culture seem to sense that dining is important, yet often it's all we can do to drag ourselves into the task. Oh, yes, many of us sigh, it would be great if we could all sit down together, and eat something real, and relax and have a real conversation. Instead we have take-out, a sandwich on the run, a slice of pizza, a soda, and call that a meal. Even for those for whom food is presumably important, time is of the essence. As I write, the trend in New York City at the best restaurants is the in-and-out business lunch. La Caravelle, that old bastion of fabulous French delights and sumptuous dining, has just introduced something owners Rita and André Jamet are calling "Lunch 1-2-3." Only have time for one course? Twenty-five bucks. Got a few more minutes? Two courses $30. And if by some miracle, you can stick around for dessert, they'll toss that in for another six dollars. Le Bernadin—one of New York's most elegant restaurants, one which I wouldn't want to step into unless I had at least three hours to spend luxuriating—promises to get business diners in and out in less than a half hour.

Tomorrow, we always say, we'll have more time.

In fact, American diners have always been in a hurry. In the late eighteenth century, the most elegant dining in America was to be found in hotel dining rooms. There, tremendous amounts of food were served, everything at once, and the hotel guests wolfed it all down as quickly as possible. Our habits were remarked upon by visiting foreigners who were bewildered by the prodigious amounts of food and annoyed by the early dining hour and dizzying speed with which people ate, not to mention the lack of conversation. Robert Burford, an Englishman visiting the United States in 1834, remarked with astonishment,

> The meals are taken in the public room where fifty to a hundred persons sit down at the same time . . . a vast number of dishes cover the table, and the dispatch with which they are cleared is almost incredible; from five to ten minutes for breakfast, fifteen to twenty for dinner, and ten minutes for supper are fully sufficient; each person as soon as satisfied leaves the table without regard to his neighbors; no social conversation follows.

Despite the lack of civilized behavior in such places, this kind of "fine dining" was reserved for the upper classes. Although restaurant service changed when restaurants began using menus and *service à la Russe* in the nineteenth century, Americans were in no less of a hurry.

During Prohibition, many restaurants closed, and fine dining went into hiding along with alcohol. There were a few select speakeasies that had great food—New York's The '21' Club, for instance. After World War II, and the return of prosperity, Americans were in the mood to celebrate, and restaurant dining reappeared.

Still, fine dining remained a class divider into the fifties and sixties. In the best restaurants, menus were in French, which intimidated the uninitiated. Although this type of bullying has disappeared from cities that by now have banished such type of restaurants, in the heartland, they still exist. Fans of Garrison Keillor's public radio show *A Prairie Home Companion* are treated to hilarious satirical treatment of these eateries in the recurring skit "Cafe Boeuf," in which the captain, Maurice, revels in abusing the Garrison Keillor character, Carson Wyler. Wyler, for instance, calls to make a reservation. "Yes, I remember you," says Maurice. "With the red socks. You were here last week. You asked for pot roast."

"And it was very good," says Wyler.

"It is not called pot roast, monsieur. It is pot-au-feu. Also known as [gibberish] or in Provence it is known as [gibberish]. But we do not call it pot roast." (French muttering.)

"I'm sorry."

"Can you say 'pot-au-feu'?"

"Pot-au-feu."

"Non non non non. Not 'pot o' few'—it is pot-au-feu. Or it is [gibberish], or in Provence, it is [gibberish]."

In America, we're now learning how to dine. We approach dining either with utter dismissal or with awe and reverence—and there's very little in between. We're almost like a young girl who has gone to charm school but missed a few key lessons.

For some reason, we can't help but refer to our best restaurants—or at any rate our restaurants with the best reputations—as "temples of gastronomy," "gastronomic meccas," and the like. There a sense of religiosity associated with the hautiest dining. It's shrouded in mystery to us, and we revere it. Yet we don't try to understand it—or even really experience it—we feel it's beyond us. And toward the end of our meal, the chef appears in the dining room, dressed in whites, betoqued; he solemnly makes the rounds, stopping here and there for a word with the initiated; one hopes one will be blessed by his presence at one's table. The chef is the demigod of cuisine, or at least the high priest. (Does a toque not resemble a mitre?)

We respond to it all by acting as we would in a church or other sanctuary: We dress nicely, sit quietly—in short—behave. And then we leave an offering.

In fact, our best restaurants insist that we dress formally. I once did a series of interviews with David Bouley, before he closed his eponymous restaurant in 1996. We met at Union Square Farmers' Market, and as Bouley examined produce, nibbling on leaves of organically grown lemon thyme, he told me, in essence, "What I care about is that someone appreciates the food. I don't care if a farmer comes in wearing jeans and a tee-shirt—as long as he appreciates what I'm doing in the kitchen. That's what's important to me." The next day, before my husband (then boyfriend) and I were to lunch there, Thierry asked me if he had to wear a tie. "Certainly not," I said, and repeated Bouley's comment. We arrived, Thierry beautifully dressed, but without a tie, and the captain promptly handed him one. And there's nothing more embarrassing than a restaurant tie, unless it's receiving the Napkin of Shame.*

Amazing that the chef/owner could give lip service to

---

*In a better restaurant, when you spill something on the tablecloth in front of you, and in between courses a waiter whisks away your plate, nonchalantly spreads a napkin of the same color as the tablecloth (usually white) over your messed-up place before putting the silver back down. That's the Napkin of Shame.

not caring about a dress code, but enforce a policy like that. I imagine Bing Crosby must have felt the same way when he was barred from New York's Le Pavillon for not wearing a tie, which was, as Henri Soulé reportedly said, "an insult to my restaurant." Or the woman who was banned from La Côte Basque, which up until the late 1960s had a no-pants-for-women rule, for wearing pants when she had her broken leg in a cast. The cashier insisted that she'd have to remove her pants if she wanted to eat there, and when the woman asked how she might do that, she was told, "In her coat." Much to the cashier's chagrin, the woman peeled off her pants on the spot and dined in her fur coat.

I was once driving through France's Rhône Valley, in the neighborhood of the legendary restaurant La Pyramide—formerly a Michelin three star, and currently holding two. My colleagues and I were wearing jeans as we happened to drive by La Pyramide just at lunchtime, so we went in and asked them if, first of all, they could accommodate our group, and second, if it were a problem that we were wearing jeans. The answer—yes, they could seat us and no, our jeans were not a problem. They were absolutely thrilled to have us.

But in the United States, the best restaurants' dress policy intimidates and excludes. Oh, no, you might be ready to argue. It's simply that one should dress in a way that shows respect for the chef, for the food. I would agree. But I don't agree with a forced show of respect, and I think that if restaurants have to insist, there's something wrong with their conception of themselves. It's almost as if the restaurant itself had a frail ego.

Restaurants have become more and more important to us in the past twenty-five years. Before the late 1970s, going out to a restaurant usually meant going out to a Continental restaurant (or as Rozanne Gold puts it, "doing the Continental"), where the service was often pretentious, the food bad and pretentious, and the atmosphere stuffy and pretentious. By the late 1950s, points out Gold's husband, Michael Whiteman, "The idea of fancy was red velvet banquettes, red flocked wallpaper, crystal chandeliers and thick carpets and a maître d' in a tuxedo who abused you."

By the early 1960s, as Julia Child was becoming big, the French restaurant became *the* place to be.

Whiteman says that in the 1960s, and especially in New York, if you took all the menus from all the Continental restaurants, and tore off the top part bearing the name, they would all be the same.

Then, we most typically went to a restaurant on our way to something else—a concert or a show—or on our way back from something else. If we had an evening out, we had to eat, so we'd stop either at one of these Continental places or perhaps a "family restaurant." If we wanted to see friends, we'd invite them over for dinner.

In the 1970s, everything started to change. Whiteman points out that as baby boomers started coming of age, they moved to cities, which up to that point had been "just a place that people left." In cities, space was at a premium, and young people had to live in small apartments that weren't conducive to entertaining at home. As a result, the restaurant became the place where one socialized. This was especially true for younger people; older people in the cities had always eaten out. We became, says Whiteman, an "eating out culture where dinner became a *form* of entertainment rather than an adjunct to something." This paved the way for a restaurant boom in the late 1970s.

By the 1980s, restaurants became the most popular form of entertainment. Hundreds of fabulous restaurants opened on both coasts and cities everywhere in between. It was a mini-renaissance that coincided with the New American

Cuisine movement and the stock market boom. Americans were rich, we felt rich, and we went out. A lot.

Restaurants in the eighties were flashy. Food was so stylish it often became ostentatious. Conspicuous consumption was it.

The business lunch and expense accounts strongly influenced dining in the eighties: It made a lot of things possible no one would have been able to afford otherwise. "Oh, that's an expense account place," I remember someone saying about Gotham Bar & Grill in 1986. I'm wondering how many great restaurants I'd have missed without the benefit of my or someone's expense account.

In Manhattan, Gotham Bar & Grill was where Alfred Portale built his ultrastylish tall food; meanwhile, Barry Wine tucked beluga caviar into beggar's purses at The Quilted Giraffe. In Los Angeles, studio executives schmoozed each other in restaurants; the big schmoozing went on at Trump's, Morton's, Spago, 385 North, Michael's, Chinois-on-Main, The Ivy, Ivy-at-the-Shore, 72 Market Street. Young producers and writers table-hopped at City Restaurant. In San Francisco, the focus was more on the food, with Masa's, Square One, Hayes Street Grill, Fleur de Lys.

Finally, going out to dinner became an end in itself—it was no longer what you did after a movie or before the theater. An evening out has come to mean, for millions of us, an evening in a restaurant. We'll catch the movie on video, and theater is mostly for New York tourists.

Dining out has become our theater. The restaurant has it all: setting—known in restaurant land as "décor," costumes (not only the waiter's designer duds—Ralph Lauren at Michael's in Santa Monica, Tommy Hilfiger at An American Place, etc., but the costumes of the patrons); props (the food, the candles, the wineglasses); characters (the server, the wine steward, the captain, the chef, the patrons); a score, if it's a musical (live or recorded music, if any); a playbill (the menu), and a plot with a beginning (appetizer), middle (main course), and an end (dessert). Sometimes it's even more elaborate, as in a Shakespeare play, five acts: the amuse bouche, the appetizer, the main course, the cheese course, dessert. And it's as hard to get a reservation at an "in" restaurant as it is tickets to the hot shows.

Dining has become theater to the point that restaurateurs have introduced highly theatrical elements into their restaurants. One New York seafood eatery bills itself as "home of the famous dancing shrimps." Diners walk on water to get into Crustacean, a Vietnamese seafood restaurant in Beverly Hills, traversing a 60,000 gallon aquarium to enter the restaurant.

John Hess told me in an interview that he was struck by something *New York Times* restaurant critic Ruth Reichl had written recently in reviewing a Manhattan restaurant. "The dishes don't always work," she had written, "but it's never boring."

"That's a terrible thing to say," said Hess. "You don't go there to be entertained; that's not the purpose. That's fashion."

This sort of theatricality began back in 1934, with the opening of the first Trader Vic's in Oakland, California. The idea caught on, and owner Victor J. Bergeron opened another in San Francisco in 1951. San Francisco's Trader Vic's boasted real shrunken heads in the outer entry. Patrons sipped flamboyant tropical drinks with gardenias floating in them, or shared enormous cocktails served in bowls with three-foot-long straws. Individual burners on each table kept the rumaki warm.

Yet Trader Vic's was no kitschy joke; it was expensive and aspired to serve well-prepared food. It purported to be a Polynesian restaurant; in fact the menu offered Chinese,

Javanese, and Tahitian specialties, as well as a few French dishes.

Forum of the Twelve Caesars took theme dining up a notch. In fact, New York has always loved theme dining. Café des Artistes, which had opened in the Hotel des Artistes in 1917, hired a resident of that hotel, Howard Chandler Christy, to paint lush murals throughout the restaurant in 1932. The '21' Club, which had opened during Prohibition as an exclusive speakeasy, became, after Prohibition, an exclusive speakeasy *theme* restaurant. Before Faith Stewart Gordon sold it in 1995, the much beloved Russian Tea Room, with its samovars, paintings, and Ballet Russe costumes, its borscht and its caviar and shots of iced vodka, all added up to a theme. Of course the line between a restaurant with a concept and a theme restaurant is a very thin one. But Nobu, the East Coast relative of the very low-key, even nondescript Los Angeles Japanese restaurant Matsuhisa, feels a little like Disneyland. Les Célébrités, one of New York's best restaurants, is decorated with paintings by celebrities. Then there is Republic, the proletarian-theme noodle shop that opened on Union Square in the late nineties.

The Los Angeles of my childhood had Lawry's, on the same stretch of La Cienega Boulevard, or "Restaurant Row," that would later house Matsuhisa and 385 North. Lawry's was a prime rib restaurant that featured a "spinning salad." Waitresses in uniforms that looked like those in *The Harvey Girls* would bring salad ingredients tableside, whirl the lettuce around in a bowl while adding the dressing. Somehow, the dressing didn't wind up on the walls.

In any case, when the theatrical elements eclipse the food in importance, theme dining becomes theme-park dining. In 1982 The Hard Rock Cafe opened in Los Angeles, with an exterior with half a Cadillac crashed into the roof. Today we have not only Hard Rocks in thirty-six American cities, but Planet Hollywoods, too. These tourist attractions have taken over Manhattan's Fifty-seventh Street, while that street's beloved Russian Tea Room is closed at the moment, having been sold to restaurant tycoon Warner LeRoy. LeRoy also owns Tavern on the Green, which for much of its history has also been a theme-park restaurant. At the time of this writing, theme-park dining is exploding, with the imminent openings of grandiose Martian and magic theme restaurants in Manhattan, cartoon and movie theme restaurants in Southern California (with price tags of $15 to $28 million to build them), and even Montage, a 30,000 square-foot cinema theme restaurant in Rockville, Maryland. There are more than 500 theme restaurants across the country.

For years, Los Angeles's best restaurant *was* a theme restaurant: Scandia. Of course a restaurant serving a foreign cuisine always walks a fine line. But at Scandia, the concept was so played up that it felt very thematic, with a Viking ship suspended from the ceiling, Viking horns adorning every other cranny, and so forth. The feeling was very different at the nearby Konditori restaurant in Beverly Hills, which served the same kind of food but in much more subdued surroundings and with less hooplah—and for far less money. The gravlaks, however, was just as delicious.

My favorite L.A. theme restaurant was actually called Theme Restaurant. It's the space-age-looking piece of architecture that sits in the center of L.A.X. I was sad to see it was recently redesigned and its name changed to Encounter.

Joe Baum defended the idea of theme dining, reminding me that when it opened in 1959, Four Seasons was a theme restaurant, the theme being the changing of the seasons, or even more broadly, change. For each season not only did the menu change, but so did the decor, the dishes, the servers' uniforms.

★ ★ ★

Service has always been an important part of the dining experience. In the 1970s, casual service replaced the haughtiness of the preceding era's Continental and French restaurants. "Hi, I'm Stan, and I'll be your waiter this evening" eventually became a cliché summation of casual service.

When Michael's opened, Michael McCarty very much wanted to break the service barrier. For starters, he wanted to eliminate preferential treatment for certain customers. "All up until that point," he pointed out, "you'd flash twenty bucks and you could bump anybody you wanted." He instituted a policy with which no one with a reservation would have to wait for a table, and such bribery went out the window. And if an important movie producer came in without a reservation, expecting a table, that was just too bad—he had to go wait at the bar. "We had certain ground rules," McCarty explained. "Nobody [with a reservation] waited. That was it. You never waited, and so you had to exclude a lot of people to keep it . . . that way. Money wasn't the issue."

Nor did his waitstaff wear the customary tuxedo; outfits by a young designer named Ralph Lauren—pink shirts, green ties, khaki pants, and topsiders—were in step with the feeling of the restaurant.

Staff training became important. In serious establishments, now, the servers actually taste the food, and often have opportunities to sample the wines. Yet this went over the heads of many Americans, whose definition of service meant fast service.

For me the nadir of relaxed service took place in New York around 1994 at a now-defunct restaurant called 9 Jones. That was the night a server felt so comfortable that she paused to correct my pronunciation of a French word. (Wrongly, I might add.)

The casual dining style of the 1970s was best expressed in the fern-bar-type restaurant. In Los Angeles, The Melting

Pot and Cafe Figaro were typical examples—there were lots of them on Melrose Avenue in West Hollywood and on the Sunset Strip. You could get things like crab salad open-faced on a bun with melted cheese and sesame seeds—real pseudo-gourmet stuff. Typically these eateries were decorated with framed posters, hanging plants, ceiling fans, pottery, stained glass; the operative esthetic was "funky." A guy (or gal) would come to take your order, saying, "Hi, I'm Toby, and I'll be serving you today. Would you like to hear the specials?"

The granddaddy of this type of establishment was Café Nicholson in New York City, which opened in 1949. Michael and Ariane Batterberry called the style of restaurant "American Eclectic" in *On the Town in New York,* and described it as "a kind of cross between the Palm Court of the Plaza and Grandma's attic." As they portrayed it, "It was characterized by brick walls, skylights, palm fronds and giant house plants, columns, leaded windows, tiles, bentwood chairs, marble-topped tables, Tiffany glass, and, beyond that, anything from stuffed gay nineties costumes to the signs of the cabala."

Dining, of course, does not mean only dining out. One dines at home, as well. Or one should, anyway. But family dining at home is becoming a disappearing phenomenon. Even as our interest in food is on the rise, as many as 78 percent of North American families are believed to eat dinner with the television on at least once or twice a week, and in the United States the average length of time we spend at the dining-room table is a half hour. More and more of us settle for take-out food standing up at the kitchen counter or opening a box of cereal. And when we get in bed at night, we read cookbooks, and dream, perchance, of food.

When we do cook at home, dining is an entirely different kind of affair than it is in a restaurant. Usually it consists of just one course, and everything gets heaped on one plate. This even holds true in a household such as my mother's; she and my stepfather eat out in good restaurants at least a couple times a week, and there they always have at least two, and probably three courses. At home it seems not to occur to them, except when entertaining in a more formal way. They eat very well at home: On a recent visit, the first night we had roasted free-range chicken with a red wine-shallot sauce, saffron basmati rice with peas, pencil-thin asparagus from the farmer's market, and a Signorello Pinot Noir. All was served on one plate, and it was over in a flash. The next night, lamb rib chops, cooked perfectly, spinach, leftover rice, and roasted beets. All on one plate, delicious, over in a flash. *Bobby Flay's From My Kitchen to Your Table,* a new cookbook published in 1998 by the New York chef who also wrote (with Joan Schwartz) *Bobby Flay's Bold American Food,* exhorts readers to "take a big, bold step and forget about serving separate courses."

Since I grew up eating in the American style, this never seemed odd to me. Then I moved in with a Frenchman, and spent some time in France, where one spends hours at the table at home.

At my in-laws' house in the Bordeaux region, my mother and father-in-law, who are not food people particularly, always have an entrée (in France this is the first course, the entry into the meal), a main course, served with a vegetable or potatoes, always followed by a salad, cheese (there's always a selection in a covered box in the fridge), fruit, and perhaps some simple dessert or yogurt. This is not to say that everything they eat is necessarily better than what my parents eat. The cheese is always better. But the vegetables are sure to be overcooked; if bought at the market, they started out beautiful, but sometimes they're frozen; the entrée may be fabulous shellfish, perfectly prepared, or it may be a can of soup. The salad is usually just plain Bibb, certainly not organically grown, dressed with a vinaigrette made with canola oil, since they don't like olive oil (I think their idea of olive oil is the very rough stuff that used to be around before extra-virgin became popular) and good red wine vinegar. If there's mayonnaise in the picture, it's homemade, *bien sûr*. My father-in-law always opens a bottle of the red wine he buys by the liter from a cooperative in nearby Lugon, bottles himself, and puts away for a few years. He considers it ordinary *(appellation Fronsac contrôlée)*, and pays the equivalent of less than two dollars for it, but wine of that quality would easily fetch twenty dollars if the bottle sported a shiny label from the Napa Valley.

But whether the food is better or not, it is served in stages that encourage lingering and savoring. The all-on-one-plate phenomenon doesn't happen in other cultures. Not in France, Italy, Sweden, China, Japan, or Mexico. It's peculiarly American.

Besides separating out courses, plating is another main difference between dining at home and in a restaurant. At home, food is usually served family-style; that is, passing platters around the table. In a restaurant the food emerges from the kitchen already plated. People who came of cooking-age in the 1980s, however, began trying to plate in the kitchen, especially those who were swept up with *nouvelle cuisine* mania. I remember trying to fan things out on plates in my kitchen, laying meats over pools of sauce, and wiping splatters off the sides of plates with a damp towel.

The biggest difference, though, between restaurant and home dining is the food: The food at home usually isn't pretentious. We apologize for it, tell ourselves it's not as good as in a restaurant, but I imagine we often enjoy it more.

10

THE FARMERS' MARKET MOVEMENT

THE BIGGEST CHANGE IN AMERICAN GASTRONOMY IN the last forty years has been in the realm of ingredients—what's available to chefs and what's available to the home cook. That change has been effected thanks, in large part, to the renaissance of farmers' markets and a revival of thousands of varieties of heirloom produce.

A hundred years ago, well over a third of all Americans lived on farms. And for those who didn't, farmlands, and consequently the farmer's market, were inevitably nearby—even in someplace as cosmopolitan as Philadelphia, with its Reading Terminal Market (among others); New York City, home of the Washington Market; Boston (Quincy Market); or Chicago (Maxwell Street Market)*.

But urbanization quickly took over America as the twen-

*Officially designated as a public market in 1912.

tieth century got underway, and as fewer Americans lived on farms or near them, we now depended upon vast food distribution systems, first through the railways and then additionally through cross-country trucking and a rapidly developing interstate highway system. Mom-and-pop groceries went the way of the family farm, and by the 1950s most Americans bought their food, all in one stop, at the supermarket.

One by one, farmers' markets disappeared until, by the early 1970s, they were an endangered species. In the meantime, the supermarket may have made it easier for housewives to jump in the station wagon and do one-stop shopping between soap operas and folding the laundry, but it also killed the possibility of finding good ingredients. In addition, it cut off an important source of social interaction, isolating would-be participants in the sterile supermarket environment, where human contact was limited to "Where are the paper towels?" and "That'll be $23.49; have a nice day." An informal study in the late 1970s showed that supermarket shoppers experienced only one-fourth of the social encounters that farmers' market shoppers did.

Directed to the masses, the supermarket had to carry what legions of people would be sure to buy, and that did not include farm-fresh produce with short shelf lives, vegetables perceived to be of only ethnic interest, or expensive exotic fruits. Ordinary tree-ripened or vine-ripened fruit began disappearing in favor of specimens picked green and allowed to "ripen" in ethylene gas en route or on the supermarket display. And the idea of what was "gourmet" bore little relationship to what people crave today. Smoked oysters, canned asparagus, and tinned pâté de foie gras were considered "fancy." When I was a child, my mother received a gift of a plastic cylinder of the type that men's underwear come in, filled with snail shells. There must have been snails involved somehow (dehydrated, hidden at the bottom?) and some packet of seasoning mix. In any case, it sat in our pantry for probably ten years before it was finally thrown away.

"Some forms of progress are not necessarily progress for the public," John Hess told me in an interview. "It's a surprising thing, but refrigeration is a very mixed blessing for the consumer." Hess cited fish as an example. To research his book *Vanishing France* (1972), Hess was surprised to find in his travels that the fish was fresher where there was no refrigeration. He had first noticed it when Paris's old market at Les Halles was closed and moved outside the city to Rungis. "At Les Halles," he explained, "they didn't have very large storage spaces for refrigeration, for fish for example, so . . . the fish had to be sold." When he questioned the merchants newly installed at Rungis, where they had to have refrigeration since it was eighteen miles outside of the city, he said, "they admitted that the fish was not as fresh because they had to keep it." Hess then visited markets in Morocco and Turkey, "inland markets like Marrakech, where the fish was fresher than it was in New York. Because it had to be. It was brought in at night over the mountains, and it has to be sold in the morning. By midday the fish has to be gone, so they lower the prices until it's gone. They don't have refrigeration. That fish is eaten by nightfall. I observed with my own nose that the fish was fresher in these places than it was in New York."

For fans of freshness, the renaissance of the farmers' market has been the single best piece of gastronomic news of the last forty years. At century's end, in large cities and small towns all across the United States, farmers' markets have sprouted up, changing the way we eat, giving us fresh food for the first time in decades and introducing—or reintroducing—us to hundreds of varieties of produce.

But more important, the farmers' markets have begun to change our relationship with the foods we eat. As a culture we had forgotten about the sources of our food. Vegetables were characterless commodities that came from huge, impersonal agricultural concerns, giant farms that freely used pesticides in order to produce something that looked good, looked uniform, shipped well, and had a long shelf life.

The health food movement was influential in reminding people that fresh food, untainted with lots of chemicals, was a desirable thing. DDT, a widely-used pesticide, was banned in the United States in 1997 after it was discovered that it caused cancer—before that, no one had thought about it much. People began to reject the idea of depending on huge corporations for foods that were overly processed, overly packaged, less nutritious, and more expensive than fresh foods. Health food stores were one answer: Here people could help themselves to minimally processed bulk goods out of bins. Shopping at farmers' markets was even more appealing than shopping in health food stores, which tended to concentrate on grains, dried legumes, dried fruits, and the like, rather than fresh produce. The farmers' market would boast the added benefit of giving patrons a sense of community.

Today people can shop for food at colorful, lively, open-air markets. There are almost three thousand of them across the country in 1998, and new ones are always being planned. Shoppers can chat with farmers who actually grow the food they're buying, which in some markets may be either certified organically grown or at least grown without the use of pesticides.* One finds a wide variety of naturally

*Certified organically grown produce has to be grown in soil that's been pesticide-free for a certain number of years before a harvest can be labeled "organically grown." Farmers at markets will sometimes tell customers their produce was grown without the use of pesticides, but they can't necessarily guarantee how long the soil was pesticide-free before they started growing that particular crop. At this writing, new federal organic rules were being worked out by the Clinton administration.

ripened fruits, farm-fresh vegetables, herbs, eggs, milk, homemade baked goods, locally produced cheeses, fresh-off-the-boat fish, meats, flowers, plants, wool, and prepared foods. The farmers' market has once again become a place to bump into friends, chat with farmers, have a fresh lemonade in the summertime or hot apple cider in the fall, catch up on news, exchange recipes, and meet local chefs. It has let us forge a much healthier relationship with the food we prepare and eat. "Besides," pointed out Robert Lewis, the co-founder of New York's Greenmarket, "you can meet someone of the opposite sex there."

For many, including me, it also inspires us to cook. And this is the way things should be: One sees a bunch of baby turnips blushing violet in the spring or a dappled sweet dumpling squash in the autumn, one's dying to taste them, so one buys and goes home and cooks. Hillary Baum, who has been active in the farmers' market movement since the mid-1980s,* pointed out that despite the exponentially growing number of cookbooks published each year, people are learning to cook more spontaneously—without following recipes—because they are inspired to do something with ingredients they find in the markets.

Restaurateurs in areas such as New York City, where the regional wholesale farmers' markets had disappeared, and even in some such as Los Angeles, which still has Grand Central Market, have come to rely on public farmers' markets. At a visit recently to the spectacular market in Santa Monica, California, I was stopped in my tracks by the most beautiful bunches of broccoli rape I had ever seen, bright green, with pencil-thin stalks. I asked the farmer about them, and she told me she had brought them for Nancy Silverton at Campanile, one of Los Angeles's top restaurants. Silverton had picked up what she needed and left the

*And who happens to be Joseph Baum's daughter . . .

rest for the public to buy. Across the way was Lily's Eggs, a farm stand selling duck eggs ($5 a dozen) and green eggs from Araucana hens ($6.50 a dozen); when I asked abut these, I learned Campanile was buying these, too. In Manhattan, many chefs shop early in the morning at Union Square Greenmarket.

One of the main reasons restaurants rely on the markets is that here they can find, besides fresher produce, a much wider variety of unusual produce. When I visited the Union Square Greenmarket with chef David Bouley, one farmer whose stand we visited had an impressive selection of potatoes. "Last year we had seventeen [varieties]," she told me. "This year we have fifty-one."

A market I visited in Napa, California, in September 1996 boasted the most amazing array of tomatoes—in almost every color of the rainbow—from six or seven different farmers. There were fat, juicy Red Brandywines; large, purplish Black Sea Man tomatoes; tiny yellow pears; gorgeous striped yellow-and-green Zebra tomatoes; large, firm, well-balanced orange Garden Peach, and delectable, sweet-as-candy Green Grape tomatoes. My shopping bag overflowed. That night I sliced them up, crumbled Laura Chenel's local goat cheese on top, added salt and some generous grindings of black pepper, and drizzled a wonderful local olive oil over all. What a feast!

If industrialization and supermarket culture had reduced our choices to hard, pale, Styrofoam tomatoes and a potato palette limited to Idaho, white rose, and round reds, where did all these varieties come from?

It used to be that farmers grew a wide range of varieties of vegetables and fruits. But as industrialization took over and shipping and predictable growing behavior became imperative, farmers replaced unusual varieties with hardy hybrids that shipped well. Small farmers who grew Brandywine tomatoes or Prairie Spy apples could no longer find outlets for the tiny quantities they grew in relation to the new giant "factory farms"; what would a supermarket chain do with a couple of bushels of something unusual? It needed to stock its stores with large quantities of produce that was uniform.

As the century marched on, the hybrids took over, until by the early 1970s, thousands of heirloom varieties were in danger of disappearing altogether.

It was then, in 1972, that Diane Whealy and her husband Kent were planting their first garden in Decorah, Iowa. While doing so, Diane often thought about her grandfather's farm just outside of nearby St. Lucas. Her grandfather, Baptist John Ott, had long ago entranced his grandchildren each year with his spectacular morning glories that he trained all over the porch on strings going in different directions. But Diane had also loved his vegetable gardens. He always had four or five plots scattered throughout his yard, each with a different focus: one for vine crops, one for corn, one for beans. When Ott became terminally ill that year, Whealy thought to ask him about his seeds—and he had indeed saved the seeds his parents had brought over from Bavaria when they immigrated. Before he died, he turned over to her three types: the morning glory (which she called "Ott's morning glory"), the German pink tomato, and a green snap bean he called "nuttle."

The Whealys became interested in heirloom seeds, imagining that others would probably have similar seeds in their families. Why not exchange them and bring some of these unusual varieties back? They started organizing gardeners and looking for gardeners who might be holding heirloom seeds, and in 1975 they funded the nonprofit Seed Savers Exchange. "We started out with three seeds and now we have eighteen thousand," Diane Whealy told me. Many were true family heirlooms; sometimes the family had no one to pass them on to. Others were seeds the Whealys had purchased as seed catalogs discontinued them. They also took a trip to Russia and Eastern Europe to collect seeds; in Russia they found a few unusual tomato varieties: Silvery Fir Tree, an early-maturing variety with foliage that looks like the carrot; Black Plum, a black tomato; and Russian Persimmon, an orange-colored tomato.

Today Seed Savers has 8,000 members throughout the country, and another 1,000 who haven't officially joined but who send in heirloom seeds. Members exchange seeds through a yearbook with over 13,000 seed listings; in 1995 they also created an educational seed catalog for gardeners who don't want to be as involved but are looking for seeds. "Our goal is not to be a seed bank," says Whealy, "but to get the seeds back in people's gardens." For this work Kent Whealy received a MacArthur Fellowship in 1989.

Many of Seed Savers's members are seed companies looking to expand their offerings into historical and heirloom varieties; from there the seeds make their way to gardeners and farmers throughout the country—including those who sell the heirloom varieties at farmers' markets.

Not every farmers' market had disappeared by the mid-seventies. New Orleans's French Market was and is the oldest continuously operating public market in the United States, established in 1794. Central Market in Lancaster, Pennsylvania, has been operating more than 200 years, specializing in products grown or produced by the region's Amish population.

Seattle's Pike Place Market, generally regarded as the nation's premier public market, began in 1907. In reaction to the high markups that food middlemen were pocketing, the Seattle City Council organized farmers to come and offer their produce direct to consumers. During World War II, a time when legions of farmers' markets closed down, Pike Place almost perished as well. Nearly half of its farmers were Japanese-Americans who were sent to internment camps, losing their businesses. Although Pike's Place hung on for the next quarter century by a thin piece of cornsilk, an urban renewal plan almost brought about its demise in 1971. Citizens stepped in with a grass-roots political initiative called Save the Market, which was resoundingly successful.

When I last visited Pike's Place in early November 1995, I saw slender homegrown sweet carrots, golden beets, Italian black collards, purple Peruvian and yellow Finn potatoes, stalks of Oregon Brussels sprouts, cauliflower mushrooms, hedgehog mushrooms, chanterelles, lobster mushrooms, and much more. But the highlight of the market is the seafood: beautiful, sleek Alaska salmon, small, firm king salmon, fabulous Dungeness crab, happily in season while I was there, all hawked by very dramatic fishmongers.

But aside from Pike's Place and a few other notable exceptions, the modern farmers' market phenomenon began in the mid-1970s with the creation of a few new farmers' markets across the country.

The movement began most energetically in New York and California. In New York, John Hess, of all people, provided a good dose of inspiration for the movement. Hess had been working for nine years at the Paris bureau of *The New York Times,* and began writing articles critical of the city's plan to abandon the public market at Les Halles and move it outside the city to Rungis. "I made the observation," he told me in an interview, "that Paris ate less well because the produce was a day older than when the wholesale market was right in the heart of town." Of Les Halles, Hess said, "It was a wonderful market. . . . The merchants would take first choice during the early hours, and then the people would come into the market and buy what was left." The competition was beneficial.

The same thing, Hess argued, had happened in New

York. Hess had worked at the old Washington Market in the 1950s, and as he described it, the produce came mostly from across the river in New Jersey; it was brought to market and distributed to merchants from there. "That was driven out in the fifties and sixties," Hess recalled. "Governor Rockefeller's big project—the World Trade Center and all of those high-rise buildings around there—they destroyed the Washington Street Market, buildings dating from the late eighteenth and early nineteenth centuries." At that point, plans were underway to get rid of Fulton Fish Market and the Bronx Terminal Market, and Hess wrote articles denouncing the plans as "unwise and wrong." He went up to Syracuse and visited the Dutin Farmers' Market, founded in 1973 by Irwin Davis. Davis, who was also head of the Metropolitan Planning Association in Syracuse, had traveled in Europe, been impressed with the markets there, and decided to start one. At this point, Barry Benepe happened to approach Hess, introducing himself as an urbanist and an architect, and told him he had written a paper describing the economic value of markets in towns. "And I said to him," recalled Hess, "we don't need studies; we need farmers' markets."

In the meantime, the City of New York had dismantled the region's two wholesale markets, one at the Bronx Terminal Market and the other at the Brooklyn Terminal Market, when these Markets were privatized between 1973 and 1975. There had been a section of each Market known as the Farmers' Square or Farmers' Market; their closing was, according to Robert Lewis, Chief Marketing Representative for New York State's Department of Agriculture's Direct Marketing program, "over the protests of farmers." The wholesale markets had been the principal resource for restaurants for farm-fresh produce; when I interviewed Lewis in 1998 he was trying to reestablish them. "It's a travesty . . . that these markets were demolished," he said, "because they were the last link between local farms and stores." There, said Lewis, restaurants had been able to find a much grater range of varieties of produce than they can today.

Lewis, a regional and ecological planner, had met Barry Benepe in 1975; he too had been impressed by Hess's articles. "We were very moved by them," he told me. The articles struck a particular chord with Benepe, who specialized in human-scale planning such as bike paths. Together Lewis and Benepe founded New York's Greenmarket in 1976. They shared the goals of "Bringing back the real food, so to speak, that had been lost from the conventional industrialized food system" and delivering it "directly to the front door of city residents so they'd have access to the wonderful flavors and tastes of tree- and vine-ripe varieties." They were also motivated by a concern for the survival of small farms in the region, as well as revitalizing urban spaces—a primary consideration to the two regional planners. "Markets, of course, are ancient phenomena and ancient institutions," Lewis pointed out. "There are theories about the origin of democracy coming from open-air markets in Athens. It's positive to think of the market as a very, very important institution historically, and obviously from which cities evolved. It's got this serendipitous experience that we need; it's got the experience of the senses and discovery and human contact."

By 1976 their dream had become a reality. But it didn't happen without a fight: Benepe and Lewis had to slash their way through plenty of red tape and more overt opposition before they succeeded. Hess says of Benepe: "He did a tremendous thing for the city . . ." Today there are 200 markets in New York's Greenmarket program, with 20,000 acres of land being farmed for the markets.

★ ★ ★

In California, the farmers' market movement was motivated by somewhat different concerns. The late 1970s saw a glut in California's stone fruit market. Even though farmers were getting only ten cents per pound for peaches and plums, they were being sold in supermarkets for sixty-nine cents, raising the ire of antihunger groups and consumers. There was a general feeling that the public could get better food less expensively if farmers could sell to them directly, cutting out the middleman. The state Department of Agriculture and Food worked with antihunger activists to try to get legislation enacted to make it legal for farmers to sell direct to the public, but according to Marion Kalb, director of the Southland Farmers' Market Association, they bumped up against a powerful large corporate agriculture lobby, and the proposed legislation was defeated. The Department of Food and Agriculture and the antihunger activists took another tack, and in 1979 managed to establish regulations exempting farmers who participated in the farmers' markets from standard packing and labeling requirements, effectively opening the door to selling direct to consumers. For the first time it was possible for farmers to mix sizes within a box.

At that point, the only two farmers' markets in California were San Francisco's Ferry Plaza Market, which had existed since 1943, and the Davis Farmers' Market in Southern California, which had opened in 1976. The San Francisco market had been founded to aid food distribution during the war; at some point later, the city had bought it.

In the Los Angeles area, the first farmers' market was founded in 1980, in the city of Gardena. Seven churches were involved in organizing the market, which borders on South Central Los Angeles and serves the population of that community. The first few farmers' markets in Southern California, in fact, were established in low-income areas: Pacoima, Compton, and Adams & Vermont. Today there are 118 in the southland; the Santa Monica Farmers' Market is the showpiece of the L.A. area markets.

In Northern California, not long after the statewide regulations were changed, Lynn Bagley had been shopping regularly at Santa Rosa Farmers' Market in Sonoma County when she hit upon the idea of starting one herself in nearby Marin County. At the time Bagley was working for U.S. Congressman John Burton, doing graduate work part time at San Francisco State University in Chinese medicine. Burton was a very liberal, social-minded legislator who was, as Bagley put it, "involved in helping people who are one way or another being screwed by the system." Bagley shared his political views. In any case, Bagley was attracted to the farmers' market because of her holistic health background. "One of my strongest interests," she told me, "was using food as medicine or food for nutrition and therefore medicine," and markets appealed to her because the food was of such high quality. At first she thought she'd just work on her pet market project on weekends. Then she went to work in earnest, in 1982, when Burton announced that he would retire. (He has since come out of retirement; today Burton is California state senator and speaker of the Senate.)

Bagley started the Marin Farmers' Market in July 1983, in San Rafael, with a lot of help from Marin County Food Bank, an organization that provides food to nonprofit organizations. The Food Bank brought in a number of people who were on probation and ordered to perform community service work to help Bagley man the phones to garner support for the market. "It was very grass roots," recalled Bagley. "We called every second house in the Zip code and told them to tell their neighbors. . . . I held a number of public meetings both in farm areas and the community. I called everyone who had anything to do with food or gardening and built my mailing list by word of mouth." Soon the market was one of the most successful in California;

today it's known for having some of the highest quality produce in the country.

As America's newfound interest in food came into the fore in the 1980s, all the emphasis in the new cooking was on ingredients. The restaurant-going and home-cooking public developed a fascination with ingredients that coincided with the gathering momentum of the farmers' market movement and greatly helped to make it as boomingly successful as it has become. People sought to buy some of the new vegetables and fruits they were tasting at restaurants, and they were able to do so for the first time at the farmers' markets.

Here the heirloom seed movement became very important. Diane Whealy sees a strong tie between the heirloom seed and farmers' market movements. "When an heirloom seed has been grown in one location year after year," she explained, "it adapts to the climate, and you're going to have a very strong plant." This works to the advantage of a farmer trying to farm organically, because a variety that strong doesn't require as much fertilizer or pesticide.

From the point of view of the markets, all the new varieties have drawn people in. "A lot of what makes markets fun for the customer," said Bagley, "is that they can try new products there at the market and farmers can show them how to use them and tell them how to cook them. . . . The heirloom products are more easily sold and more successful there because of that type of interpersonal communication. And from the farmers' point of view, it's a good test market, and they can get feedback right there from the customer. I think the heirloom movement got started, in a sense, at the farmers' markets."

For many people, the freshness of the food, lower prices, interaction with the farmers, and newfound sense of community have been fortuitous fringe benefits of the market.

★ ★ ★

There's an interesting dichotomy between the original aims of the movement's New York and California branches. New York's Greenmarket was inspired by urban revitalization, the need for human-scale spaces, and other regional planning considerations, plus a concern for disappearing small farmers. The urban revitalization aspect of it isn't surprising, since cities in New York state tend to be more centralized, more urban, shall we say, than cities in California, which tend to be newer and less likely to need revitalization.

The California movement grew more out of grass roots activists working against hunger.

But even markets that weren't driven by the antihunger movement are now serving the lower-income populations of their regions. In 1986, nutrition coupons that could only be used at farmers' markets were distributed to lower-income families in Massachusetts. A number of other states followed Massachusetts's lead, and in 1989 the WIC Farmers' Market Nutrition Program was founded. Today it includes thirty-five states, including Washington, D.C., and two Native American tribal nations. This has helped attract farmers to markets in lower-income areas they otherwise wouldn't have been able to serve.

Each region's farmers' market movement reaped benefits it hadn't necessarily bargained for. For instance, in places where local businesses had objected to the presence of a market, fearing competition, it has inevitably turned out that the crowds attracted by it have actually increased business. Rather than fight the market, some forward-looking supermarkets wound up sponsoring markets in their parking lots.

The farmers' market movement has even had the happy and unexpected consequence of improving the selection of products in our supermarkets. Customers who shop at farmers' markets have become accustomed to very fresh, high-quality produce, and supermarkets have had to meet their higher expectations. As a result, organic produce, locally grown produce, and organic or local farm-fresh dairy products are sometimes available. Robert Lewis pointed to Ronnybrook milk—old fashioned, farm-fresh milk in glass bottles—which appeared in many New York supermarkets after customers first became acquainted with it at some of the city's Greenmarkets.

Related to the farmers' market movement is the chef-to-farm connection, which started in California, but has spread across the country. With the focus shifting onto ingredients, restaurants have had to work hard to keep themselves supplied. They couldn't count on their regular wholesalers to provide heirloom varieties and exotic produce. A number of chefs and others have started programs to address the problem. In 1983 Sibella Krause founded the Farm Restaurant Project while she was working as a cook at Chez Panisse. The object was to establish links between Bay Area restaurants and growers of high-quality produce. Out of that came the Tasting of Summer Produce in 1983, which was held annually through 1989. This event brought together abut 150 top local producers to meet potential buyers, establishing a permanent strong link between Bay Area farms and restaurants.

Cakebread Winery in Napa Valley began its American Harvest Workshop in 1986, partly with the goal of gathering chefs, sommeliers, and journalists together to encourage education and discourse on bringing food and wine together. But another important goal of the workshop has been to introduce chefs to some of the region's producers of ingredients: cheese, produce, seafood, and game. Although certainly the idea of generating publicity has also played a part in Cakebread's plans, the Workshop has been quite a positive force for many of the Bay Area's producers who might have had more difficulty reaching a national customer base—that is, connecting with chefs.

And that has been good for the general public, as well. For instance, abalone, a mollusk that is one of California's indigenous treasures, had almost disappeared from the Pacific. I met Luc Chamberlain of Abalone Acres—located in Marshall, California—in 1996 at Cakebread's ten-year reunion workshop. Chamberlain described himself as an "aqua ranger"; he farms abalone (rather than fishing for it wild). When he buys the seeds from a hatchery, they are a mere one-quarter inch in size; he lets them grow to three to four inches, lifting them up out of the water once a week to feed them four different types of seaweed. "I really believe in sustainable agriculture," he told me. "That's why I use four kinds of kelp." Wild abalone, he explained, are harvested when they're seven inches, which they reach when they're between ten and twelve years old. It's illegal to remove them any smaller than that. Chamberlain's farmed abalone fetched $22 per pound in the shell, retail; $40 per pound for the meat. The connections he made at Cakebread were good for Chamberlain ("I can sell everything we can produce," he said), good for the chefs he supplied, and good for the general public.

Farmers' markets have also been great for cities, which had been declining steadily in terms of quality of life since the 1970s; this has of course greatly satisfied those who created farmers' markets expressly with that goal in mind.

But some in the farmers' market movement—Lynn Bagley among them—see establishing markets for the purpose of urban revitalization as less than desirable. When the establishment of a market is dictated by the redevelopment departments of cities, she explained, the market that goes in is not a market for the sake of a market. Rather, she said, "The purpose is to use the market to develop the downtown. When you add too many agendas, the market loses something." In California, she said, this has caused an unnatural growth of markets. "Rather than multiply the number of farmers going to the markets, when you don't have enough supply, then you get monopolies, and the idea of meeting the farmers gets lost; you get [to meet] an employee. It's gone a little too fast and it's stretched the farmers' market world here in California a little too thin." The Marin Farmers' Market attracts farmers from the San Fernando Valley, a suburb of Los Angeles, some 450 miles away. In some areas of the country, market rules limit the distance away from the market the farmers can come from, but not in California. "It's worth it for some of them," explained Bagley. "They send a truck and put people in hotels," hitting a number of the region's markets over the weekend. Some farmers manage to go to thirty, forty, or even fifty markets a week. "It's not exactly what we had in mind," said Bagley.

Still, when all is said and done, it's difficult to see the resurgence of farmers' markets as anything but a terrifically positive force in terms of Americans' relationship with what goes on their plates.

11

THE PURSUIT OF HAPPINESS

THE BEGINNINGS OF AMERICA'S LOVE AFFAIR WITH FOOD coincided with the start of the sexual revolution. Just as we were discovering the pleasures of the table, we were also discovering the joy of sex; our palates were unchained when our sexuality was liberated. Julia Child became popular at an odd time in terms of the women's movement. In the late sixties and early seventies, women wanted to escape from the kitchen, but Julia Child showed women—and men—that what happened in the kitchen didn't have to be drudgery, it could be an exciting place of creativity, self-expression, even fun.

As the culture became more open about sex, we also opened ourselves up to the sensual pleasures of the palate. Appetite was no longer experienced as something sinful or threatening—whether it was sexual appetite or an appetite for food.

Overcoming these attitudes was an uphill battle. But by the time the mid-1980s rolled around, it looked like casual sex was becoming the national pastime. Perhaps it's no accident that it was also during the mid-eighties that American food started getting wild, with tall food, crazy combinations, extravagant expenditures, and frivolous fusions.

Then the AIDS crisis struck and the party was over. Yet if sensual pleasures were suddenly forbidden in the bedroom, at least we were allowed them in the dining room. Sure, monogamous sex was still safe, but our society's libido began to fade, or at least went underground along with licentiousness. In the 1990s we began to crave what was safe and familiar in food, as well—and that meant comfort food. We've become more serious about our food, more sober, more *applied.*

Although we may be moving in an encouraging direction in terms of American interest in and dedication to gastronomy, it's still far too early in the game to be smug. Food historian Harvey Levenstein cited a number of elements that conspired to destroy fine dining in America in the late nineteenth and early twentieth centuries, and we'd do well to learn from history. "These included dieting, the food and health mania, the cult of simplicity, and Prohibition, which undercut the financial basis of fine restaurants," he wrote.

The Protestant work ethic, which ruined food in America for a hundred years, continues to inhibit the food revolution. Wine with food remains a radical idea for many. That we *ever* could have accepted Prohibition says quite a bit about us as a society. How far have we come since then? Anachronistic blue laws and wine shipping laws are still in place and enforced, and though a group of California wineries is lobbying to change the shipping laws, we have a long way to go. In Kentucky, Georgia, and Florida, for instance, it's a felony to ship wine directly to consumers.

I'll never forget how shocked I was moving from California to New York in 1986. I had just landed in the city and was invited to dinner at the apartment of some friends on a Sunday. I stopped to pick up a bottle of wine on the way and was absolutely stunned to find that this was impossible—New York retailers aren't allowed to sell wine or liquor on Sunday. Nor may wine be sold under the same roof as food items: That's why it's not sold in supermarkets. What is that but an outrage against civilization? Beer may be sold in grocery stores—that's why citywide, beer is the beverage of choice among forgetful New Yorkers on Sunday evenings. On that long-ago Sunday, I had to bribe a bartender in a restaurant to sell me a bottle on the Q.T.

Even though wine has become chic, few young Americans are in the habit of making wine a part of their dining experience. Of the wine drunk in America, 67.5 percent is consumed by people over forty, even though less than 42 percent of the population is forty or older.

If dieting, a health mania, and the cult of simplicity played a great role in destroying gastronomy a hundred years ago, it seems to me that today those urges are even stronger.

Dieting is certainty a current threat. Although the flapper esthetic dictated slimness, flappers were pleasantly plump in comparison to 1990s high-fashion models, whose esthetic has embraced an asexual gauntness and "heroin chic." (Junkies are notoriously uninterested in eating.) Dieting has reached scary proportions in this country. Although cases were recorded around the turn of the century, anorexia and bulimia are rampant today among teenage girls and young women. "Low-fat" and "no-fat" scream out on cereal boxes, salad dressing bottles, and even cookie packages all up and down the aisles of supermarkets. Just to eat Olestra—a synthetic fat-substitute—in their potato chips, people will risk incontinence, an occasional side effect of the product!

At the same time that Americans are snapping up synthetic fat and artificial sweeteners, we also appear to be interested in health—at least in "healthy" items that are easily purchased. A cereal called Fiber One may sound like dog food, but it offers an impressive 13 grams of dietary fiber per half-cup serving. (Though it also happens to contain artificial sweetener in the form of NutraSweet.) Organic produce and dairy products have made their way into the supermarket as well, answering a desire for products grown without pesticides; often they taste better to boot, just as produce grown on smaller farms with greater care may taste better. Yet many Americans look at certain foods as if they were medicine, eating greens, for instance, because they are healthy rather than because they're delicious. Vitamin sales are higher than ever—Americans spend a whopping $8.9 billion dollars each year on dietary supplements (including vitamins, herbs, minerals, and so-called natural medicines). Though the food and health mania was certainly strong at the end of the nineteenth century, it's hard to imagine they held a tighter grip on the public than they do today.

At the same time, the cult of simplicity—reminiscent of the ethics of Puritanism—has reemerged. A burgeoning movement called Voluntary Simplicity advocates paring one's life down to the bare essentials—getting a less demanding job, moving into smaller quarters, and saving money wherever possible—in order to live a more "balanced" life. A bible of the movement, *Your Money or Your Life,* by Joe Dominguez and Vicky Robin, suggests a variety of ways to save on food expenditures, such as "Do one big shopping every seven to ten days, rather than making several small trips," and "Make up menus ahead of time for the seven to ten days you're shopping for, basing meals on what foods are on sale." As any dedicated cook knows, it's well-nigh impossible to eat well unless one buys fresh products every couple of days; and of course it's best to cook according to what looks good in the market that day. What these authors suggest recalls the way we used to shop in the 1950s and 1960s—the way the Domestic Scientists, who by the way were also called Home Economists, wanted us to shop. To save money entertaining, the authors of *Your Money or Your Life* suggest, "Invite friends to share a meal, but don't prepare anything different from your normal fare. Rice and beans may be old hat to you, but they could be a treat for your guests." Pity the poor guests! As my friend Pierre replies when someone invites him to dinner, modestly saying, "Oh, it's nothing special," Pierre says, "No? Then why should I come?"

A series of books published by Knopf called *Chic Simple* aims at a different audience, though it pitches the same pared-down esthetic. These starkly elegant books were seemingly written for readers in their twenties with money to burn but neither the time nor the inclination to steep themselves in anything too involved. *Chic Simple: Cooking* aims to make it chic to be too busy or unmotivated to cook.

Witness the success of the *Dummies* books. After the splash of their boffo computer books *Mac for Dummies, Windows for Dummies, Internet for Dummies,* and so forth, IDG publishers brought out a whole series of *Wine for Dummies* books. In olden times, ignorance was bliss. Today, ignorance is chic. In 1996 when *Cooking for Dummies* was published, I was surprised to find that Bryan Miller, the well-regarded former restaurant critic for *The New York Times,* was the author; it seemed the tiniest bit undignified. Says my mother, "If they're so dumb, they should go out for dinner." *The Complete Idiot's Guide to Cooking Basics* had been published the previous year.

But it didn't stop there: Soon *Gourmet Cooking for Dummies* appeared on the shelves, and if I was surprised by Bryan Miller's participation, I was amazed to see Charlie Trotter's name gracing the cover (Trotter is one of the most respected chefs in the United States). Perhaps it's shortsightedness on my part, but I'd be less bothered by these books if they were for "beginners" rather than "dummies" or "idiots," appealing to inexperience rather than stupidity.

And Americans spend a much smaller percentage of our income on food than just about any other culture. People in poorer societies, of course, spend a large percentage of their smaller incomes on food for subsistence; in societies in which food is part of culture, people are willing to spend more than we are in order to eat better. We also spend a smaller percentage of our incomes on food than we used to, and the numbers are still dropping. In 1994 we spent 11.1 percent of our disposable personal income on food, down from 13.9 percent in 1970.

The hold Puritanism has always had on this country is remarkable. It was behind National Prohibition, just as it underlies the overzealousness with which "concerned" citizens will object to a pregnant woman having a glass of wine with dinner. Of course, it's the source of the federal labeling law that requires wine bottles to post a warning of the danger to the fetus. It also explains the archaic "blue laws."

And Puritanism underpinned the late nineteenth-century zeal for health, just as it does today. The Puritan ethic demands that nothing should be wasted; the notion of buying dozens of ingredients simply to make a dish taste good is anathema. Social historian Michelle Stacey pointed out in her 1994 book *Consumed* that today, when we eat for pleasure, we feel guilty. "The word 'sin,' " she wrote, "has a powerful resonance in this country, and these days it is often applied to food." How often do we hear about "sinfully rich" desserts?

The Puritan in us loves killing two birds with one stone. Obviously we have to eat, so why not eat as much fiber as possible in a breakfast cereal? Why not plan our vegetable consumption according to which greens prevent cancer? If we look at our foods as medicine, we're not as likely to become ill. We save on health care costs!

Nor should money be "thrown away" on extravagant food. Not only is it wasteful, but it promotes the deadly sin of gluttony. Culinary historian Waverly Root analyzed the problem most succinctly in a 1975 *New York Times Magazine* essay:

> The Puritan nourishes himself (grudgingly), for God has so organized the universe that he must. Possibly he suspects that the chore of eating was imposed on him as penance for his disgraceful *gourmandise* in connection with an apple. "Because thou hast . . . eaten of the tree, of which I commanded thee, saying, Thou shalt not eat of it," reads Genesis, iii, 17, "cursed is the ground for thy sake; in sorrow shalt thou eat of it all the days of thy life." Obviously man was not intended to enjoy eating, and the Puritan obediently disapproves of taking pleasure in food. He eats to maintain strength in order to get on with the serious business of earning his bread by the sweat of his brow. . . .

Root also pointed out that pride—another deadly sin—comes into the picture as well when one entertains one's friends, offering the best of one's larder and showing off one's cooking skill (or that of one's cook).

How much of this attitude remains today? I stopped into a coffee bar in Malibu in 1998, and attempted to order a frozen coffee drink with chocolate. Confused by the blackboard description, I asked the young woman behind the counter, who must have been about twenty-one years old, about its ingredients. "Are you watching calories or fat?" she asked, instead of telling me the ingredients. "Neither," I said. She looked bewildered for a moment, then must have decided she didn't hear me right. "Are you watching calories or fat?" she tried again. "Neither," I said, now grinning. I knew I appeared to her as a freak, and the other customers were beginning to regard me suspiciously, so I chose to bask in it.

American cuisine might be poised for greatness, but the question is: Are we Americans really equipped to enjoy it?

In the Preface to her 1995 book, *Endangered Pleasures,* author Barbara Holland described what happened after our fling with sex in the 1970s gave way to rampant fear of AIDS. "Now in the nineties," she wrote, "we're left to wring joy from the absence of joy, from denial, from counting grams of fat, jogging, drinking only bottled water and eating only broccoli. The rest of the time we work. A recent study informs us that Americans in 1994 worked 158 hours, or roughly a month, longer than we did in 1974." After reading that, I picked up the book with great excitement to see what Holland offered. As it turned out, she seemed to be trapped in the same Puritanical corset that has a stranglehold on most of us. Out of sixty-seven short essays, each describing an endangered pleasure, not one directly involved sex, not even the one titled "Bed," except for the sentence describing the perfect bed: "It should encourage sleep, love-making, reading, or television-watching . . ." Holland touched on food in only three essays ("Lunch," "Dinner," and "Seasonal Food"), but dinner she called "an obligatory meal." It seems food and sex as pleasures for Holland aren't merely endangered, they're extinct.

Food, however, has become part of the American vernacular—with a vengeance. We love to talk about food, love to gossip about chefs, love to read reviews in travel magazines of restaurants whose interiors we'll never see. We're probably as fascinated with the movements and habits of chefs as we are with Britain's royal family. The cover of Karen Gantz Zahler's 1997 cookbook *Superchefs* promises "Signature Recipes from America's New Royalty." Enough said.

When it comes to food, we're quick to embrace anything that's new and different, even if it's a mishmash. Americans love novelty; we love upheaval and change. It's manifested in our attitude toward politics and politicians. We love to throw out a whole Congress and elect a new one just for the sake of it. While other cultures revere age and experience in those who would lead them, Americans are suspicious of those too long in politics, so we propose term limit legislation, voicing the view that we should get them out of there and try someone new. We love youthful, handsome politicians the way we love youthful, handsome chefs and beautiful new dishes. Americans love the frontier, the pioneering spirit, invention. We honor chefs more for their creativity and originality than for perfection of execution.

While our love for what is new and different in food is borne out of our adventurous nature, it's also a symptom of our short attention span. Magazine editors always want to feature what's new and hot—who wants to read an article, they think, about a chef who's been at it for ten years and has finally hit her stride? It's also true that few editors at travel magazines or general interest magazines are real food people. But the result, as Joyce Goldstein points out, is that many young chefs garner lots of press before they're ready for it. It's a system that doesn't reward the steady development of a chef's career, and that can't help our fledgling cuisine come into its own.

American cuisine is still young. And as a culture, we don't have enough experience yet to be able to discern for ourselves what's good and what isn't. We're wowed by presentation, and by lots of different elements on a plate, yet most of us haven't yet calmed down enough to think about whether the flavors work together or whether any of it makes sense.

But somehow, despite everything, Americans intuitively understand something about good food: The marketplace works. Perhaps we don't know exactly why, but we do not keep returning to the restaurants that are not good. Usually. The restaurants doing crazy fusion are forced to do something real, or else they go out of business. No one voluntarily eats foie gras with mango, peaches, rosemary, and a port reduction twice. But we do want to eat perfectly cooked roast chicken and garlic mashed potatoes twice—and thrice and a hundred times. We're just like a one-year-old who has just learned how to walk: Mostly what we want to do is toddle around exploring this and that. Old toys are not interesting; anything new is fascinating. And then suddenly, all we can think of is running into Mommy's arms.

If the waiter in the Paris bistro who automatically pegged me for a hamburger hound had visited Los Angeles or Seattle or Miami or New York City—or any of a dozen or more other U.S. cities in the last five years—he'd never have made that crack. For even if we can be impressed by all the wrong things about a restaurant, this country has seen remarkable change in terms of the culinary sophistication of even the average person—so much so that what has happened here at least resembles a revolution.

Perhaps we still don't know how to relax, how to savor. One wonders when or whether we ever will.

Often it seems to me that what's happening here is not merely a love of food, an interest in gastronomy that we've come to embrace; rather it's a voraciousness that is purely American. When the founding fathers penned the Declaration of Independence, they settled on a major edit in the original text, changing the ultimate birthright of Americans from the pursuit of "property" to "the pursuit of happiness." The authors of the Declaration foresaw something significant about Americans and the American character, and it's fitting that "the pursuit of happiness" won out over our more Puritanical streak. Similarly, it looks as though the pursuit of pleasure is winning out over the more austere attitudes about how we nourish ourselves. And we feel we're entitled to pursue all that wonderful, tremendous variety.

In a similar vein, one of the things that has always made American society such a dynamic one is the tension between democracy and individual liberty—two ideals with an uneasy alliance, since often the goals of one stand opposed to the aims of the other. We're free to express ourselves as we will, to pursue the career of our choice, to practice whatever religion we believe in—that's individual liberty. But the framers of the Constitution also worried about the tyranny of a minority—that the rights of individuals posed a threat to the majority—and that's why our governmental structure is filled with checks and balances.

The same tension is played out in the realm of our cookery: The tuna melt of the diner, *Joy of Cooking* meatloaf, the McDonald's hamburger—democratic food, as it were—these are the polar opposite of tall food, of the nine-course tasting menu, of Hudson Valley foie gras and Michigan morels—the food of individual liberty and of privilege. Yet here it's the democratic food that threatens the food of privilege. When the industrialization and commercialization of our food supply at the end of the nineteenth century allowed people to eat vegetables and fruits they hadn't had access to before, that was positive—and democratic. Yet the canned string beans and frozen broccoli they gained were a far cry from the fresh versions those wealthy enough to afford them could enjoy thanks to the interstate transportation system that developed around the same time—that was individual liberty. Likewise, in the nineteenth century, only the affluent could afford to eat lettuce. This wasn't right: It wasn't democratic. So iceberg lettuce was developed, and as a result, everyone could have lettuce. Inferior lettuce. In both cases the democratic, and, incidentally, inferior alternative supplanted the preferable choice.

In other countries, great cuisines have depended upon the presence of an aristocracy or a nobility to develop. It's true of France, whose *grande cuisine* was developed at court, of Italy, whose *cucina alta* evolved in noble kitchens, and of China, for outside of the mandarins' banquets the poorer part of the nation has subsisted primarily on rice.

In the United States, although we don't have an aristocracy per se, we do have economic and cultural elites. And increasingly, gastronomy is a realm in which these elites like to express themselves. Our elites are less and less drawn to literature, to music, to theater, and more and more to the table, the kitchen, the wine cellar. Thus in 1995 Oprah Winfrey flew a well-known restaurant critic on her private jet to Europe so he might show her all of his very favorite eating spots. And one of the favorite pastimes of the well-heeled is the cooking-school-as-vacation—in 1997 Ed Bradley traveled to Florence to take a cooking course with Giuliano Bugialli.

One of the most prestigious of these cooking schools is that of Lorenza de Medici—whom one notes is a member of Italy's aristocracy, and interestingly in terms of food history, a descendant of Catherine de Medici, the woman who kick-started France's rise to gastronomic power by bringing a number of ingredients and top cooks there from Italy in 1533. But the topper is L'Ecole des Chefs. If accepted, applicants pay $2,450 (plus transportation and accommodation) for the privilege of spending five or six days as an intern at a Michelin three-star restaurant in France, working eight- to twelve-hour days in the kitchen.

Even though we read less, in the last fifteen years we've grown tremendously in a certain kind of cultural sophistication. In fashion, for example, it used to be that New York followed Paris and Milan, and other American cities were either a couple years behind New York or not fashionable at all. When I left Los Angeles in 1986, there was no fashion sense in that city, not even in Hollywood. Now Paris follows New York, and not only does Los Angeles not lag behind, it creates its own style—as do smaller cities such as Seattle and Minneapolis. As a society, we're a lot less geeky than we used to be.

Travel plays a big part in our growing sophistication. Being sophisticated today means having traveled and knowing what other cultures have long known about food and its role in culture. Culinary sophistication means having a seasoned palate, and slowly but surely we're gaining seasoning.

Back in November 1977, just as America was beginning to awaken to the possibilities of food in our lives, an article in the *New York Times* titled "Narcissism in the 'Me Decade' " appeared alongside a piece cataloging all the fancy food gifts available that holiday season (Sheila Lukins and Julee Rosso had just opened their gourmet shop, The Silver Palate, and were offering "exquisite plump and colorful apricots, prunes, oranges and lemon slices in a port-wine compote packed in stunning glass apothecary jars . . .").

The "me decade" in fact lasted two decades: probably until about the time the stock market crashed in 1989. These two decades correspond exactly with the time span in which the most intense evolution in American eating habits was going on. Maybe we had to spend some time thinking about ourselves, indulging, breaking out of our Puritan shackles and democratic limitations long enough to get something going.

Who prepares our food also says a lot about who we are, or at least about our attitudes toward food. Before the 1980s, becoming a cook or even a chef was something that no one of a certain class, that is the professional classes and upper classes, would ever consider. It was a *trade,* like being an auto mechanic or secretary. And people of these classes aspired to university, not trade school.

Women cooked at home, men barbecued, and lower middle class men, French guys, and other immigrants worked as cooks.

Now cooking is a glamour profession. Mark Miller, Alice Waters, and Robert Del Grande paved the way for academics to make their place in the kitchen; today doctors and lawyers, unsatisfied with their careers, are flocking to cooking schools looking for a different kind of life. Martha Stewart was an institutional stockbroker before she became a caterer.

Partly this is because we've come to see cooking as an art form, not just a craft. And it's respectable for members of the upper middle class to apply themselves to an art, whereas it's not as socially impressive to engage in a craft.

So *is* cooking an art form? It would be impossible to make the blanket statement that it always is—flipping a burger at a diner isn't usually art. Yet few would argue that what David Bouley and Thomas Keller and Jean-Georges Vongerichten and many other chefs are making is not art. Unlike most of the other plastic arts, though, their art is destroyed—consumed—almost immediately after its creation. In this sense cooking is more like one of the performing arts. Once a song has been performed live, that performance is gone forever (unless it's been recorded); likewise, once an actor has performed a soliloquy from *Hamlet,* it's gone. But much as the written music may still exist or the script from a play may still exist, the chef may produce a recipe that's permanent. It's not the same thing as the original creation, the original dish, however; it's just a skeleton, a sketch. Once someone else executes the recipe, it changes somewhat; and in fact it's even unlikely that Thomas Keller turns it out exactly the same way the next time he cooks it.

Art has also come to mean an expression of self, therefore I'd argue that home cooks who put their heart into what they're doing are making art, even if they're not inventing new dishes. The *Oxford English Dictionary* gives the following as its primary definition of art: "Skill in doing anything as the result of knowledge and practice." Applying this definition would make our hamburger flipper an artist, though most of us wouldn't consider him one. Closer, probably, would be the *OED*'s fifth definition: "The application of skill to subjects of taste, as poetry, music, dancing, oratory, literary composition, and the like. . . . Skill displaying itself in perfection of workmanship, perfection of execution as an object in itself." Of course much of cooking is technique, but so too is there technique in painting, in photography, in writing. There's craft in every art.

Cooking can also be an act of love. When I spend a half hour cutting fine julienne from a dozen vegetables and braising them in homemade chicken stock for my difficult-to-please toddler, that's love. Especially when there's a fifty-fifty chance he'll turn away from it in displeasure. Everyone knows the way to a man's heart is through his stomach. And to someone who loves to cook, doing so for one's friends may feel like an expression of love. I'm constitutionally unable to cook for someone I don't like.

It can also be an act of seduction. The image of the single man cooking the fabulous dinner for his date, complete with candlelight and wonderful wine has even become cliché. Within the phrase "wining and dining" is the implication of ulterior motive, whether it's on the part of a firm trying to recruit a smart young associate or the would-be lover trying to win over the object of his or her desire.

For many food lovers, even eating is an art. M. F. K. Fisher called her collected essays *The Art of Eating.*

One variety of fervent food lover is the "foodie"—whose ascent we saw in the 1980s. The foodie—the person who, whatever his or her profession, makes it his business to know about food—cooks it, keeps up on the newest ingredients, knows who's who at the farmers' market, follows chefs from kitchen to kitchen. Besides artists in music, dance, theater, and film, what other admired profession has groupies? Doctors: Lawyers? Certainly not. No doubt we treat chefs as artists, not artisans, and food not as craft, but art.

POSTSCRIPT

INTO THE MILLENNIUM

At century's end, America seems to be drifting away from things sensual in favor of things cerebral—or at any rate, things cyber. We've become more abstract, our minds move faster, our eyes flit about, our attention span is shorter, and one wonders if taking pleasure in dining can really be compatible with that.

Yet sensuality is far from dead, and today even those who have despaired of having sex are suddenly whistling a happy tune. As I waited to cross a street near my house the other day, a man stopped his car at the intersection, honking his horn wildly and yelling out the window for anyone who would listen, "I tried Viagra last night. Hooray!" Perhaps our taboo against sex is wearing thin, and perhaps we'll begin once again to allow ourselves pleasure in general. That could only be a good thing for gastronomy.

In the meantime, for all our talk about New American

this and regional American that, what kind of progress have we actually made? All these wonderful foodstuffs may be available, but does the fact that we're buying mesclun at the supermarket instead of iceberg lettuce really mean that Americans are eating any better?

"They've learned more," says Joyce Goldstein. "They know what couscous and polenta are now, which they didn't years ago. . . . The quality of produce is improved a great deal. But you look and see what's in people's carts. You look and see. For every fresh vegetable, there's forty-two packaged things in there. Or frozen food. I'm not optimistic. There will always be certain people who are interested in food. It's important to them. But to the vast American public, I don't think it's important . . ."

And though it's now easy to find mesclun and broccoli rabe and organic milk, some good basic ingredients are increasingly difficult to find. Butcher shops are disappearing. I'm lucky enough to have a real butcher shop in my neighborhood. But the only rabbits they have are frozen. Forget about duck breast, quails, or other meats that one finds easily in restaurants now. I suppose I should be thankful that there's always a good supply of lamb shanks, which *The New York Times* recently proclaimed are impossible to find at butchers since the restaurants snap them all up. And though *this* place frequently sells hangar steak, it can be notoriously difficult to find for the same reason. At my fishmonger in the late spring a sign goes up boasting "Jumbo Soft-Shell Crabs." I spoke with the proprietor, asking if he could get some small ones, since they're sweeter and more delicious. "No," he said. "No one wants those. Jumbo are better." This mentality is holding us back a little.

And we don't know the sources of much of our food. Last summer, my local greengrocer offered a display of Santa Rosa plums, my favorite variety. Since I come from California, I know well what they are: smallish, deeply creased, deep purple when ripe. The interior is soft, sweet, and yellowish, tinged with red from the deliciously tart skin. For the first few weeks of the season, I was in heaven with my plums. Then, although the sign announcing "Santa Rosa Plums" stayed on the display, the greengrocer replaced the Santa Rosas with another variety of plums—hard, purple-black, flavorless.

In France, if a market stall has three kinds of strawberries, they all will be clearly identified by variety and place of origin—one as *fraise ronde* (round strawberry) from Spain, another as *gariguette* from Agen, and the third *Mara des bois* from Périgord. Everyone knows that the *Mara des bois,* which is a new, highly perfumed variety that resembles *fraise des bois,* are the best and that the Spanish strawberries are large and relatively flavorless. Many foods are also subject to laws similar to the *appellation contrôlée* laws for wine. Cheeses have their special names; you can't get a Tomme de Savoie that was made in Provence. Even vegetables such as lentils—*lentilles du Puy*—are controlled.

In the United States, outside of farmers' markets and a handful of enlightened food stores, produce is often incorrectly identified or not identified at all regarding the place of origin. If we don't know where it was grown, not only can we not make informed judgments about the quality of flavor and texture, but we can't even be sure they're local or even from the United States. While the United States has come a long way in terms of labeling laws for packaged ingredients, we haven't even begun to address this issue when it comes to produce or meats.

And if we care about either what chemicals are used to grow our produce or the farmers' attention to safe food handling or even the environmental ramifications of trucking strawberries from Mexico or jetting in grapes from Chile, we're out of luck. I was amazed last year, on a cold December day, to take note of a small brouhaha outside of my greengrocer's. Strawberries at $4.99 a pint? someone was saying, astonished and outraged. "You dope!" I wanted to say. "They're out of season and have to be jetted in from a foreign country."

On the positive side, farmers' markets keep growing in number, size, and the variety they offer. And the bigger-is-better myth doesn't hold sway at the markets. On a recent late spring market day here in Brooklyn, a woman sampling Long Island strawberries next to me remarked with some surprise that although they were small, they were full of flavor. She happily bought two quart baskets. The San Francisco Ferry Plaza Market has big plans to expand and transform itself into a covered market modeled after the one in Florence, Italy, eventually opening for business seven days a week. Shopping at farmers' markets will likely become a way of life for more and more Americans, and as it does, the general quality of what Americans can eat if they choose will improve—one hopes at least at the same rate the fast-food chains continue to expand.

I do think our cuisine will calm down and develop sanely. Crazy fusions have short half-lives. An American cuisine will continue to grow, and one day will be a mature cuisine. One of the best things that can happen in American cuisine is for a chef to be so proud of a dish that he or she claims it as his or her own creation, whether or not it is. It's positive because it's a measure of how good a dish is, and the quality of a dish will determine its likelihood of becoming a permanent addition to the American repertoire. It has started happening in the past ten years or so—molten chocolate cake comes to mind. This is a very positive sign.

We'll discover the one or two cuisines we might have overlooked; new fusions will develop. At the moment, the cuisine of India is garnering interest and Indian-French fusion is on the lips of foodies. I predict an interest in spices—not just chilies, but cardamom, saffron, cumin, and so forth—will come to the fore. I also imagine that we'll become more and more adept at using herbs to build layers of flavor, both in restaurants and at home. As we exhaust what used to seem like an endless world of ingredients to discover, we'll learn to focus on complementary flavors rather than throwing a bunch of elements together helter-skelter.

And people who care about food will come to care more about wine. I also predict that American wines will eventually move away from their overblown style and begin to emphasize qualities that add to the synergy between food and wine.

Fortunately, there are a great number of food professionals and others working toward improving the way Americans eat.

Oldways Preservation and Trust, a nonprofit organization dedicated to encouraging the preservation of traditional foodways throughout the world, founded Chef's Collaborative 2000 in 1993. The Collaborative is a group of more than a thousand chefs; its mission is to develop and encourage sustainable food choices for the next century. It sponsors educational programs for children, teaching them to cook, appreciate foods from around the world, and understand where their food comes from. The Collaborative's chefs are "committed to advancing sustainable agriculture by buying locally grown produce and by designing their menus around seasonally fresh foods."

Community-supported agriculture, a nascent movement, is also growing. In some programs, youths from low-income areas are planting vegetable gardens and selling their harvests to members who subscribe. In others, community members pool together to support one particular farm, receiving deliveries of organic produce each week from that farm.

Alice Waters has been very politically active, trying to bring Edible Schoolyard, her wonderful gardening in the schools program, to a wider public. Children are naturally curious about how food grows and how it is prepared. As the imperative grows to teach science in a meaningful way, I think we'll find that the garden and the kitchen are fabulous laboratories of practical application. My only specific memory from kindergarten is the day our teacher brought in a jar of heavy cream, passed it around the room, letting us each give it a few good shakes. At last it became butter, which we gleefully spread on crackers and ate. What magic in that transformation! To this day it remains the single most powerful thing I learned in school.

One thing I'm fairly sure we can look forward to is the widening availability of organic produce, which is not just a silly whim of consumers who, as some in agribusiness have suggested, want to "have it all." Industry watchers predict that in the twenty-first century "organic" will become the most important word in our food vocabulary.

In 1996, Jean-Claude Vrinat, owner of Michelin three-star Taillevent in Paris, chose to celebrate the restaurant's fiftieth anniversary in, of all places, New York, at Gramercy Tavern. ". . . Taillevent's cuisine changes almost not at all," wrote Molly O'Neill after the fact. "The restaurant prepares dishes . . . that would have been familiar to the fourteenth-century gourmand for whom the restaurant is named." She went on:

> This path to perfection has interesting ramifications for America, where constant change is a national obsession. By choosing an American restaurant to salute both his French and American patrons, Vrinat has acknowledged that American cooking has come a long way. Whether we can go the distance, and accept tedium and repetition as the route to transcendence, will be interesting to see.

Repetition, we can certainly handle—we do keep coming back, not only to many traditional preparations and spins on them, but also to some new "classics." Americans, on the other hand, will never stand for tedium; fortunately, it doesn't seem necessary.

We have an opportunity to go beyond the ingredient revolution and venture more profoundly into the world of flavor, and to look beyond French technique and learn techniques from cuisines such as China's or India's, as opposed to just borrowing their ingredients.

Perhaps one day we'll even return to the past, to an American past, and relearn the joys of ripe fruit in season, vegetables that taste like something. With luck we'll come to understand that we don't need to fly asparagus in from Chile or red peppers in from Holland just to have some color on the plate in midwinter.

Some chefs and journalists worry that the globalization of gastronomy will continue until all we're left with is one cuisine. "Something that will more or less become standardized," as Wayne Nish puts it, "almost the way hotel food in the fifties and sixties became the same throughout the entire world." Young chefs, he explains, are picking up whisks and knives in Australia and reading about what chefs in New York, London, or Hong Kong are doing and imitating it. "I think it's contributing to a new international style," he says, "and I don't know that it's all that good. I fear that it could result in a sameness and at the same time a loss of the regional characters that were so strong and so identifiable, so great."

Still, when it comes to the basics, there's much to be accomplished gastronomically in the United States. With bread, cheese, and wine—in many cultures the heart of every meal—we've only just started. We should have some exciting times ahead.

Our best hope is to get people back into their kitchens—

not to amass a million ingredients and spend two days making Veal Orloff, but briefly, to make something simple and delicious—*something that tastes like what it is.* As more and more people start shopping at the farmers' market, meeting those who grow their food, smelling herbs, tasting ripe fruit; as high-quality organic produce becomes more widely available in supermarkets, to do so will become easier and more natural. To make food that tastes like what it is can be easily accomplished, with minimal effort, if the product is good.

Can we even sit at table as long as it takes to truly enjoy a meal? That's the challenge. Certainly there are more and more Americans who are living on fast food and microwaved entrées, and it seems for many of us that we have less and less leisure time. But for some years family has become increasingly important to this culture. I believe that the concepts of family and good food are not only compatible, but that we'll come to see them as inseparable. While many believe that the fate of good food in America is tied up with the frenetic pace of our society and is therefore doomed, I believe that on the contrary, the fate of good food is tied up inextricably with the notion of family.

And if family is to thrive, we're bound to slow down, to embrace the ideal of eating well. Of dining.

NOTES

INTRODUCTION

PUBLISHED AND OTHER SOURCES

p. 3 **more than a third of Americans are obese** Nicholas Wade, "Genetic Cause Found for Some Cases of Human Obesity," *New York Times,* 24 June 1997.

p. 7 **. . . the earliest settlers** John L. Hess and Karen Hess, *The Taste of America,* 224.

p. 7 **Americans are one more generation removed** Ibid., xv.

CHAPTER 1
HOW WE LOST GASTRONOMY

PUBLISHED AND OTHER SOURCES

pp. 11–12 **sometimes a single crab was large enough to feed a family of four** Editors of *American Heritage, The Magazine of History, The American Heritage Cookbook and Illustrated History of American Eating and Drinking,* 16.

p. 12 **strawberries much superior to those in England** Ibid., 14.

p. 12 **they pit-cooked beans** Waverly Root and Richard de Rochemont, *Eating in America: A History,* 31.

p. 12 **they roasted peanuts** Ibid., 31.

p. 12 **it was the Cherokees who invented** Ibid., 29.

p. 12 **thinking them fit only for hog feed** Ibid., 52.

p. 13 **"a superb piece of corned beef"** Jean-Anthèlme Brillat-Savarin, *The Physiology of Taste,* trans. Anne Drayton, 77–78.

p. 13 **the city's chefs had access** Kay Shaw Nelson, "Philadelphia's Culinary Heritage," *Gourmet* (March 1976): 32.

p. 13 **"In the eighteenth century housewives were"** Waverly Root, "Early American Cookery," *Gourmet* (February 1976): 21.

p. 13 **they infused it with horseradish** Ibid., 21.

p. 13 **the colonies were consuming the second greatest amount** Sidney W. Mintz, *Sweetness and Power: The Place of Sugar in Modern History,* 188.

p. 14 **"was a cuisine which, even excluding desserts"** Harvey Levenstein, *Revolution at the Table: The Transformation of the American Diet,* 7.

p. 14 **"every other wild animal."** Quoted in Dale Brown and the Editors of Time-Life Books, *American Cooking,* 41.

p. 14 **As far as he was concerned** Ibid., 42.

p. 14 **"macaroni, Parmesan cheese"** Ibid., 42.

p. 14 **Jefferson's wine habit** Marion Burros, "Monday's Menu Looks to Virginia and Mr. Jefferson," *New York Times,* 15 January 1997.

p. 15 **wild turkeys, ducks** Brown, *American Cooking,* 51.

p. 15 **the food served in private homes** Root and de Rochemont, *Eating,* 313.

p. 16 **he complained that European butter had no salt** Evan Jones, "Mark Twain," in *The American Heritage Cookbook,* 62.

p. 16 **frogs** Ibid., 370–71.

p. 16 **first patent for tin cans** Root and de Rochemont, *Eating,* 158.

p. 17 **"The decline of a nation commences"** Levenstein, *Revolution,* 93.

p. 17 **he created a breakfast cereal** Michelle Stacey, *Consumed: Why Americans Love, Hate, and Fear Food,* 14.

p. 17 **Cheerios, America's biggest-selling cereal** Patrick Henry Bass, "Open Box, Pour Cereal, Add Milk. Call It Dinner," *New York Times,* 18 June 1997.

p. 17 **Americans have increased their dinner-time cereal consumption** Ibid.

p. 17 **William James and his brother Henry James** Levenstein, *Revolution,* 87.

p. 17 **published by the Department of Agriculture** Laura Shapiro, *Perfection Salad: Woman and Cooking at the Turn of the Century,* 74.

p. 18 **"Elaborate methods of food preparation"** Levenstein, *Revolution,* 83.

p. 18 **"This was the era"** Shapiro, *Perfection Salad,* 3–4.

p. 19 **"Peas and beans"** *The Boston Cooking School Magazine* (October/November 1899): 166.

p. 19 **"Bread should be toasted"** Ibid., 168.

p. 20 **the first boxcar of fresh fruit** Levenstein, *Revolution,* 31.

p. 20 **In 1894 the eighteen-year-old W. Atlee Burpee Company** James Trager, *The Food Chronology,* 344.

p. 20 **accessible only to the relatively wealthy** Levenstein, *Revolution,* 31.

p. 20 **it is she we can thank for the sweet orange goop** Shapiro, *Perfection Salad,* 204.

p. 21 **"It's got many of the attributes"** Stephanie Pierson, "Seeing Red," *Saveur* (January/February 1995): 38.

pp. 21–22 **With the Crisco white sauce** Shapiro, *Perfection Salad,* 215.

p. 22 **depends on vegetable shortening** Julia Child, Louisette Bertholle, and Simone Beck, *Mastering the Art of French Cooking,* 139.

p. 22 **"The same forces"** Harvey Levenstein, *Paradox of Plenty: A Social History of Eating in Modern America,* 27.

p. 22 **Milk, cheese, and green vegetables** Ibid.

p. 23 **General Foods introduced Birds Eye** Jean Anderson, *The American Century Cookbook,* 239.

p. 24 **20 million victory gardens produced 40 percent of the vegetables** Evan Jones, *Epicurean Delight: The Life and Times of James Beard,* 114.

p. 24 **In 1945 American consumption of vegetables hit a record high** Levenstein, *Paradox,* 88.

p. 26 **Locke-Ober's, began to use frozen foods** Levenstein, *Paradox,* 128.

p. 26 **Ray Kroc opened the first McDonald's** McDonald's web site, www.mcdonalds.com; INTERNET.

CHAPTER 2
WHY JULIA CHILD CAPTURED OUR IMAGINATION

INTERVIEWS

Joseph Baum, interview by author, 5 December 1997.

Barbara Pascal, interview by author, 19 November 1997.

Michael Whiteman and Rozanne Gold, interview by author, 21 January 1998.

Judy Marcus, interview by author, 13 August 1997.

Chuck Williams, interview by author, 11 July 1995.

PUBLISHED AND OTHER SOURCES

p. 30 **"sitting primly at table"** Editors of *Esquire,* "Outdoor Hospitality," insert 2, *Esquire's Handbook for Hosts.*

p. 30 **"Another weighty vote"** Ibid.

p. 30 ***Betty Crocker's Picture Cookbook* sold well** Robert Clark, *James Beard: A Biography,* 159.

p. 31 **"There was a notion among youths . . ."** Douglas Dales, "Future of Chefs Is Served up as Woe; Food Experts Find Few Taking Up Art," *New York Times,* 1 September 1957.

p. 32 **bemoaning the death of elegance in cuisine.** Craig Claiborne, "Elegance of Cuisine Is on Wane in U.S.," *New York Times,* 13 April 1959.

p. 32 **(fn) took issue with the idea that Pierre Franey** Hess and Hess, *Taste of America,* 62.

p. 32 **(fn) "It may be doubted that the late Henri Soulé"** Ibid., 204.

p. 33 **100,000 in its first year of publication** Noël Riley Fitch, *Appetite for Life: The Biography of Julia Child,* 292.

p. 35 **"food had indeed attained nearly epic seriousness"** Clark, *James Beard,* 180.

p. 37 **filet of sole amandine** Trager, *Food Chronology,* 555.

p. 37 **"a reformed vegetarian"** Alan Hooker, *Alan Hooker's New Approach to Cooking,* 48.

p. 37 **The Ranch House opened in 1950** Alan Hooker, *California Herb Cookery: From the Ranch House Restaurant,* 6.

p. 38 **relied heavily on "silantro"** Hooker, *Alan Hooker's New Approach,* 255.

p. 38 **Craig Claiborne, who had been hired two years earlier** Clark, *James Beard,* 180.

p. 38 **"perhaps the most exciting restaurant"** Craig Claiborne, "Food News: Dining in Elegant Manner," *New York Times,* 2 October 1959.

p. 39 **"the first really seasonal restaurant"** James Beard, *Love and Kisses and a Halo of Truffles: Letters to Helen Evans Brown,* ed. John Ferrone, 248.

p. 41 **"Oak leaf lettuce, cos salad and Bibb"** Claiborne, "Food News: Dining in Elegant Manner," *New York Times,* 2 October 1959.

p. 41 **"I believe in making stroganoff"** Quoted in Robert Sheehan, "Four Seasons: A Flourish of Food," *Fortune,* February 1960: 213.

p. 45 **Beard's first article appeared in 1942** Clark, *James Beard,* 124.

p. 45 **by 1948 he was a regular contributor** Ibid., 123.

p. 45 **succeeded in landing one in the spring of 1949** Ibid., 124.

p. 45 **he lost the job less than a year later** Ibid., 135.

p. 46 **"No vegetable exists which is not better slightly undercooked."** Quoted in Jones, *Epicurean Delight,* 242.

p. 46 **early American cooks such as Mary Randolph** Karen Hess (lecture presented at a meeting of Culinary Historians of New York), 28 April 1998.

p. 46 **"Cook vegetables as short a time as possible."** Irma S. Rombauer, *The Joy of Cooking: A Facsimile of the First Edition,* 94.

p. 47 **"Last year, for example"** James Beard, *Delights and Prejudices: A Memoir with Recipes,* 318.

p. 49 **"Maybe French chefs"** Ted Patrick and Silas Spitzer, *Great Restaurants of America,* 286.

p. 50 **The signs in this country** Ibid.

p. 50 **"We can no longer depend upon"** "California Acts to Better Cruisine," *New York Times,* 27 August 1961.

p. 50 **"When you get a cook now, he doesn't know the difference between sauce bearnaise and cherries jubilee."** Ibid.

p. 51 **The White House had been accused** "Envoy's Chef Spurns Call to White House," *New York Times,* 23 February 1961.

p. 51 **"The menu was seasonal"** Craig Claiborne, "White House Hires French Chef," *New York Times,* 7 April 1961.

p. 52 **the meal began with New England Clam Chowder** René Verdon, *The White House Chef Cookbook,* 149–50.

CHAPTER 3
REGULAR FISH AND SACRED COWS

INTERVIEWS

Julia Child, interviews by author, 14 August 1995; 23 June 1997.

Susan Stamberg, interview by author, 5 December 1997.

Barbara Pascal, interview by author, 19 November 1997.

Barbara Kafka, interviews by author, 20 August 1997; 26 August 1997.

Jo Brans, interview by author, 22 May 1997.

Joyce Goldstein, interview by author, 10 September 1996.

Gloria Burg, interview by author, 8 August 1997.

Chuck Williams, interview by author, 11 July 1995.

Chip Fisher, interview by author, 14 August 1995.

Laura Furman, interview by author, 25 August 1997.

PUBLISHED AND OTHER SOURCES

p. 57 **her roast duck exploded in the oven** Fitch, *Appetite for Life,* 130.

p. 58 **Bertholle's participation was limited** Ibid., 330–31.

p. 58 **under contract to Ives Washburn** Ibid., 196.

p. 58 **insisted they find an American** Ibid., 197.

p. 59 **Washburn and Les Trois Gourmandes parted ways** Ibid., 198.

p. 59 **Avis DeVoto got the book to Boston publisher Houghton Mifflin** Joan Reardon, *M. F. K. Fisher, Julia Child and Alice Waters: Celebrating the Pleasures of the Table,* 126.

p. 59 **sent them a contract along with a $200 advance** Fitch, *Appetite for Life,* 198.

p. 59 **her manuscript, which by the end of 1957 consisted of over 700 pages** Ibid., 241.

p. 59 **in which Bertholle would receive 18 percent** Ibid., 221.

p. 59 **"We are not going to publish an encyclopedia"** Ibid., 241.

p. 59 **too costly to publish in relation to its projected sales** Reardon, *M. F. K. Fisher, Julia Child,* 140.

p. 59 **to a connection at Knopf** Ibid., 140.

p. 60 **"As nobody else could do as well"** Jones, *Epicurean Delight,* 258.

p. 60 **"I think the Knopf book is wonderful"** James Beard, *Love and Kisses,* 295.

p. 60 **reviewers all across the country soon followed suit** Jones, *Epicurian Delight,* 258.

p. 60 **In the first five years it sold 300,000 copies,** Editors of *Time,* "Everyone's in the Kitchen," *Time* (25 November 1966): 74.

p. 60 **the first hardcover edition would go on to sell 650,000 copies** Karen Lehrman, "What Julia Started," *U.S. News & World Report* (22 September 1997): 58.

p. 61 **"food B.C.—Before Child"** "Julia Child," written and narrated by Susan Stamberg, *Morning Edition,* National Public Radio, WNYC, 15 August 1997.

p. 61 **"We ate this . . . the night Josh was born"** Ibid.

p. 62 **"Under Julia's tutelage . . ."** Jo Brans, *Feast Here Awhile: Adventures in American Eating,* 58.

p. 62 **"There probably never has been . . . this decade."** Craig Claiborne, *New York Times Cookbook,* ix.

p. 63 **"really in the 'business' of food"** Fitch, *Appetite for Life,* 318.

p. 63 **choosing to believe** Ibid.

p. 64 **plugging Pepperidge Farm** Hess and Hess, *Taste of America,* 62–63.

p. 64 **thinly disguised, pilfered** Ibid., 139.

p. 64 **inauthentic** Ibid., 150.

p. 64 **inaccurate** Ibid., 160.

p. 64 **cartoonishly mundane** Ibid., 159.

p. 64 **using flour to excess in sauce recipes** Ibid., 153, 162.

p. 64 **"The same old library paste, *ad nauseam*"** Ibid., 162.

p. 64 **bad advice about cooking with wine** Ibid., 163.

p. 64 **"the gourmet plague"** Ibid., 164 and elsewhere.

p. 64 **fondness for Golden Delicious apples** Ibid., 44.

p. 64 **aspics made with gelatin** Ibid., 182.

p. 64 **McDonald's French fries** Ibid., 199.

p. 64 **canned broth** Ibid., 183.

p. 64 **calling herself "The French Chef"** Ibid., 174.

p. 66 **"Les Eschalottes"** *Gourmet* (November 1967): 113.

p. 73 **"By all means"** George and Virginie Elbert, *Simple Cooking for Sophisticates,* 99.

p. 73 **"Homemade Butter"** Ibid., 47.

p. 74 **Bazaar Français had been offering** George Dullea, "Culinary Landmark Closes," *New York Times,* 22 August 1975.

p. 75 **"From here on in"** Ibid.

p. 79 **The cover story** Karen Lehrman, "What Julia Started," *U.S. News and World Report,* 22 September 1997.

CHAPTER 4
XENOPHOBES NO MORE: THE FOREIGN INFLUENCE

INTERVIEWS

Vavy Kittivech, interview by author, 10 February 1998.

Karen Hess, interview by author, 6 June 1998.

Barbara Kafka, interviews by author, 20 August 1997; 26 August 1997.

Caroline Bates, interview by author, 14 December 1997.

Judy Marcus, interview by author, 13 August 1997.

Warren Winston, Esq., interview by author, 30 January 1997.

An-My Lê, interview by author, 1 June 1998.

Michael McCarty, interview by author, 3 April 1996.

Rozanne Gold and Michael Whiteman, interview by author, 21 January 1998.

Roy Yamaguchi, interview by author, 13 February 1998.

Allen Susser, interview by author, 24 January 1996.

Norman Van Aken, interview by author, 26 January 1996.

Juanita Plana, interview by author, 24 January 1996.

Carole Kotkin, interview by author, 24 January 1996.

PUBLISHED AND OTHER SOURCES

p. 86 **In the sixteenth century** Maguelonne Toussaint-Samat, *History of Food,* 83.

p. 86 **at least the dish appears** Karen Hess, *Martha Washington's Booke of Cookery,* 87–88.

p. 86 **as was the cookie *(koekje)*** Karen Hess, Introduction to *American Cookery* by Amelia Simmons, xi.

p. 86 **frankfurters were German *wienerwurst*** Jean Anderson, *American Century Cookbook,* 351.

p. 87 **"The forerunner is believed to be Steak Tartare"** Ibid., 348.

p. 87 **(fn) in 1619** Jessica B. Harris, *The Welcome Table: African-American Heritage Cooking,* 25.

p. 87 **beginning before the Pilgrims** Ibid.

p. 87 **a number of "culinary tendencies"** Ibid., 21–22.

p. 87 ***Tchingombo,* Umbundu for "okra"** Ibid., 19.

p. 88 **"The Africans brought . . ."** Joe Randall and Toni Tipton-Martin, *A Taste of Heritage: The New African-American Cuisine,* xiii.

p. 88 **They overcame adversity** Ibid.

p. 88 **"Wherever African-Americans did the cooking"** Karen Hess, *The Carolina Rice Kitchen: The African Connection,* 5.

p. 89 **spaghetti and macaroni** Harvey Levenstein, *Paradox of Plenty,* 122.

p. 89 **Throughout the 1950s** Maldwyn Allen Jones, *American Immigration,* 265.

p. 90 **". . . the most distinctive"** Michael and Ariane Batterberry, *On the Town in New York: From 1776 to the Present,* 220–21.

p. 90 **Italian, German** Ibid., 219–22.

p. 90 **they were produced outside** Anderson, *American Century,* 161; and Trager, *Food Chronology,* 451.

p. 91 **first recorded mention** Trager, Ibid., 451.

p. 91 **bagels only appeared** Grace Lichtenstein, "Taming Szechwan Food in Hashbrown Country," *New York Times,* 24 August, 1976.

p. 92 **San Francisco had boasted** Doris Muscatine, *A Cook's Tour of San Francisco,* 284.

p. 92 **6,000 Japanese residents** Ibid., 286.

p. 92 **weren't any Japanese restaurants to speak of** Ibid.

p. 92 **except Yamato** Ibid., 289.

pp. 92–93 **Julia Child's husband Paul** Fitch, *Appetite for Life,* 225–26.

p. 93 **"a Japanese dish resembling eggs foo yung."** Helen Evans Brown, *Helen Evans Brown's West Coast Cook Book,* 173.

p. 93 **Japanese cookery is becoming** Ibid.

p. 94 **"In San Francisco today"** Muscatine, *A Cook's Tour,* 287.

p. 94 **Sukiyaki, teriyaki** Jacqueline Killeen, ed., and Roy Killeen, *101 Nights in California,* 27, 62.

p. 94 **San Francisco's Mingei-Ya** Ibid.

p. 94 **first sushi bar in New York in 1957** Jean Anderson, *American Century,* 313.

p. 94 **first sushi bar opened in Manhattan in 1963** James Trager, *Food Chronology,* 575.

p. 94 **Benihana** Ibid., 578.

p. 94 **Hiroaki "Rocky" Aoki** Ibid.

p. 95 **In California where the Chinese community** Maldwyn Allen Jones, *American Immigration,* 213.

p. 95 **Chinese Exclusion Act was repealed in 1946** United States Immigration and Naturalization Service Datebook Stastistics, INS web site, www.ins.usdog.gov/stats/index.html; INTERNET.

p. 95 **few lived in families** Leslie Brenner, "The New New York," *New York Woman,* (April 1991): 77.

p. 96 **more at home in Portugal** Margaret Visser, *The Rituals of Dinner: The Origins, Evolution, Eccentricities, and Meaning of Table Manners,* 143.

p. 96 **Kan's in San Francisco** Muscatine, *A Cook's Tour,* 103.

p. 96 **sliced abalone over Chinese ravioli** Ibid., 104.

p. 97 **Imperial Palace** Ibid., 109.

p. 97 **smoked tongue** Ibid.

p. 97 **sautéed shark fin** Ibid.

p. 97 **"You might have"** Ibid., 110.

p. 97 **In 1958, Boston saw** Trager, *Food Chronology,* 579.

p. 98 **"Today our people most recently from Mexico"** Helen Evans Brown, *West Coast,* 180–81.

p. 98 **"an authentic Mexican restaurant"** Michael and Ariane Batterberry, *On the Town,* 222.

p. 98 **James Beard made carnitas** Beard, *Love and Kisses,* 15.

p. 98 **He roasted the pork** Ibid., 364.

p. 100 **(fn) "Berkeley seemed to be"** Todd Gitlin, *The Sixties: Years of Hope, Days of Rage,* 209.

p. 100 **(fn) ". . . the Haight-Ashbury merchants"** Ibid., 208.

p. 101 **"Skin 1 or 2 eels"** James Beard, "Cooking with James Beard: Broiling and Grilling," *Gourmet* (February 1969): 56.

p. 101 **Quenelles with Shrimp Sauce** "Gourmet's Menus: Sunday Luncheons," *Gourmet* (August 1969): 40.

p. 102 **"I doubt there is another"** Donald Aspinwall Allan, "Spécialités de la Maison," *Gourmet* (August 1969): 7.

p. 102 **owner of a restaurant in Montana** Lichtenstein, "Taming Szechuan Food," 34.

p. 102 **one well-stocked wine shop** Ibid.

p. 102 **small carp and bacon in vinegar sauce** " 'Home on the Range' Spices the Three-Hour Banquet," *New York Times,* 22 February 1972.

p. 103 **"It is China's haute cuisine"** Jay Jacobs, *New York à La Carte,* 188–89.

p. 103 **"In the seventies we invented all these dishes"** Quoted in Ruth Reichl, "The Vanishing Haute Cuisine," *New York Times,* 17 June 1998.

p. 106 **"well-fried beans"** Diana Kennedy, *The Cuisines of Mexico,* 282.

p. 109 **We have all met the type** Caroline Bates, "Spécialités de la Maison: California," *Gourmet,* (January 1978): 12.

p. 110 **One way to blow his cover** Ibid.

p. 110 **fugu—blowfish** Jay Jacobs, "Spécialités de la Maison: New York," *Gourmet* (March 1977): 54

p. 112 **Tsunoda's family had been** Ellen Brown, *Cooking with the New American Chefs,* 31.

p. 112 **in the late 1970s Tsunoda** Ibid., 32.

p. 117 **"The change in the number"** Calvin Trillin, *The Tummy Trilogy: with a New Foreword,* xi.

CHAPTER 5
THE CALIFORNIA VISION

INTERVIEWS

Alice Waters, interview by author, 6 September 1996.

Rozanne Gold and Michael Whiteman, interview by author, 21 January 1998.

Michael McCarty, interview by author, 3 April 1996.

Caroline Bates, interview by author, 14 December 1997.

Lois Dwan, interview by author, 14 August 1997.

Sibella Krause, interview by author, 13 February 1998.

Rose Dosti, interview by author, 26 January 1996.

Margrit Biever, interview by author, 9 September 1996.

Robert Mondavi, interview by author, 9 September 1996.

Joseph Phelps, interview by author, 29 May 1998.

Joyce Goldstein, interview by author, 10 September 1996.

Roy Yamaguchi, interview by author, 13 February 1998.

PUBLISHED AND OTHER SOURCES

p. 126 **Delmonico family bought a piece of land** Lately Thomas, *Delmonico's: A Century of Splendor,* 23.

p. 127 **food that changed with the seasons** Caroline Bates, "Spécialités de la Maison: California," *Gourmet* (March 1974): 52–54.

p. 128 **Rosetta Clarkson who had been** Clementine Paddleford, *How America Eats,* 45.

p. 129 **"Rosetta Clarkson was an English teacher"** Ibid.

p. 129 **"There is always a good quiche"** Donald Aspinwall Allan, "Spécialités de la Maison," *Gourmet* (February 1970): 5.

p. 129 **"Never *à l'orange*"** Ibid., 6.

p. 130 **I recently enjoyed** Allan, "Spécialités de la Maison," *Gourmet* (August 1971): 8.

p. 135 **Henry David Thoreau was lamenting** James Trager, *Food Chronology,* 242.

p. 135 **founded by a French chef from New Orleans** Frances de Talavera Berger and John Parke Custis, *Sumptuous Dining in Gaslight San Francisco, 1875–1915,* 83.

p. 136 **first documented Chinese restaurant** Trager, *Food Chronology,* 243.

p. 136 **When the Poule d'Or changed** Berger and Custis, *Sumptuous Dining,* 83.

p. 136 **its gold-mining customers had fondly anglicized it** Doris Muscatine, *Cook's Tour,* 62.

p. 136 **frogs' legs** Berger and Custis, *Sumptuous Dining,* 83.

p. 136 **founded in 1864** Ibid., 136; Trager *Food Chronology,* 270.

p. 136 **Georges Voges** Trager, *Food Chronology,* 270.

p. 136 **Palace featured the far-superior** Helen Evans Brown, *West Coast,* 143.

p. 136 **Ernie's (opened in 1935)** Trager, *Food Chronology,* 482.

p. 137 **It's all very well** Lucius Beebe, "Along the Boulevards," *Gourmet* (October 1965): 13.

p. 137 **pleased with finding shad roe** Ibid.

p. 139 **"A rich food"** Helen Evans Brown, *West Coast,* 110.

p. 139 **"Avocados are a favored first course"** Ibid., 111.

p. 139 **"almost a staple with cocktails"** Ibid., 180.

p. 139 **"In fact, so devoted"** Ibid., 120.

p. 140 **"favorite combination"** Ibid., 137.

p. 140 **"one of the prizes of the Pacific"** Ibid., 158.

p. 140 **"one of California's most famous dishes"** Ibid., 173.

p. 147 **"We were declaring war"** Phillip S. Cooke, ed., *The Second Symposium on American Cuisine,* 22.

p. 147 **Number two, cook** Ibid., 22–23.

p. 151 **"did not like dishes finished by a *maître d'hôtel*"** Jean & Pierre Troisgros, *The Nouvelle Cuisine of Jean & Pierre Troisgros,* trans. Roberta Wolfe Smoler, 9.

p. 151 **"He did not like complicated platters"** Ibid.

p. 152 **"The list of French wines . . ."** Caroline Bates, "Spécialités de la Maison: California," *Gourmet* (March 1974): 14.

p. 152 **"When it comes to wines"** Caroline Bates, "Spécialités de la Maison," *Gourmet* (May 1974): 11.

p. 152 **"The only disappointments"** Ibid., *Gourmet* (September 1974): 10.

p. 153 **"California's winemakers"** Ibid.

p. 153 **"such rarefied labels as Joseph Swan Zinfandel"** Ibid.

CHAPTER 6
FOOD AS CHIC

INTERVIEWS

Philippe Boulot, interview by author, 11 June 1997.

Frieda Caplan, interview by author, 6 January 1998.

Erik Blauberg, interview by author, 27 May 1997.

PUBLISHED AND OTHER SOURCES

p. 164 **he complained** John Mariani, "Chef's Choice: Are tasting menus decadent displays or savory samplers?" *Diversion* (June 1997): 25.

p. 167 **"My pleasure in them"** M. F. K. Fisher, "Serve it Forth," in *The Art of Eating,* 27.

p. 168 **"Almost every person has something"** Ibid., 26.

p. 171 **"The same late-twentieth-century consumers"** J. M. Coetzee, "Meat Country," *Granta 52* (Winter 1995): 50.

p. 173 **Celery graced** Susan Williams, *Savory Suppers and Fashionable Feasts: Dining in Victorian America,* 110.

p. 173 **Oranges became fashionable** Ibid., 108.

p. 173 **a newly introduced exotic fruit** Ibid.

p. 174 **"What is often called Hunanese"** Quoted in Ruth Reichl, "The Vanishing Haute Cuisine."

p. 176 **"A fine sake"** Florence Fabricant, "Chilled and Subtle, Surprising New Sakes Beckon," *New York Times,* 3 December 1997.

p. 181 **"We don't grow herbs and vegetables"** Daniel V. Thompson, "A Gourmet's Greenhouse—Part II," *Gourmet* (February 1970): 20.

p. 185 **Fleur de sel was routinely ignored** Amanda Hesser, "From the French Marshes, a Salty Treasure," *New York Times,* 6 May 1998.

CHAPTER 7
IT'S DELICIOUS, BUT IS IT *CUISINE?*

INTERVIEWS

Larry Forgione, interview by author, 13 January 1998.

Rozanne Gold and Michael Whiteman, interview by author, 21 January 1998.

Barbara Kafka, interviews by author, 20 August and 26 August 1998.

Joyce Goldstein, interview by author, 10 September 1996.

Phillip S. Cooke, interview by author, 10 February 1998.

Bea Beasley, interview by author, 4 June 1998.

Roy Yamaguchi, interview by author, 13 February 1998.

Allen Susser, interview by author, 24 January 1996.

Norman Van Aken, interview by author, 26 January 1997.

Charles Palmer, interview by author, 11 July 1996.

Wayne Nish, interview by author, 25 June 1998.

Erik Blauberg, interview by author, 27 May 1997.

Phillipe Padovani, interview by author, 1995.

Michael McCarty, interview by author, 3 April 1996.

Alice Waters, interview by author, 6 September 1996.

Waldy Malouf, interview by author, June 1998.

Rose Dosti, interview by author, 26 January 1996.

PUBLISHED AND OTHER SOURCES

p. 191 **More than other countries** James Beard, *The Fireside Cookbook,* 11.

p. 191 **"by train, plane, automobile, by mule back, on foot"** Clementine Paddleford, *How America Eats,* v.

p. 192 **"check-up of what's cooking"** Ibid., 28.

p. 192 **"Mrs. Chamberlain told me"** Ibid.

p. 192 **The other third of our cooking** Ibid.

p. 193 **a judge in New York** Carol Truax, "Father at Home," *Gourmet* (March 1965): 17–18.

p. 194 **"Call the cookery American"** Alvin Kerr, "Spécialités de la Maison," *Gourmet* (June 1965): 6.

p. 194 **"Only fresh vegetables"** Ibid.

p. 194 **"Now, after 350 years"** Dale Brown, *American Cooking,* 6.

p. 195 **In the years since** James Beard, *James Beard's American Cookery,* xi.

p. 200 **"Frankly we didn't know"** Cooke, ed., *The Second Symposium on American Cuisine,* ix.

p. 202 **"I truly wonder if I'm in America"** James Villas, keynote address, (presented at Second Symposium on American Cuisine, New Orleans, 7 March 1982).

p. 202 **"Only then"** Ibid.

p. 203 **"less and less interested"** Ibid., 25.

p. 203 **"The extraordinary diversity"** Ibid., 26.

p. 203 **"trapped by the predominance of French"** Ibid.

p. 203 **". . . It's very difficult for me"** Ibid., 65.

p. 204 **"There are those kids"** Ibid.

p. 205 **"It took me many years"** Paul Prudhomme, *Chef Paul Prudhomme's Louisiana Kitchen,* 14–15.

p. 206 **article by Jack Bishop** Jack Bishop, "Not So Fast: Vegetables the Italian Way," *New York Times,* 6 March 1996.

p. 216 **"probably will never have one"** Sidney W. Mintz, *Tasting Food, Tasting Freedom: Excursions into Eating, Culture, and the Past,* 121.

p. 217 **"None of the standard theories"** Raymond Sokolov, *Why We Eat What We Eat: How the Encounter Between the New World and the Old Changed the Way Everyone on the Planet Eats,* 147.

p. 221 **"Cuisine is when food tastes of what it is."** Quoted in John L. and Karen Hess, *Taste of America,* 172.

CHAPTER 8
THE AMERICAN MENU

INTERVIEWS

Michael McCarty, interview by author, 3 April 1996.

Alexandra Leaf, interview by author, 30 June 1998.

Elaine Deane, interview by author, 3 June 1998.

PUBLISHED AND OTHER SOURCES

p. 227 **"the confusion that inevitably follows"** M. F. K. Fisher, "An Alphabet for Gourmets," *The Art of Eating,* 596.

p. 227 **The waiter waits** Ibid.

p. 230 **"His agents combed"** Michael and Ariane Batterberry, *On the Town,* 47.

p. 230 **Michael and Ariane Batterberry place it** Ibid., 63.

p. 230 **Margaret Visser asserts it was 1830** Margaret Visser, *Rituals of Dinner,* 202.

p. 231 **"around mid-century"** Stephen Mennell, *All Manners of Food: Eating and Taste in England and France from the Middle Ages to the Present,* 150.

p. 231 ***Service à la Russe* came** Batterberry, *On the Town,* 62–63.

p. 231 ***Traiteurs,* for instance** Mennell, *All Manners of Food,* 138.

p. 231 **Sellers of stocks and bouillons** Ibid.

p. 231 **an upstart named Boulanger** Ibid., 138–39.

p. 232 **Restaurants came into being for the first time** Batterberry, *On the Town,* 45–46.

p. 232 **restaurants must have a menu** Visser, *Rituals of Dinner,* 197.

p. 232 **An 1838 Delmonico's menu lists *Potages* (Soups)** Reprinted in Thomas, *Delmonico's,* endpapers.

p. 236 **"How do you feel about the trend"** Phillip S. Cooke, ed., *Second Symposium,* 61.

p. 237 **"Ordering from a menu used to be routine"** William Grimes, "Menus: Challenging the Old Order," *New York Times,* 4 February 1998.

p. 240 **"The bistro boom"** Ibid., "Is America Ready for Bunny Ragout?," *New York Times,* 29 October 1997.

p. 241 **A menu of Astor House** Lately Thomas, *Delmonicos,* 35–36.

p. 242 **"cultural critics have been slow"** Ibid., "Menus: Challenging the Old Order."

p. 242 **"By dismantling old categories"** Ibid.

CHAPTER 9
DINING AND THE AMERICAN PALATE

INTERVIEWS

Rozanne Gold and Michael Whiteman, interview by author, 21 January 1998.

Larry Forgione, interview by author, 13 January 1998.

Frieda Caplan, interview by author, 6 January 1998.

Jim Caudill, interview by author, 8 September 1998.

Thierry Pérémarti, interview by author, 16 February 1998.

Mario Mieli, interview by author, 7 June 1998.

David Bouley, interview by author, 21 June 1991.

John Hess, interview by author, 6 June 1998.

Joseph Baum, interview by author, 5 December 1997.

Michael McCarty, interview by author, 3 April 1996.

p. 250 **"Americans are way ahead"** Quoted in Ellen Brown, *New American Chefs,* 53.

p. 251 **"impish creatures"** Quoted in Laura Shapiro, *Perfection Salad,* 56.

p. 252 **"taste better to mothers"** James Trager, *Food Chronology,* 539.

p. 252 **As long ago as 1880** Sidney W. Mintz, *Sweetness and Power,* 188.

p. 252 **"It might be argued"** Waverly Root and Richard de Rochemont, *Eating,* 41.

p. 254 **"When Americans eat Chinese food"** Quoted in Ruth Reichl, "The Vanishing Haute Cuisine."

p. 254 **"God, the American palate"** James Beard, *Love and Kisses,* 259.

p. 258 **made by Bob Trinchero** Stanley Hock, *Harvesting the Dream: The Trinchero Family of Sutter Home,* 38.

p. 258 **Americans loved it** Ibid., 44.

p. 260 **New Orleans, the national capital of obesity** from a 1998 Centers for Disease Control Study, cited in Nanci Heilmich, USA Today web site, www.usatoday.com/life/health/diet/obesity/bdob.013.htm; INTERNET.

p. 261 **the portion sizes were too small** Noël Riley Fitch, *Appetite for Life,* 261.

p. 262 **"In Hispanic countries"** Margaret Visser, *Rituals of Dinner,* 271.

p. 263 **Coffee is brought** Ibid.

p. 263 **"everyone is too replete"** Ibid., 197.

p. 264 **"The meals are taken"** Quoted in Michael and Ariane Batterberry, *On the Town,* 46.

p. 265 **"Yes, I remember you"** Garrison Keillor, *Prairie Home Companion,* Minnesota Public Radio web site, www.mpr.org; INTERNET.

p. 267 **"an insult to my restaurant"** Ibid., 315.

p. 267 **In her fur coat.** Ibid.

p. 272 **theme-park dining is exploding** "Belly Up to the Baroque," *New York Times Magazine* (14 June 1998): 29.

p. 274 **"American Eclectic"** Batterberry, *On the Town,* 293.

p. 274 **"a kind of cross . . ."** Ibid.

p. 274 **as many as 78 percent** Visser, *Rituals of Dinner,* 265.

p. 274 **in the United States the average length of time** Ibid., 266.

p. 275 **"take a big, bold step and forget about serving separate courses."** Bobby Flay and Joan Schwartz, *From My Kitchen to Your Table,* 39.

CHAPTER 10
THE FARMERS' MARKET MOVEMENT

INTERVIEWS

John Hess, interview by author, 6 June 1998.

Robert Lewis, interview by author, 18 February 1998.

Hillary Baum, interview by author, 12 February 1998.

Diane Whealy, interview by author, 2 March 1998.

Marion Kalb, interview by author, 3 March 1998.

Lynn Bagley, interview by author, 2 March 1998.

Alice Waters, interview by author, 6 September 1996.

Sibella Krause, interview by author, 13 February 1998.

Luc Chamberlain, interview by author, 14 September 1996.

PUBLISHED AND OTHER SOURCES

p. 279 **A hundred years ago** Economics Research Service, "Farmers and the Land," in *U.S.D.A.: A History of American Agriculture 1776–1990,* U.S.D.A. web site www.usda.gov/history2/text3.htm, INTERNET.

p. 280 **An informal study in the late 1970s** Robert Sommer, *Farmers Markets of America,* 52.

CHAPTER 11
THE PURSUIT OF HAPPINESS

INTERVIEWS

Joyce Goldstein, interview by author, 10 September 1996.

PUBLISHED AND OTHER SOURCES

p. 300 **"These included dieting"** Harvey Levenstein, *Paradox of Plenty,* 45.

p. 301 **Of the wine drunk in America** Frank Prial, "Microbrew Generation Just Won't Pop the Cork," *New York Times,* 18 February 1998.

p. 301 **less than 42 percent of the population** U.S. Census Bureau estimate for 1998 U.S. Census Bureau web site, www.census.gov/ population/ estimates/ nation/ intfile21.txt; INTERNET.

p. 302 **Americans spend a whopping $8.9 billion dollars each year** "U.S. Nutrition Industry Seen at $17.2 Billion in Sales," *Whole Foods,* February 1997: 12–13.

p. 302 **"Do one big shopping"** Joe Dominguez and Vicky Robin, *Your Money or Your Life,* 198.

p. 303 **"Invite friends to share"** Ibid.

p. 304 **In 1994 we spent 11.1 percent** U.S. Department of Agriculture, *Agricultural Fact Book 1996,* 9.

p. 304 **"The word 'sin,' "** Michelle Stacey, *Consumed,* 22.

p. 305 **The Puritan nourishes himself** Waverly Root, "On Enjoying Food While Millions Starve," *New York Times Magazine,* 31 August 1975: 12.

p. 306 **"Now in the nineties"** Barbara Holland, *Endangered Pleasures,* xv.

p. 306 **"It should encourage sleep,"** Ibid., 65.

p. 306 **"an obligatory meal"** Ibid., 30.

p. 310 **In 1997 Ed Bradley traveled to Florence** Eunice Fried, "Ed Bradley Raises a Toast," *Wine Enthusiast* (May 1998): 62.

p. 311 **"exquisite plump and colorful apricots"** Mimi Sheraton, "For Christmas, a Shopper's Guide to Tasty Gifts," *New York Times,* 30 November 1977.

POSTSCRIPT: INTO THE MILLENNIUM

INTERVIEWS

Joyce Goldstein, interview by author, 10 September 1996.

Phillip S. Cooke, interview by author, 10 February 1998.

Wayne Nish, interview by author, 25 June 1998.

PUBLISHED AND OTHER SOURCES

p. 321 **"committed to advancing sustainable"** "About Chefs Collaborative 2000" (brochure), 1.

p. 322 **". . . Taillevent's cuisine changes"** Molly O'Neill, "The Perfectionist," *The New York Times Magazine,* 13 October 1996: 69–70.

p. 322 **This path to perfection** Ibid., 70.

Bibliography

Algren, Nelson, *America Eats.* Iowa City, Iowa: University of Iowa Press, 1992.

Anderson, Jean. *The American Century Cookbook.* New York: Clarkson Potter, 1997.

Barthes, Roland. *Mythologies.* Trans. Annette Lavers. New York: Hill and Wang, 1972.

Batterberry, Michael and Ariane. *On the Town in New York: From 1776 to the Present.* New York: Charles Scribner's Sons, 1973.

Baudrillard, Jean. *Amérique.* Paris, France: Éditions Grasset et Fasquelle, 1986.

Beard, James. *Delights and Prejudices: A Memoir with Recipes.* New York: Collier Books, 1990.

———. *James Beard's American Cookery.* Boston: Little, Brown, 1972.

———. *The Fireside Cookbook: A Complete Guide to Fine Cooking for Beginner and Expert.* Illustrations by Alice and Martin Provensen. New York: Simon & Schuster, 1949.

———. *Love and Kisses and a Halo of Truffles: Letters to Helen Evans Brown.* Ed. John Ferrone. New York: Arcade Publishing, 1994.

Berger, Frances de Talavera, and John Parke Custis. *Sumptuous Dining in Gaslight San Francisco, 1875–1915.* Garden City, N.Y.: Doubleday, 1985.

Bertolli, Paul, with Alice Waters. *Chez Panisse Cooking.* New York: Random House, 1988.

Blue, Anthony Dias. *America's Kitchen: Traditional and Contemporary Regional Cooking.* Atlanta: Turner Publishing, 1995.

Brans, Jo. *Feast Here Awhile: Adventures in American Eating.* New York: Ticknor & Fields, 1993.

Brenner, Leslie, with illustrations by Juliet Jacobson. *The Art of the Cocktail Party.* New York: Plume, 1994.

Brewster, Leitia, and Michael F. Jacobson, Ph.D. *The Changing American Diet.* Washington, D.C.: Center for Science in the Public Interest, 1978.

Brillat-Savarin, Jean-Anthelme. *The Physiology of Taste (La Physiologie du goût,* 1825) Trans. Anne Drayton. New York: Penguin, 1994.

Brown, Dale, and the Editors of Time-Life Books. *American Cooking.* New York: Time-Life Books, 1968.

———. *American Cooking: The Northwest.* New York: Time-Life Books, 1970.

Brown, Ellen. *Cooking with the New American Chefs.* New York: Harper & Row, 1985.

Brown, Helen Evans. *Helen Brown's West Coast Cook Book.* Boston: Little, Brown, 1952.

Brown, Linda Keller, and Kay Mussell, co-editors. *Ethnic and Regional Foodways in the United States: The Performance of Group Identity.* Knoxville, Tenn: The University of Tennessee Press, 1984.

Bullock, Helen Duprey, consulting ed., Margaret Klapthor, historical text. *The First Ladies Cookbook: Favorite Recipes of all the Presidents of the United States.* Revised edition. New York: GMG Publishing, 1982.

Burke, David, and Carmel Berman Reingold. *Cooking with David Burke*. New York: Alfred A. Knopf, 1996.

Camp, Charles. *American Foodways: What, When Why and How We Eat in America*. Little Rock, Ark.: August House, 1989.

Chalmers, Irene, with Milton Glaser and Friends. *Great American Food Almanac*. New York: Harper & Row, 1986.

Chamberlain, Samuel. *Bouquet de France: An Epicurean Tour of the French Provinces*. Recipes translated from the French and Adapted by Narcissa Chamberlain. New York: Gourmet, 1952.

Child, Julia. *Cooking with Master Chefs*. New York: Alfred A. Knopf, 1993.

Child, Julia, Louisette Bertholle, and Simone Beck. *Mastering the Art of French Cooking*. New York: Alfred A. Knopf, 1961.

Child, Julia, and Simone Beck. *Mastering the Art of French Cooking, Volume II*. New York: Alfred A. Knopf, 1970.

Claiborne, Craig. *New York Times Cookbook*. New York: Harper & Row, 1961.

Clark, Robert. *James Beard: A Biography*. New York: HarperCollins, 1993.

Clayton, Bernard Jr. *Bernard Clayton's Cooking Across America*. New York: Simon & Schuster, 1993.

The Compact Edition of the Oxford English Dictionary. Oxford, England: Oxford University Press, 1971.

Conaway, James. *Napa*. New York: Avon Books, 1990.

Cooke, Phillip S., ed. *The Second Symposium on American Cuisine*. New York: Van Nostrand Reinhold, 1984.

Dominguez, Joe, and Vicky Robin, *Your Money or Your Life: Transforming Your Relationship with Money and Achieving Financial Independence*. New York: Penguin, 1993. (Originally published by Viking, 1992.)

Downing, Century. *The Conspirator's Cookbook*. New York: Alfred A. Knopf, 1967. (First American edition; first British edition was privately printed, copyright 1966.)

Editors of *American Heritage, The Magazine of History*. *The American Heritage Cookbook and Illustrated History of American Eating and Drinking*. New York: Simon & Schuster, 1964.

Elbert, George, and Virginie. *Simple Cooking for Sophisticates.* New York: Hearthside Press, 1968.

Ephron, Nora. *Heartburn.* New York: Afred A. Knopf, 1983.

Esquivel, Laura. *Like Water for Chocolate.* Trans. Carol Christensen and Thomas Christensen. Garden City, N.Y.: Doubleday, 1992. (Originally published in Spanish, 1989.)

Evely, Mary. *The Vintner's Table Cookbook: Recipes from a Winery Chef.* Healdsburg, Calif.: Simi Winery, 1998.

Feibleman, Peter S., and the Editors of Time-Life Books. *American Cooking: Creole and Acadian.* New York: Time-Life Books, 1971.

Fein, Ronnie. *The Complete Idiot's Guide to Cooking Basics.* Indianapolis, Ind.: Alpha Books, 1995.

Ferrary, Jeannette, and Louise Fiszer. *The California-American Cookbook: Innovations on American Regional Dishes.* New York: Simon & Schuster, 1985.

Fisher, M. F. K. *The Art of Eating.* New York: Collier Books, 1990.

Fisher, Mrs. *What Mrs. Fisher Knows About Old Southern Cooking: Soups, Pickles, Preserves, Etc.: with Historical Notes by Karen Hess.* Bedford, Mass.: Applewood Books, 1995. First published in San Francisco: Women's Cooperative Printing Office, 1881.

Fitch, Noël Riley. *Appetite for Life: The Biography of Julia Child.* Garden City, N.Y.: Doubleday, 1997.

Flay, Bobby, and Joan Schwartz. *Bobby Flay's Bold American Food.* New York: Warner Books, 1994.

———. *Bobby Flay's From My Kitchen to Your Table.* New York: Clarkson Potter, 1998.

Foner, Nancy, ed. *New Immigrants in New York.* New York: Columbia University Press, 1987.

Forgione, Larry. *An American Place: Celebrating the Flavors of America.* New York: William Morrow, 1996.

Frank, Ken with Dewey Gram. *Ken Frank's La Toque Cookbook.* New York: Simon & Schuster, 1992.

Fussell, Betty. *I Hear America Cooking.* New York: Penguin Books, 1997. (First published by Viking Penguin, 1986.)

Gitlin, Todd. *The Sixties: Years of Hope, Days of Rage.* New York: Bantam Books, 1987.

Guérard, Michel. Trans. Narcisse Chamberlain. *Michel Guérard's Cuisine Minceur.* New York: William Morrow, 1976. (Originally published in France under the title *La Grande Cuisine Minceur,* copyright 1976, Editions Robert Laffont, S.A.).

Haller, Henry, with Virginia Aronson. *The White House Family Cookbook.* New York: Random House, 1987.

Harris, Jessica B. *The Welcome Table: African-American Heritage Cooking.* New York: Simon & Schuster, 1995.

Henderson, Janice Wald. *The New Cuisine of Hawaii: Recipes from the Twelve Celebrated Chefs of Hawaii Regional Cuisine.* New York: Villard Books, 1994.

Hess, John L., and Karen Hess. *The Taste of America.* Third Edition. Columbia, S.C.: University of South Carolina Press, 1989. (First published by Grossman/Viking, 1977.)

Hess, Karen. *The Carolina Rice Kitchen: The African Connection.* Columbia, S.C.: University of South Carolina Press, 1992.

Hess, Karen, transcribed by, with historical notes and copious annotations. *Martha Washington's Booke of Cookery.* New York: Columbia University Press, 1981, 1995.

Hibler, Janie. *Dungeness Crabs and Blackberry Cobblers: The Northwest Heritage Cookbook.* New York: Alfred A. Knopf, 1994.

Hock, Stanley. *Harvesting the Dream: The Trinchero Family of Sutter Home.* St. Helena, Calif.: Sutter Home Winery, 1998.

Holland, Barbara. *Endangered Pleasures.* New York: Harper Paperbacks, 1996. (Originally published by Little, Brown, 1995.)

Hooker, Alan. *Alan Hooker's New Approach to Cooking.* Ojai, Calif.: The Ranch House Restaurant, 1966.

———. *California Herb Cookery: From the Ranch House Restaurant.* Ojai, Calif.: Edwin House, 1996.

Hooker, Richard J. *A History of Food and Drink in America.* Indianapolis, Ind.: Bobbs-Merrill, 1981.

Idone, Christopher. *Glorious American Food.* New York: Random House, 1985.

Jacobs, Jay. *New York à La Carte.* New York: McGraw-Hill, 1978.

Johnson, Ronald. *The American Table.* New York: William Morrow, 1984.

Jones, Evan. *American Food: The Gastronomic Story.* 2d ed. New York: Random House, 1974.

———. *Epicurean Delight: The Life and Times of James Beard.* New York: Fireside, 1992. (Originally published New York: Alfred A. Knopf, 1990.)

Jones, Maldwyn Allen. *American Immigration.* 2d ed. Chicago: University of Chicago Press, 1992.

Kafka, Barbara. *The Opinionated Palate: Passions and Peeves on Eating and Food.* New York: William Morrow, 1992.

Kaytor, Marilyn. *"21": The Life and Times of New York's Favorite Club.* New York: Viking Press, 1975.

Kennedy, Diana. *The Cuisines of Mexico.* Rev. ed. New York: Harper & Row, 1986. (Originally published 1972.)

Killeen, Jacqueline, ed., and Roy Killeen. *101 Nights in California.* San Francisco: 101 Nights in California, 1968.

Klein, Richard. *Eat Fat.* New York: Pantheon Books, 1996.

Krondl, Michael. *Around the American Table: Treasured Recipes and Food Traditions from the American Cookery Collections of The New York Public Library.* Holbrook, Mass.: Adams Publishing, 1995.

Lagasse, Emeril, with Marcelle Bienvenu. *Louisiana Real & Rustic.* New York: William Morrow, 1996.

Leonard, Jonathan Norton, and the Editors of Time-Life Books. *American Cooking: The Great West.* New York: Time-Life Books, 1971.

Lesberg, Sandy. *Sandy Lesberg's One Hundred Great Restaurants of America.* New York: Crown Publishers, 1981.

Levenstein, Harvey. *Paradox of Plenty: A Social History of Eating in Modern America.* New York: Oxford University Press, 1993.

———. *Revolution at the Table: The Transformation of the American Diet.* New York: Oxford University Press, 1988.

Lewis, Edna. *The Taste of Country Cooking.* New York: Alfred A. Knopf, 1976.

Lovegren, Sylvia. *Fashionable Food: Seven Decades of Food Fads.* New York: Macmillan, 1995.

Lukins, Sheila. *U.S.A. Cookbook.* Illustrations by Carolyn Vibbert; Wine and Beer Selections made with Steve Olson. New York: Workman, 1997.

Malouf, Waldy, with Molly Finn. *The Hudson River Valley Cookbook.* Reading, Mass.: Addison-Wesley, 1995.

Mariani, John F. *America Eats Out: An Illustrated History of Restaurants, Taverns, Coffee Shops, Speakeasies, and Other Establishments that Have Fed us for 350 Years.* New York: Morrow, 1991.

Mast, Gerald. *A Short History of the Movies.* 2d ed. Indianapolis, Ind.: Bobbs-Merrill, 1976.

McCoy, Elin, and John Frederick Walker. *Thinking About Wine: Insights for the Enthusiast.* New York: Simon & Schuster, 1989.

McCullough, Frances, and Barbara Witt. *Classic American Food Without Fuss.* New York: Villard, 1997.

McGee, Harold. *On Food and Cooking.* New York: Collier Books, 1984.

McPhee, John. *Giving Good Weight.* New York: Farrar, Straus, & Giroux, 1979.

Mennell, Stephen. *All Manners of Food: Eating and Taste in England and France from the Middle Ages to the Present.* New York: Basil Blackwell, 1985.

Mennell, Stephen, Anne Murcott, and Anneke H. van Otterloo. *Sociology of Food: Eating, Diet and Culture.* London, England: SAGE Publications, 1992.

Meyer, Danny, and Michael Romano. *The Union Square Cafe Cookbook.* New York: HarperCollins, 1994.

Mintz, Sidney W. *Sweetness and Power: The Place of Sugar in Modern History.* New York: Elisabeth Sifton Books/Viking, 1985.

———. *Tasting Food, Tasting Freedom: Excursions into Eating, Culture, and the Past.* Boston: Beacon Press, 1996.

Mothershead, Alice Bonzi. Illustrations by Marilena Perrone. *Dining Customs Around the World.* Garrett Park, Md.: Garrett Park Press, 1982.

Muscatine, Doris. *A Cook's Tour of San Francisco*. New York: Charles Scribner's Sons, 1963.

Nelson, Richard. *Richard Nelson's American Cooking*. With a Foreword by James Beard. New York: New American Library, 1983.

The New York Times Company. *The New York Times Guide to Dining Out in New York, 1972 Edition*. New York: Atheneum, 1973.

O'Neill, Molly. *A Well-Seasoned Appetite: Recipes from an American Kitchen*. New York: Viking Press, 1995.

Paddleford, Clementine. *How America Eats*. New York: Charles Scribner's Sons, 1960.

Palmer, Charlie, with Judith Choate. *Great American Food*. New York: Random House, 1996.

Pappas, Lou Seibert. Preface by M. F. K. Fisher. *New American Chefs and Their Recipes*. San Francisco: 101 Productions, 1984.

Patrick, Ted, and Silas Spitzer. *Great Restaurants of America*. Philadelphia: J. B. Lippincott Co., 1960.

Penner, Lucille Recht. *The Colonial Cookbook*. New York: Hastings House, 1976.

Powell, Polly, and Lucy Peel. *'50s & '60s Style*. Secaucus, N.J.: Chartwell Books, 1988.

Price, Mary, and Vincent. *A Treasury of Great Recipes*. New York: Ampersand Press, 1965.

Prudhomme, Paul. *Chef Paul Prudhomme's Louisiana Kitchen*. New York: William Morrow, 1984.

Puck, Wolfgang. *The Wolfgang Puck Cookbook: Recipes from Spago, Chinois, and Points East and West*. New York: Random House, 1986.

Randall, Joe, and Toni Tipton-Martin. *A Taste of Heritage: The New African-American Cuisine*. New York: Macmillan, 1998.

Reardon, Joan. *M. F. K. Fisher, Julia Child, and Alice Waters: Celebrating the Pleasures of the Table*. New York: Harmony Books, 1994.

Renggli, Seppi, with Susan Grodnick. *The Four Seasons Spa Cuisine*. New York: Simon & Schuster, 1968.

Rombauer, Irma S. Foreword by Edgar Rombauer. *The Joy of Cooking: A Facsimile of the First Edition.* New York: Scribner's, 1998. (Originally published in 1931.)

Rombauer, Irma S. and Marion Rombauer Becker. *Joy of Cooking.* Indianapolis, Ind.: Bobbs-Merrill, 1975.

Root, Waverly, and Richard de Rochemont. *Eating in America: A History.* Hopewell, N.J.: The Ecco Press, 1981.

Rosso, Julee, and Sheila Lukins, with Michael McLaughlin. *The Silver Palate Cookbook.* New York: Workman Publishing, 1982.

———, with Sarah Leah Chase. *The Silver Palate Good Times Cookbook.* New York: Workman Publishing, 1985.

Rozin, Elisabeth. *Ethnic Cuisine: How to Create the Authentic Flavors of 30 International Cuisines.* New York: Penguin Books, 1992.

Schremp, Gerry. *Kitchen Culture: Fifty Years of Food Fads.* New York: Pharos Books, 1991.

Shacochis, Bob. *Domesticity: A Gastronomic Interpretation of Love.* New York: Charles Scribner's Sons, 1994.

Shapiro, Laura. *Perfection Salad: Woman and Cooking at the Turn of the Century.* New York: Farrar, Straus and Giroux, 1986.

Shere, Lindsey Remolif. *Chez Panisse Desserts.* Preface by Alice Waters. New York: Random House, 1985.

Simmons, Amelia. Introduction by Karen Hess. *American Cookery: or, The art of dressing viands, poultry and vegetables and the best modes of making puff-pastes, pies, tarts, puddings, custards and preserves, and all kinds of cakes from the imperial plumb to plain cake, adapted to this country, and all grades of life.* Reprint of 2d ed. Bedford, Mass.: Applewood Books, 1996. (Originally published: Albany, N.Y.: C. R. Webster, 1796.)

Sokolov, Raymond. *Fading Feast: A Compendium of Disappearing American Regional Foods.* New York: Farrar Straus and Giroux, 1981.

———. *Why We Eat What We Eat: How the Encounter Between the New World and the Old Changed the Way Everyone on the Planet Eats.* New York: Summit Books, 1991.

Sommer, Robert. *Farmers Markets of America.* Santa Barbara, Calif.: Capra Press, 1980.

Spitzer, Theodore Morrow, and Hilary Baum. *Public Markets and Community Revitalization.* Washington, D.C.: ULI—the Urban Land Institute and Project for Public Spaces, 1995.

Stacey, Michelle. *Consumed: Why Americans Love, Hate, and Fear Food.* New York: Simon & Schuster (Touchstone), 1995.

Stern, Jane, and Michael. *American Gourmet: Classic Recipes, Deluxe Delights, Flamboyant Favorites, and Swank "Company" Food from the '50 and '60s.* New York: HarperCollins, 1991.

———. *Real American Food.* New York: Alfred A. Knopf, 1986.

Szathmáry, Louis. *American Gastonomy.* Chicago: Henry Regnery Company, 1974. (Published by special arrangement with Arno Press, New York.)

Tannahill, Reay. *Food in History.* Rev. and Updated ed. New York: Crown Publishers, 1989.

Thomas, Lately. *Delmonico's: A Century of Splendor.* Boston: Houghton Mifflin, 1967.

Toussaint-Samat, Maguelonne. Trans. Anthea Bell. *History of Food.* Cambridge, Mass.: Blackwell Publishers, 1992.

Trager, James. *The Food Chronology.* New York: Henry Holt and Co., 1995. (Owl Book Edition, 1997.)

Trillin, Calvin. *The Tummy Trilogy: with a New Foreword.* New York: Farrar, Straus & Giroux, 1994.

Troisgros, Jean & Pierre. Trans. Roberta Wolfe Smoler. *The Nouvelle Cuisine of Jean & Pierre Troisgros.* New York: William Morrow, 1978. (Originally published under the title *Cuisiniers à Roanne,* copyright 1977 by Editions Robert Laffont, S.A.)

Turner, James S. *The Chemical Feast.* New York: Grossman Publishers, 1970.

U.S. Department of Agriculture, *Agricultural Fact Book 1996,* Washington, D.C.: GPO or on-line.

Verdon, René. *The White House Chef Cookbook.* Garden City, N.Y.: Doubleday, 1967.

Villas, James, with a Foreword by James Beard. *American Taste: A Celebration of Gastronomy Coast-to-Coast.* New York: Arbor House, 1982.

Visser, Margaret. *The Rituals of Dinner: The Origins, Evolution, Eccentricities, and Meaning of Table Manners.* New York: Penguin Books, 1992. (First published in the United States by Grove Weidenfeld, 1991, and in Canada by HarperCollins, 1991.)

Wallace, Lily Haxworth, editor-in-chief. *The New American Cook Book.* New York: Books, 1941.

Walter, Eugene, and the Editors of Time-Life Books. *American Cooking: Southern Style.* New York: Time-Life Books, 1971.

Waters, Alice. *Chez Panisse Menu Cookbook.* New York: Random House, 1982.

Williams, Susan. *Savory Suppers and Fashionable Feasts: Dining in Victorian America.* New York: Pantheon Books, 1985.

Wilson, José, and the Editors of Time-Life Books. *American Cooking: The Eastern Heartland.* New York: Time-Life Books, 1971.

Zahler, Karen Gantz. *Superchefs: Signature Recipes from America's New Royalty.* New York: John Wiley & Sons, 1996.

———. *A Taste of New York.* New York: Addison-Wesley, 1993.

Ziemann, Hugo, and F. L. Gillette, with Patti Bazel Geil, R.D. and Tami Ross, R.D. *White House Cook Book.* Revised and Updated Centennial Edition. Minneapolis, Minn.: Chronimed Publishing, 1996.

Zola, Émile. *The Belly of Paris.* Trans. Ernest Alfred Vizetelly. Los Angeles: Sun & Moon Press, 1996.

Index